An Early History of
Akwesasne

The Works of
Franklin B. Hough
1822-1885

Frankin B. Hough by Jade Thompson

An Early History of
AKWESASNE

The Works of
Franklin B. Hough
1822-1885

Darren Bonaparte

The
WAMPUM
Chronicles

Akwesasne Mohawk Territory
2020

An Early History of Akwesasne: The Works of Franklin B. Hough 1822-1885
© 2020 by Darren Bonaparte. All rights reserved. Except for brief quotations in a review, this book may not be reproduced in any form without written permission from the publisher.

Quoted sources, when not in the public domain, are copyrighted by their original authors or publishers. All rights reserved.

Illustrations are copyrighted by the artist who created them. All rights reserved.

Cover Illustration: *Part of the St. Lawrence River at the St. Regis Mohawk Indian Reservation* (1818) by F. R. Hassler. Courtesy of the William L. Clements, University of Michigan.

Back Cover Illustration: *St. Regis, Indian Village (St. Lawrence)* (1841) engraved by H. Griffiths after a picture by W. H. Bartlett, published in *Canadian Scenery* (1841).

Layout: Dan Poirier, Astro Printing, Cornwall, Ontario.

For information about permissions, or to inquire about bulk purchases, address all correspondence to either of the following addresses:

Darren Bonaparte
P. O. Box 1026
Akwesasne NY 13655

Darren Bonaparte
P. O. Box 459
Akwesasne QC H0M 1A0

The Wampum Chronicles
c/o the Mohawk Territory of Akwesasne
Website: wampumchronicles.com
E-mail: wampumchronicles@hotmail.com

Dedication

*To my wife, Jennifer,
and to the spouses of authors everywhere,
for the special price they pay.*

*This book was written and compiled during the pandemic of 2020,
an incredibly challenging time for my wife and her coworkers at the Cornwall
Community Hospital, as well as for all others on the "front lines" of this global
emergency. Your courage and dedication will not soon be forgotten.*

Contents

Acknowledgments	viii
Introduction	ix
I Hough's *St. Regis*	1
Franklin B. Hough's 1853 Maps of Akwesasne	2
"...to snatch from oblivion the reminiscences of the olden time..." Franklin B. Hough and the Early History of Akwesasne	3
"St. Regis" by Franklin B. Hough. *A History of Saint Lawrence and Franklin Counties, New York, from the Earliest Period to the Present Time.* 1853.	17
Further References to Akwesasne	119
"St. Regis" in Retrospect	130
Photograph of three Akwesasne men with the Seven Nations of Canada Treaty	135
II His Later Work	137
Franklin B. Hough Returns to Akwesasne	138
"The St. Regis Indians." by Franklin B. Hough. *The New York Times.* January 11, 1856.	144
"St. Regis" by Franklin B. Hough. *The Census of the State of New York for 1855.* 1857.	148
Documents from the Franklin Benjamin Hough Papers	153
Indenture for Islands in the St. Lawrence River 1796	159
An Appeal by Gautinonty, a Chief of Oswegatchie 1805	165
Notes on Governance at Akwesasne and Kahnawake c. 1856	166
Documents in the Possession of Reverend Eleazer Williams	168
Biographies Written by Reverend Eleazer Williams	173
Lewis Cook (Colonel Louis Cook)	174
William Gray	184
Thomas Williams	185

Life of Te-ho-ra-gwa-ne-gen, alias Thomas Williams, a Chief of the   200
Caughnawaga Tribe of Indians in Canada. by Reverend Eleazer Williams.
Edited by Franklin B. Hough. 1859.

Colonel Louis Cook in Hough's Later Books   218

"St. Regis Reservation" by Franklin B. Hough. *U. S. Bureau of Education*   228
Special Report. 1888.

"Franklin B. Hough." by Henry S. Graves. *Dictionary of American Biography,*   235
Volume 9. 1932.

Acknowledgments

I would like to thank my friends William Starna, Janeth Lazore Murphy, and René Garcia for their helpful comments and encouragement.

I would also like to thank the William L. Clements Library, University of Michigan for permission to use a map from their collection on the cover. *Part of the St. Lawrence River at the St. Regis Mohawk Indian Reservation* was created by F. R. Hassler in 1818.

Thank you to my daughter, Jade Thompson, for her excellent pen-and-ink illustration of Franklin B. Hough. It is based on an 1860 engraving by J. C. Buttre that appeared in the book, *A History of Lewis County, in the State of New York, from the Beginning of its Settlement to the Present Time.*

Thank you to my son, Elijah Thompson, for locating an important file, and Laryssa Cole, for making sure it got to me.

Thank you to the rest of my family and friends who have always been supportive of my adventures in the realm of history.

Introduction

The student of Akwesasne history quickly learns to appreciate the scholarship of Franklin B. Hough. Long considered the finest historian of New York's "North Country," Hough wrote a chronicle of the community's first century, from its origins as a Jesuit mission of New France, to the "reservation period" of the 1850s. Colonial wars, native confederacies, mercurial leaders, controversial treaties, and devastating epidemics —that's a lot of history tied up in one little town. Hough was to Akwesasne what Lewis Henry Morgan was to the Iroquois Confederacy: his scholarship put the community on the academic map, and it has remained there ever since.

This landmark work is a chapter of a much larger book, *A History of St. Lawrence and Franklin Counties, New York, from the Earliest Period to the Present Time,* published in 1853. It has been reprinted many times over the years, but with each copy weighing in at over seven hundred pages, it can well afford to let one of its chapters be a book of its own. The full text of Hough's "St. Regis" is reprinted here, supplemented with additional materials he collected and wrote from the time of his first visit until the end of his notable career more than three decades later.

Several chapters have been written to introduce the various texts, and to tell the story of the historian's visits to Akwesasne. Franklin B. Hough may have arrived with his fair share of the cultural biases of his time, but he became fascinated with the community and its legendary past. This was something he could only learn "on the ground," from the people who knew it. The respectful way he approached them earned their trust.

It has been a privilege to share his discoveries with a new generation.

I

Hough's *St. Regis*

Franklin B. Hough's 1853 Maps of Akwesasne
from *A History of St. Lawrence and Franklin Counties, New York*

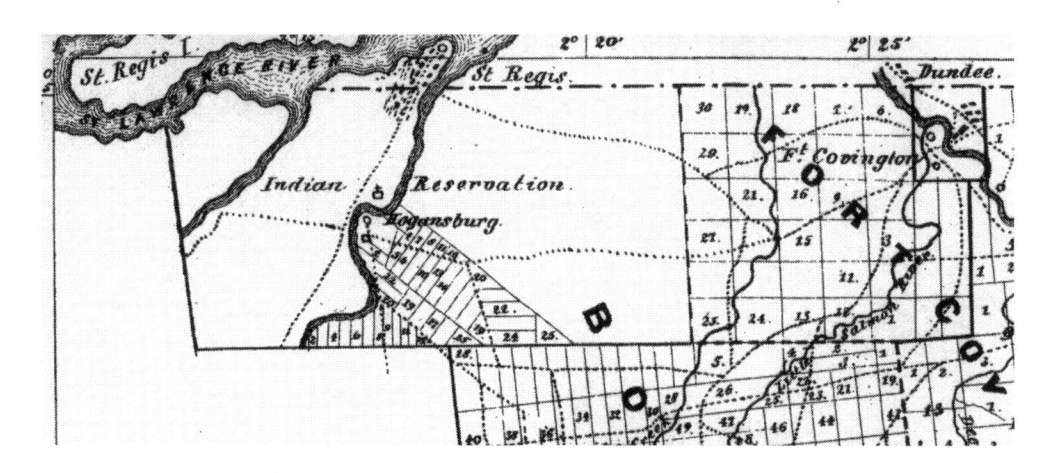

St. Regis Reservation from Franklin B. Hough's map of Franklin County.
The area beneath "Dundee" on the right of the map is the "mile square" at French Mills (Fort Covington) reserved to Akwesasne in the Seven Nations of Canada Treaty of 1796.

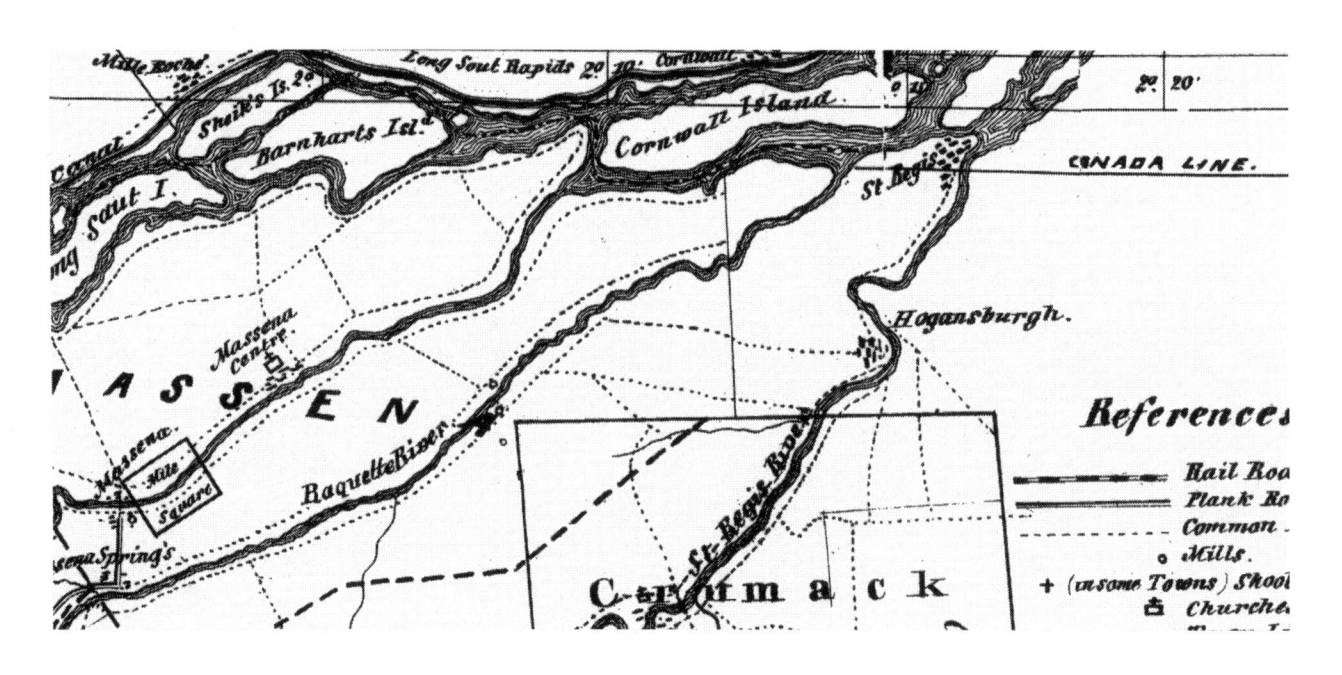

St. Regis Reservation from Franklin B. Hough's map of St. Lawrence County.
The area beneath "Massena" in the lower left corner of the map is the "mile square" on the Grass River reserved to Akwesasne in the same treaty.
The meadows leading up to it from the St. Lawrence were also reserved.

"...to snatch from oblivion the reminiscences of the olden time..."
Franklin B. Hough and the Early History of Akwesasne

Once upon a time in Akwesasne, a young visitor came to learn its story. It was the spring of 1852. The outside world knew very little about the Mohawk community on the banks of the St. Lawrence river.

It is not that it lacked for things to make it stand out. Akwesasne was where four Adirondack rivers met the mighty Saint Lawrence amid a multitude of islands. It was the only native community divided by the border between the United States and Canada. It had one of the earliest Roman Catholic churches in the region, a venerable stone edifice where hymns were sung in Mohawk by a Mohawk choir.

Nor could anyone be unaware of its people, who roamed the "North Country" like they owned the place. Akwesasne men felled trees as lumberjacks in the Adirondacks. Others poled rafts of logs to saw mills down rivers. Some served as guides to hunters and fishermen.

The St. Regis Mission, named after Saint Jean-François Régis of the Society of Jesus, was established halfway through the eighteenth century. By 1852, the region was no longer the vast wilderness of towering trees that it was a century before. New towns were popping up in every direction. County lines were drawn, two of which converged at Akwesasne, a popular place for boundaries. And since you have counties, you might as well have county histories. Enter Dr. Franklin Benjamin Hough.

The young man who came to Akwesasne to document its past had quite a history of his own. He was born Benjamin Franklin Hough to Dr. Horatio and Martha Hough in the town of Martinsburg, New York, about twenty-five miles southeast of Watertown, on July 20, 1822. His father died when he was eight years old. This was when his first and middle names were reversed, and he went by Franklin from that point on. He graduated from Union College in Schenectady in 1843, taught school for a year, and then became the principal of a school in Ohio.

Three important events marked Hough's life in 1846. He married Sarah Maria Eggleson of Champion, New York. He wrote his first book, *A Catalogue of Indigenous, Naturalized, and Filicord Plants of Lewis Counties, New York*. And he decided to follow in his late father Horatio's footsteps and study medicine.

His wife gave birth to their daughter, Lola, while he was enrolled at what is now Case Western Reserve School of Medicine in Cleveland, Ohio He graduated in 1848.

Tragedy struck when the new doctor's wife passed away in June of that year.

Hough married Mariah Kilham in 1849. They would have eight children between 1850 and 1872. He practiced medicine for a few years in Somerville, New York, but in 1852, he set his practice aside for a time to pursue his love of science and history.[1] He was then twenty-nine years old, and his love of historical preservation did not extend to the soles of his shoes:

> He was a man of splendid physique, as may be inferred from the following incidents mentioned in his autobiography. After recounting his visit to a locality rich in choice minerals, he writes, "I found myself loaded with forty or fifty pounds of treasures with which I walked back over the twenty-five miles I had come!" In another place he mentions walking all night a distance of forty-five miles to his home.[2]

His first major project was to complete his research into the history of St. Lawrence and Franklin counties, and publish the results. This was an ambitious project, the likes of which had not been seen in northern New York. He gave a lecture on the subject in Ogdensburgh in 1851, and felt the positive response it received warranted a comprehensive book. The research for this tome was what brought him to Akwesasne.

Hough's journal is preserved among his papers at the New York State Library in Albany.[3] It tells us that he arrived in the area on Saturday, the first of May. Since he was new to area, he found himself a good guide:

> Called upon Mr James Campbell of Massena about midway between Racket River Bridge and Hogansburgh. Spent the night with Judge Campbell and was very much delighted with his company. He promises to make the tour of Franklin County with me and will doubtless be of very great service in my inquiries.

The following day he set out for Hogansburg, the small village two miles south of the village of St. Regis, and then on to the village itself:

> Sunday 2 May 1852
> Went out in the morning to Hogansburgh where I had my team put out and walked down to St. Regis Village arriving just in time to attend their meeting. For an account of my visit there see a news paper acct.
> I met with great success in enlisting the Catholic priest in my favor and hope to get from them a full account of the Mission. Returned to Hogansburgh.

The route he took is known as St. Regis road. The village of St. Regis is two miles north of Hogansburg. It was then and is now the most densely-populated part of the community. Hough's impressions of the village would become the opening passages of what he would eventually write about Akwesasne in his book:

> On a beautiful and elevated point which juts into the St. Lawrence, where that river is crossed by the forty-fifth parallel of latitude, and between the mouths of the St. Regis and Racquette rivers, stands a dilapidated and antique looking village, whose massive and venerable church, with tin covered spire; whose narrow and filthy streets, and the general appearance of indolence and poverty of its inhabitants, and especially the accents of an unaccustomed language, almost convey to the casual visitor an impression that he is in a foreign land.[4]

In his journal, Hough mentioned a newspaper account of his visit, written from his home in Somerville five days later. It ran on the front page of *The St. Lawrence Republican* of Ogdensburgh on May 25, and was as rich in detail as his journal entry was sparing:

Correspondence.
For the St. Lawrence Republican
Somerville, N. Y. May 7, 1852

Dear Sir,–I improve the earliest opportunity to inform you of the result of my visit of inquiry at the Indian village of St. Regis. My design was more to learn what historical materials existed and where they might be procured, than to obtain them at this time. I was received with great kindness by the Rev. F. Marcoux, to whom I am greatly indebted for his endeavours to promote the object my visit. This gentleman has, for more than twenty years, been settled in this Mission, in charge of the Catholic church, and possesses a great influence with the natives. He assured me that it would give him great pleasure to answer every inquiry which I could make by letter, and have the materials ready against the next time when I might visit the village in June next. The Jesuit College, at Montreal, contains every fact in relation to the founding of this mission, together with those of La Galette, &c., and I shall take with me, from St. Regis, letters to the members of that order in Montreal, which, I have hopes, will lead me to materials of great interest. The Jesuits were model historians, for they treasured up the passing events of their times, which have now become history. The Rev. gentleman also promised to make inquiries among the Indians, and call a kind of council, to give me their traditions and war stories, which they are very willing to relate.

    These, of course, must pass for what they are worth. I attended their church, and was much impressed with the novelty of the scene. The internal decorations are very fine, and adapted to the taste of the natives.

The room is spacious, and the ritual conducted with all the pomp and ceremony which I have ever witnessed in a cathedral. Most of the Indians sat on the floor, and, throughout the service, conducted themselves with decorum. During much of the service, the responses were chanted by the males and females of the congregation, alternately, in the Mohawk dialect of the Iroquois language, and with much attention to musical rules. The Priest was assisted by twelve attendants, mostly natives, and dressed in the robes of their office. The history of the famous bell of St. Regis can all be readily obtained, and differs essentially from the story published several years ago in the county papers. I have hopes of learning, from some source, the inscription that was cast upon it.

This mission was founded in 1759. The first church was built of logs and covered with bark. It stood near the bank of the St. Regis river; the second stood in the priest's garden, and contained the bell; the present one was built in 1792, and is the oldest in the northern country, except at Quebec, Montreal and, perhaps, at Kingston.

About 1828, a deputation of the chiefs visited France, and were received with great ceremony by Charles X, who presented them with three splendid paintings, two of which are here and one at Caughnawaga. One of them, over the altar, is the portrait of St. Regis, the patron saint of the mission, and the one to the left, near the pulpit, is a splendid and finished full-length portrait of St. François Xavier. Both were executed in France.

The festival of St. Regis occurs on the 16th of June. I regretted that it was impossible for me to attend the election of chiefs on the first Tuesday of May.

My efforts to snatch from oblivion the reminiscences of the olden time, which are fast fading from the memory of the "oldest inhabitant," are meeting with every encouragement, and from no one more than a resident of Massena, who has long held offices of trust, both civil and military, in Franklin county. From his vigorous frame and broad shoulders, the Indians gave him the name of Lag-a-gath-ta (strong and able to carry), and his mind and memory are quite as vigorous as his body. His official business formerly extended to every town in Franklin county, and, in 1820, he was acquainted with every inhabitant. Lag-a-gath-ta will make the tour of Franklin county with me, and be the lamp to my path, or, in other words, carry the lantern.

The Indians have names for every stream and lake of any magnitude, and I hope to obtain them with their signification. A few of them I have already. St. Regis is called by the natives "Ake-sas-ne," and signifies, "when the partridge drums;" Grass River is "Mik-ent-si-a-ke," meaning "with fishes," or the "fishes home;" the Raquette is "Ni-o-nas-te" or "swift river;" Black River is "Ni-ka-hi-on-ba-kow-a" or "big river." I am not sure that the foregoing orthography is reliable; it will be correctly obtained at my next visit. The word 'Oswegatchie' is, by the Indians, pronounced "Swekatsi." I shall take pleasure in recording the history of this people, and hope to be able to obtain an account that will possess more than a local interest.

Franklin B. Hough[5]

The Rev. F. Marcoux mentioned in the article was François-Xavier Marcoux. He was the second Marcoux to serve as priest at St. Regis, the first being Joseph Marcoux. Lag-a-gath-ta was no doubt Judge James Campbell mentioned in his journal.

Hough returned to Akwesasne in June for four more days. He conducted interviews, copied documents, and made observations. This time out, he put more detail into his journal:

> Wednesday June 16 1852
>
> St Regis day. Started from Judge Campbell's early in morning and went to the village of Hogansburgh where I called upon John S Eldridge and Mr Fulton went thence to St Regis and stopped at the Catholic Priest's. Spent the day from 10 o'clock to 7 with Marcoux the priest and a group of Indians writing down the early history of the St Regis tribe.
>
> Was told that the Indians propose to adopt me into their tribe and give me a name Took supper [with] Marcoux and lodged at night with an Indian family in the village just above the British custom house

As he stated in his article, he intended to get a proper orthography and translations of the place names on his return visit. Those that appear in his book differ significantly from what he had recorded in May, such as *Ak-wis-sas-ne,* "where the partridge drums." It was his keen interest in the community's name that prompted them to bestow a Mohawk name on him, as he noted in a footnote in the book:

> On the occasion of the author's visit to St. Regis in June 1852, the natives desired to give him a name, and proposed among others, that of their village. Objections being made, they decided upon, O-kwa-e-sen, a partridge, they regarding that bird somewhat at a national emblem, like the eagle to the United States. The idea was doubtless suggested by the particular inquiries made about the origin of their village. The custom of naming those who have business with them in common, and in former times when the drinking of rum was more prevalent, the ceremony of christening and adoption was conducted with excessive demonstration of joy. At present it consists in singing and shouting around the candidate, and the shaking of hands. At times a rude dance is performed, but this people have lost every recollection of the national feasts and dances, which are

still maintained among the pagan party of the Iroquois at Onondaga and other Indian settlements, in the interior of the state.

They informed the author that they should consider him as belonging to the Ro-tis en-na-keh-te, or little Turtle band, that being the smallest and feeblest one among them.[6]

It may have pleased the community to see someone taking an interest in the community's Mohawk name once again. In colonial times, British officials took great pains to record it as best they could and employed it in their speeches. By the middle of the nineteenth century, those who dealt with Akwesasne in an official capacity used only *St. Regis*.

Hough learned that there was more to the Mohawk name than its literal translation: "In winter time, the ice from the rapids above, coming down under the firm ice at this place, often occasions a sort of tremor or earthquake in miniature, and is attended with a noise very much like the drumming of a partridge."[7]

He continued his investigation the following day. He witnessed a religious observance in the morning, and then was introduced to the elderly daughter of one of Akwesasne's notable chiefs:

Thursday 17 June 1852
Left the house of Katehearon (where I spent the night) about 7 o'clock. Observed a procession in the street consisting of the priest, two or three clerks and a miscellaneous crowd of females without order praying as they walked. Followed them into the church and met Mr Marcoux as he came out of the vestry. Spent the forenoon with him and with him as an interpreter had an interview with several of the Indians and among others the daughter of Col Louis Grey. Consulted the archives of the American Indians and in PM met with Judge Campbell and had a long talk with him and the priest about the war &c. Went thence to Hogansburgh and had a conversation with Mr Eldridge.

It is important to note here that "Col Louis Grey" was actually Colonel Louis Cook, an individual Hough had clearly never heard of, but whose life he would go on to document in great detail. He confused him with William Gray, an associate of Cook, who served as the council's clerk and interpreter. Hough identified the daughter of Cook as Mary Ka-wen-ni-ta-ke in his book.

The next person Hough was to encounter at Akwesasne was already something of a historic figure in his own right, even at the time he met him. The rest of his journal entry for that day contains his interesting story:

Called a short time on the Rev Eleazer Williams an Episcopalian minister of Indian parentage, (commonly so believed) who is teaching a little school in the edge of the town of Fort Covington. He is 65 years of age and very intelligent. I [seldom] meet with a man who has a more ready flow of language or who is more interesting in conversation.

There is a strange story reported that he is a Bourbon by descent. And as near as I can get hold of the story it is as follows. His earliest recollections is that of his being at the head of Lake George when a child. He was brought up among the Indians and has [always] been considered a descendent of the Rev Mr Williams who was taken a prisoner at Deerfield.

In 1839(?) when Prince de Joinville was travelling in the country he made inquiries for a person whom he understood had been brought up among the Cognawagas having been conveyed thither and given to the indians to save his life from the hands of the terrorists of the French Revolution

This child was said to be the legitimate son of Louis XVI. Who is or was at the time reported to have died in prison.

Having learned of this Williams the prince from some reason was led to suspect that he was the one and having expressed a desire to see him some pains was taken to obtain an interview which was effected on a steamer on Lake Michigan. The prince spent a long time with him in private conversation and it is aid expressed his conviction that he was the man. He is said to have been led to this from certain marks or scars upon his face.

Mr. Williams showed me a dress of splendid Brocade silk with a long trail, which he says he received from France as the dress of his mother the Queen. It is really a most splendid quality of silk as far as I can judge, whatever may have been its history. Mr Williams promised to write out at length all he knew of the Indians which will be at my service

Spent the night at Fort Covington at the [Northern] Hotel.

Reverend Eleazer Williams is known as the "Lost Dauphin" even today. Williams had many detractors in his time, but there were some who entertained his fantastic story. It made him something of a celebrity, and he gave frequent lectures in American cities. Nobody wanted to believe that the child of beheaded King Louis XVI and Marie Antoinette died a miserable, wasting death in a French prison. Better that he was smuggled to America by the Scarlet Pimpernel and raised by Indians!

Hough made no mention in his book of Williams's claims. Instead he acknowledged him for the materials he wrote, and selectively incorporated them into his own text. But in his personal notes found among his papers in Albany, he had this to say about Williams:

> The reputed Bourbon. I was aware of the Bourbon story before the book printed but believing that it had in it little to recommend it let it pass

> unnoticed. Some have blamed me for this but they are of that romantic class whom I little respect.
>
> E Williams labored to impress upon me the reality of his reputed royal birth; showed me the silk dress said to have belonged to the queen his mother (?) and related to me the interview with de Joinville. He was evidently extremely anxious to receive notice from me, and is vain, egotistical, and intriguing; affects the dress of the Catholic priests by wearing a robe, &c.
>
> He is very unpopular among the whites of French Mills and at Malone where he is generally known as a man destitute of a sense of responsibility in the payment of his debts and fulfillment of his promises.[8]

What was it that kept Hough from discrediting Williams in print? It was no doubt the detailed biographies Williams wrote of the aforementioned Colonel Louis Cook and William Gray, as well as his own father, Thomas Williams, another of Cook's contemporaries. Since Williams knew them personally, his accounts were of enormous historical value, especially after Hough learned how intimately involved these people were in events of the late eighteenth and early nineteenth centuries. He would later enhance Williams's work with further archival research that confirmed their illustrious pasts, and then incorporated the results in the chapter he wrote about Akwesasne.

The three manuscripts ended up in Hough's papers in Albany, along with copies he took of various letters in Williams's possession when he visited him again in 1856.

Hough's judicious handling of Williams was a fine example of his efforts, in his own words, "to snatch from oblivion the reminiscences of the olden time." Hough was a historian's historian, someone so dedicated to research that he named a child after an acquaintance who loaned him books. It was his zeal for the past that led him to discover the story of Colonel Louis Cook, an unsung hero of the American Revolution, and a man we might not know much about today had the studious young doctor not taken a chance on the crafty old reverend.

To resume with the events of 1852, Hough visited Williams a second time on June 19, but not much detail is offered in his journal:

> Saturday 19 June
> Spent the morning in writing. The forenoon in making inquiries of Mr Jabez Parkhurst Mr Wallace &c. about the early history of Fort Covington Went to Bombay Corners and spent several hours at work on the town records of Bombay &c. Called again on the Rev Eleazer Williams. Went on to Hogansburgh where I spent the evening and night. Put up at the white tavern to the right of the river

Hough extended his visit to Akwesasne another day, returning to the village to continue his work. By his account, the chiefs of the community thought enough of his approach to history to seek his opinion on at least one of their own historic claims:

> Sunday 20 June 1852
>
> Spent the morning in writing. In forenoon went to St Regis and put up my horse at the [house] near where the tavern was burned last winter, and not far from Mr Gwynn's Custom house. Attended Church in the forenoon. At noon dined with the priest and spent a couple of hours in conversing with him (pen in hand) and in consulting the parish records. Attended Mass and a funeral in the afternoon.
>
> After Service met quite a number of principal men (chiefs of the British and American parties) some 6 or 8 in number together with the Priest, School master and one or two others. The object of this was to give some account of the Oswegatchie tribe whose successors the St Regis claim to be.
>
> They have a vague and indefinite report or belief among them that they have a title to a piece of land opposite to Chimney Island. I told them all I knew about the Oswegatchies.
>
> They offered me a very liberal share if I should become instrumental in aiding them in recovering their rights. I do not believe they have any that can be sustained. It is very certain they have nothing but a very vague tradition of the subject which would scarcely stand the test of law.

Hough may have been dismissive of their claim at the moment, but he did look into the matter. He included a significant account of the "Oswegatchies" in the first chapter of his book, which did indeed link them, in part, to the people at Akwesasne.

Summer began with good news for the young historian. On June 27, *The St. Lawrence Republican* published an editorial that enthusiastically supported his efforts:

THE HISTORY OF ST. LAWRENCE AND FRANKLIN COUNTIES

> Our readers are aware that a very elaborate and extensive work of the above title, is in progress of preparation by Dr. Hough, of this village. We have had an opportunity of examining a specimen, containing a few engravings and pages of printing, bound the size it will be when complete. The paper is very fine, the binding excellent, the type clear, the pages large, and the engravings of the most costly and elegant kind. Should the work be finished, we doubt not that it will commend itself to every reader. The inhabitants of nearly every village in the two counties, are contributing, we understand, very fine engravings for the work which will greatly enhance its value. Dr. Hough has just returned from the Indian village of St. Regis, with several pages of Indian names of locations, and many interesting incidents of their early history. We infer that he has met with his usual

> success in searching out the obscure traditions of this interesting people. We are informed that the Dr. intends to visit the Jesuit College in Montreal, to glean from its archives the dates and facts concerning the old mission, along the St Lawrence. The Indians at St. Regis, as well as their priest, took great interest in his enquiries.
>
> We further learn that they, as a mark of friendship, gave him a name and adopted him into their tribe, according to their ancient forms and ceremonies.
>
> It remains with the inhabitants of St. Lawrence and Franklin counties to decide whether this laudable enterprise shall be sustained, for the terms of the prospectus are such that the work cannot be published until a sufficient subscription can be obtained to defray the expense of the publication. The cost of a book of this kind is very great, therefore all who feel an interest in seeing the annals of their own towns recorded and the incidents of early settlements of their neighborhoods, must signify their desire by subscribing for a copy of this book. To say to the author that his plan is a good one, and that perhaps a book will be taken when out of the press, is no encouragement. That deception has been practiced by agents in obtaining subscriptions for books, we do not doubt, but this case is quite different. The circulation is local and the patronage cannot be expected to extend beyond the limits of the two counties, and the author is well known.
>
> We hope that he will be sustained in an undertaking, that will reflect the honor upon the age and shed a flood of light on the origin, progress, and condition of the counties when written. We are convinced from what we have learned, that the author will not hazard a farthing on its publication. The materials for the work are coming together with a rapidity and abundance which is due only to the zeal, industry and energy expended upon it.[9]

The appeal was successful. It garnered the proper amount of subscriptions to cover production costs, and in 1853, Hough published *A History of St. Lawrence and Franklin Counties, New York, from the Earliest Period to the Present Time.* It was over seven hundred pages long, richly illustrated with engravings, and had several foldout maps.

The chapter devoted to Akwesasne, or St. Regis, as he preferred to call it, was the second one in the book, and contained an enormous amount of information beyond what has been described here. It has stood the test of time as an authoritative source on the early history of Akwesasne, and has been quoted extensively by scholars since it came into print.

The entire chapter about Akwesasne is reprinted in this book, so it will be left to the reader to discover the contents of Hough's account, rather than give a detailed overview here. But it should be noted that the author continued to be fascinated by Akwesasne and its legendary chiefs, and sought further information in archives, long after the book was published. He returned to Akwesasne during his work for the New York State Census in 1855, 1865, and 1875. He wrote of these visits and published what he wrote, noting the changes he had seen. These have been gathered for this book, and will appear sequentially after the chapter from *A History of St. Lawrence and Franklin Counties*. Several other documents found among Hough's papers will be found here, such the materials he acquired from Eleazer Williams, as well as a few things found in his other publications.

Hough's research at Akwesasne paralleled the work of Lewis Henry Morgan among the Seneca, but since he was more interested in conventional history than the social sciences, as Morgan was, he has not been celebrated as a similar pioneer in the field of anthropology.

The late anthropologist Arthur Einhorn lived in Lowville, the town where Hough's home is a national historic landmark. In his 1976 article, "Franklin B. Hough, An Incipient Anthropologist of the Early Nineteenth Century," Einhorn noted Hough's contributions to the field of archaeology, ethnography, ethnohistory, and linguistics:

> It is apparent that Hough touched in varying degrees on many aspects of what we today define as anthropology. With his historical orientation he ably used archives, did fieldwork, asked the right questions, gathered data, and presented a diachronic picture of a region. While he exhibited incipient anthropological behavior, his general interests were too varied to concentrate in one area.[10]

Einhorn wondered what might have been had Hough focused more on anthropology. But his enormous contributions to so many other fields, due to his varied interests, speak for themselves. The respect he continues to be shown as the premiere historian of New York's "North Country," a Civil War surgeon, and the "Father of Forestry," among other things, does not suggest he is lacking in reputation.

Today's Akwesasne is a thoroughly modern community. The dirt road and village lanes that Dr. Hough once walked upon have pavement and concrete curbs. The log houses are gone, but the old stone church still towers over the modern homes that take their place. There are government offices and small shops, and pedestrians share the road with vehicles of every sort. Time has not stood still for this community. A lot has happened since O-kwa-e-sen came calling, some of it just as eventful as the times he told us about. He would have found it fascinating.

That story is yet to be written. Those who would undertake such a task can learn a lot from the tireless efforts of Franklin Benjamin Hough.

1   "Franklin Benjamin Hough." Henry S. Graves. *Dictionary of American Biography, Vol. 9.* Dumas Malone, Editor. Charles Scribner's Sons, New York. 1932. 250-252. Wikipedia's entry for Franklin B. Hough contained more personal information. https://en.wikipedia.org/wiki/Franklin_B._Hough Hough's first wife's full name was Sarah Maria Hough, as found on her grave stone. https://www.findagrave.com/memorial/66241749/sarah-maria-hough
2   Franklin Benjamin Hough Papers, 1840-1885. SC7009. Finding Aid. Fred Bassett, Senior Librarian, Manuscripts and Special Collections. New York State Library, Albany, N. Y. April 1987. Revised October 1996.
3   Franklin B. Hough Papers, 1840-1885. SC7009. Box 8. File 4. Journal. Somerville, N. Y. 1852. New York State Library, Albany, N. Y.
4   *A History of St. Lawrence and Franklin Counties, New York, from the Earliest Period to the Present Time.* Franklin B. Hough. Albany: Little & Co. (1853) 110.
5   Correspondence. *St. Lawrence Republican.* May 25, 1852.
6   Hough, *History.* Ibid., 113.
7   Ibid. It is the ruffed grouse that makes a drumming sound with its wings, not the partridge. The partridge is not indigenous to the North America, whereas the ruffed grouse is common at Akwesasne.
8   Hough Papers, NYSL. Box 74. Item 1. History of St. Lawrence and Franklin Counties, vol. 1, annotated galley, 1853.
9   "A History of St. Lawrence and Franklin Counties." Franklin B. Hough. *The St. Lawrence Republican.* June 27, 1852.
10 "Franklin B. Hough: Incipient Anthropologist." Arthur Einhorn. *American Anthropology: The Early Years.* 1974 Proceedings of the American Ethnological Society. Robert G. Spencer, gen. ed. John V. Murra, ed. Princeton, New Jersey. (1974) 23-35.

"St. Regis"

from

A History of St. Lawrence and Franklin Counties, New York, from the Earliest Period to the Present Time
by Franklin B. Hough, A. M., M. D.,
Corresponding Member of the New York Historical Society
Albany: Little & Co., 53 State Street
1853

CHAPTER II.

It's situation – Origin – Labors of Father Gordon, a Jesuit – Legend of the bell – Capture of Deerfield – Their action in the revolution – Treaties of various Indian tribes – Account of the Seven Nations of Canada – Their proceedings previous to the treaties – Doings at the first treaty – Account of subsequent treaties – Part taken in the war – Great mortality – Internal organization – Present condition – Names of places – Lives of several Indian chiefs, ..

ST. REGIS.

On a beautiful and elevated point which juts into the St. Lawrence, where that river is crossed by the forty-fifth parallel of latitude, and between the mouths of the St. Regis and Racquette rivers, stands a dilapidated and antique looking village, whose massive and venerable church, with tin covered spire; whose narrow and filthy streets, and the general appearance of indolence and poverty of its inhabitants, and especially the accents of an unaccustomed language, almost convey to the casual visitor an impression that he is in a foreign land.

Such is the Indian village of St. Regis, whose origin and history we are about to relate. Its founders in selecting this site, evinced the possession of a taste at once judicious and correct, for it may well be questioned whether the shores of the St. Lawrence, abounding as they do in charming and lovely localities, affords anywhere a spot that will surpass this in beauty of scenery, or pleasantness of location. The village stands on a plain, moderately elevated above the river, which having for more than forty miles been broken by cascades and dangerous rapids, here becomes tranquil.

To the west, the ground swells into a gentle hill, which overlooks the village and river to a great distance; beyond which it again descends into a spacious plain, which for time immemorial has been the favorite ground for ball-playing, a pastime to which the natives are strongly attached, and in which they engage with much zeal.

The surrounding fields, are an open common, without separate enclosures, and are used as a public pasture by the inhabitants. Around the cabins of the villagers are usually small enclosures, devoted to the cultivation of corn, and culinary vegetables, which by the right of occupancy have come to be considered the private property of individuals, and as such are bought and sold among the natives, although the law recognizes no such private ownership, and holds them all as tenants in common, denying them the right of buying or selling land, except to the government. [111]

Opposite to the village, lay several very fertile and beautiful islands, which are owned and cultivated by the villagers, and upon which is raised the grain upon which they subsist, and the grass which serves for their cattle during the winter months. The public points in the village, and the summits of the hill are crowned by the cross, which indicates the religious faith of the greater part of the inhabitants, and reminds us that the colony owes its origin to a religious movement. Such is St. Regis, as it appears to the stranger; a village which under Anglo-Saxon enterprise, would ere this have attained a preeminence equal to any place on the river, but which now exhibits nothing but an air of decay and listlessness, peculiar of the Indian character, when it assumes the habits of civilization.

To one who traverses the streets, and observes the general aspect of its inhabitants, a leading trait will be notices as their controlling principle, and he will recognize INDOLENCE in every feature, and in every action.

With this preliminary, we will proceed with our account of the origin of this village, which was formed by an emigration from the mission at Caughnawaga, or the Sault Saint Louis, about nine miles above Montreal. The latter at a remote period of American history, in its turn, was formed by a portion of the tribe of Indians, who were induced by the French to emigrate to their vicinity and embrace the Catholic faith.

About a hundred and thirty years ago, three children, (a girl about twelve or thirteen years of age, and two younger brothers,) were playing together in a barn, in the town of Groton, Massachusetts, and being absent from the house longer than was expected, their mother became solicitous about them, and went to find them. The girl was lying on the floor, with a broken limb, and the boys were missing.

She related that seeing some Indians coming, she fled to the upper part of the barn, and fell by accident from the beams above, and that they had seized the two boys, and carried them away. The stealthy manner of this seizure, and, the time that had elapsed, forbade pursuit, with any hope of success, and the distracted parents were left to mourn the loss without consolation of hope. The probable motive for the seizure of these children, was the expectation that a bounty would be offered for their ransom; or perhaps they might be exchanged for French prisoners.

As afterwards appeared, these boys were taken by Caughnawaga Indians to their village near Montreal, where they were adopted as their own children, growing up in habits, manners, and language, as Indians, and in due time they married the daughters of chiefs of that tribe. The names of these chiefs were Sa-kon-en-tsi-ask and Ata-wen-ta. But they possessed the superiority of intellect, and enterprise, which belonged to their race, and this led to a series of petty quarrels, growing out of the jealousy of the young Indians of their age, which disquieted the village, and by the party spirit which it engendered, became a source of irritation and trouble in the settlement, and of anxiety on the part of the missionary, who labored in vain to reconcile the difficulties between them.

Failing in this, he advised the two young men, (one of whom they had named Ka-re-ko-wa) to remove with their families to a place by themselves, where they might enjoy tranquility, and be beyond the reach of annoyance from their comrades.

This advice they adopted; and taking with them their wives, and followed by their wives' parents, these four families departed in a bark canoe, with their effects, to seek in a new country, and in the secluded recesses of the forest, a home.

They coasted along up the St. Lawrence, and at length arrived at the delightful point on which the village of St. Regis now stands, where they landed and took possession.

The name of these youths, was TARBELL, and their descendants have always resided at St. Regis, and some of them have been distinguished as chiefs and head men of the tribe. One of these named Lesor Tarbell, and a son of his name, was a prominent chief, about fifty years since, and very much esteemed by the whites, for his prudence, candor, and great worth of character.

The name of Tarbell, is said to be very common in Groton, to this day.

Another traditional version of the account, differs in some particulars from that just related, and is as follows:

Three lads, and an elder sister, were playing together in a field, when they were surprised by a small party of Indians. One of the boys escaped, but the rest were seized, and marched that day about fourteen miles into the woods towards Canada, when it coming on dark, they came to a halt, and camped for the night. Thinking their prisoners secure, the Indians were less watchful than usual, and finally all fell asleep.

The girl, about twelve years old, kept awake, and seeing the rest asleep, her first thought was to awaken her brothers, and attempt to escape, [113] but fearing to disturb the Indians, should she attempt this, and thus prevent any possibility of escape, she crept carefully out from among them, and struck off in the direction of her home, which she at length reached after undergoing great hardship.

One of the lads on growing up went off to the north west, the other married, and subsequently with his wife, and one or two other families, moved off, and made the first settlement at St. Regis.

From the abundance of partridges which the thicket afforded, they called it, AK-WIS-SAS-NE "where the partridge drums," and this name it still retains.[1]

These families were living very peaceably together, and had made small clearings for corn fields, when they were joined by Father Anthony Gordon, a Jesuit from Caughnawaga, with a colony of these Indians in 1760.

The year of this settlement is known by the fact that they were met near Coteau du Lac, by Lord Amherst, who was descending the St. Lawrence, to complete the conquest of Canada. Gordon named the place ST. REGIS.

With the belief that a biographical sketch of this saint, would be acceptable to our readers, in connection with this account, we will take the liberty of inserting it as it is given by a catholic author.

> "JEAN FRANÇOIS REGIS, of the society of Jesus, was born Jan. 31, 1597, at Foncouverte, a village in the diocese of Narbonne in Languedoc, France, and was a descendant of an ancient and noble family. At an early age he became strongly impressed with religious sentiments, and while a youth, was one of the first to enter the Jesuit School at Beziers, where he led a very exemplary life. At the completion of his earlier studies, he undertook the charge of instructing menial servants in Tournon. In 1631, his studies being finished, he visited Foncouverte to [114] settle some family affairs, and there attracted much notice from the zeal with which he preached to the people, and solicited alms for the poor. He spent several years in missionary labors in France, always conspicuous for his zealous labors among; the poor, over whom he acquired great ascendency. This excited such persecution from the higher classes, that he solicited an appointment as a missionary to the Hurons, and Iroquois of Canada, but finally remained at home, much to his own disappointment. He continued his labors among the lower classes till his death, Dec. 31, 1640, at the age of 43 years, of which 26 were spent as a Jesuit. This tomb at La Louvase, in Languedoc, is regarded by the catholic population of France, as a shrine, and miracles are believed by them to have been performed at it. He was canonnised by pope Clement XII, in 1737, at the joint request of Kings Louis XV of France, and Philip V, of Spain, and of the clergy of France, assembled at Paris, in 1735. His festival occurs on the 10th of June. {*See Butler's Lives of the Saints*, 18*mo edition, vol. vi, p.* 261, 287.}

A painting of St. Regis, exists in the church at the mission of that name. It was presented by Charles X, as hereafter stated.

It is not known how long the four families had been residing at this place, when they were joined by the others, nor the numbers of the latter, further than the vague tradition that "there were many canoe loads." Probably they numbered several hundred souls.

The cause assigned for this emigration, was a desire to get the natives away from the corrupting influences of rum, and the train of vices to which they were particularly exposed from their proximity to Montreal. It was hoped that by this means being withdrawn from the temptations to which they were constantly liable, that a benefit would be derived.

In our account of Picquet's mission, we have seen that the missionaries at the Indian establishments felt and deplored the contaminating influences of the Europeans, and that the mission of St. Louis, was for this cause obliged to be moved some distance up the river, to get the natives out of the way of the moral miasm of Montreal, and the further emigration to St. Regis, may without doubt be attributed to the same cause.

In these acts, these ecclesiastics evinced a commendable regard for the moral welfare of their flocks, which challenges our admiration. In order that the end desired might not be defeated, it was considered essential that the new colony should be made up of a native population entirely; that no military post should form a part of them, and that traffic especially in spirituous liquors should be entirely interdicted.

Among the first duties of Gordon was the erection of a church, which was built of logs and covered with barks.

This humble and primitive temple of worship, was made to serve the double purpose of a church and a dwelling, and one end of the hut was partitioned off for the residence of their priest.

There being no bell, when the hour of worship arrived, an Indian went through the village from hut to hut, and announced with a loud voice [115] the hour that they might assemble for prayer. This practice reminds one of the Mahomedan custom, of proclaiming the hour of prayer from the Minarets of mosques.

In about two years this church was burned, and with it the first two years of the parish records.

The first record extant, bears date Feb. 2, 1762, when Margarita Theretia an Abenaki woman, married, and of unknown parentage, was baptized.

Since that date, the parish records are very perfect, they have been kept in the Latin and French languages.

Soon afterwards a small wooden church was erected on the ground now occupied by the priest's garden, which was furnished with a small cupola, and contained *a bell*.

It has been generally believed that this bell was the same as that taken in 1704, from Deerfield, in Massachusetts, but after careful inquiries, the author has arrived at the conclusion that that celebrated bell never was at St. Regis, but that it is none other the smaller of the two that hangs in the steeple of the church of St. Louis, in Caughnawaga.

About fifteen years since, a bell belonging to the church of St. Regis, was broken up at Ogdensburgh, for recasting, and the Indians were very jealous lest some part should be abstracted, and are said to have appointed some of their number to watch the operation, and see that every part was melted. This metal now forms a part of the larger bell in the church at St. Regis.

That the Deerfield bell could not have been taken directly to St. Regis, is evident, from the fact that fifty-six years elapsed between its capture and the founding of St. Regis.

The latter place was first begun by emigrants, in 1760, from Caughnawaga, the larger portion of the tribe remaining behind. It can scarcely be believed, that those that remained would allow themselves to be deprived of the only bell their church possessed, especially as the mission at the Saut St. Louis has been continued without interruption.

While on a visit to Caughnawaga, in October, 1852, the author found in the village a direct and consistent tradition of the bell, which is still used in their church, and among the records in the hands of the priest, a manuscript in the French language, of which we shall give a translation. The bell is a small one, and once possessed an inscription, which has been effaced.

The legend purports to have been found some fifteen years since, in an old English publication, and is regarded by the priest of the mission (Rev. Joseph Marcoux), who has for many years resided there, as in the main points reliable. If this view of the subject be correct, the legend loses none of its interest, except being transferred from the church of [116] St. Regis to the church of the Saut St. Louis. This village is on the south side of the St. Lawrence, opposite the village of Lachine, at the head of the Saut St. Louis, and nine miles above Montreal.

Legend of the Bell of Saut St. Louis (Caughnawaga), near Montreal.

"Father Nicolas having assembled a considerable number of Indians who had been converted to the catholic faith, had established them in the village which now bears the name of the Saul St. Louis, upon the River St. Lawrence. The situation of this village is one of the most magnificent which the banks of that noble river presents, and is among the most picturesque which the country contains.

The church stands upon a point of land which juts into the river, and its bell sends its echoes over the waters with a clearness which forms a striking contrast with the iron bells which were formerly so common in Canada, while the tin covered spire of the church, glittering in the sunlight, with the dense and gloomy forests which surround it, give a character of romance to this little church, and the legend of its celebrated bell.[2]

Father Nicolas having, with the aid of the Indians, erected a church and a belfry; in one of his sermons explained to his humble auditors, that a bell was as necessary to a belfry, as a priest to a church, and exhorted them to lay aside a portion of the furs that they collected in hunting, until enough was accumulated to purchase a bell, which could only be procured by sending to France. The Indians exhibited an inconceivable ardor in performing this religious duty, and the packet of furs was promptly made out, and forwarded to Havre, where an ecclesiastical personage was delegated to make the purchase. The bell was accordingly ordered, and in due time forwarded on board the *Grande Monarque*, which was on the point of sailing for Quebec.

It so happened that after her departure, one of the wars which the French and the English then so often waged sprung up, and in consequence the Grande Monarque never attained her destined port, but was taken by a New England privateer, brought into the port of Salem, where she was condemned as a lawful prize, and sold for the benefit of her captors.

The bell was purchased by the village of Deerfield, upon the Connecticut river, for a church then about being erected by the congregation of the celebrated Rev. John Williams.

When Father Nicolas received news of the misfortune, he assembled [117] his Indians, related to them the miserable condition of the bell, retained in purgatory in the hands of heretics, and concluded by saying, that it would be a most praise worthy enterprise to go and recover it.

This appeal had in it as it were a kind of inspiration, and fell upon its hearers with all the force of the eloquence of Peter the Hermit, in preaching the crusades.

The Indians deplored together the misfortune of their bell, which had not hitherto received the rite of baptism: they had not the slightest idea of a bell, but it was enough for them, that Father Nicolas, who preached and said mass for them, in their church, said that it had some indispensable use in the services of the church.

Some of their number, who had heard a bell, said that it could be heard beyond the murmur of the rapid, and that its voice was more harmonious than that of the sweetest songster of the grove, heard in the quiet stillness of evening, when all nature was hushed in repose. Their eagerness for the chase was in a moment suspended, and they assembled together in groups, and seated on the banks of the river, conversed on the unhappy captivity of their bell, and each brought forward his plan which he deemed most likely to succeed in effecting its recovery.

All were melancholy, and inspired with a holy enthusiasm; many fasted, and others performed severe penances to obtain the deliverance of the bell, or the palliation of its sufferings.

At length the day of its deliverance approached. The Marquis de Vaudreuil, Governor of Canada, resolved to send an expedition against the British colonies of Massachusetts and New Hampshire. The command of this expedition was given to Major Hertel de Rouville, and one of the priests of the Jesuit college, at Quebec, was sent to procure the services of Father Nicolas to accompany the expedition.

The Indians were immediately assembled in the church: the messenger was presented to the congregation, and Father Nicolas in a solemn discourse pointed to him as worthy of their veneration, from his being the bearer of glad tidings, who was about departing for his return to Quebec, to join the war. At the end of the discourse, the whole audience raised with one voice the cry of war, and demanded to be led to the place where their bell was detained by the heretics.

The savages immediately began to paint themselves in the most hideous colors, and were animated with a wild enthusiasm to join the expedition.

It was in the depth of winter when they departed to join the army of M. de Rouville, at Fort Chambly. Father Nicolas marched at their head, with a large banner, surmounted by a cross, and as they departed from their village, their wives and little ones, in imitation of women of the crusades, who animated the warriors of Godfrey of Bouillon, they sang a sacred hymn which their venerated priest had selected for the occasion.

They arrived at Chambly after a march of great hardship, at the moment that the French soldiers were preparing to start on their march up Lake Champlain.

The Indians followed in their rear, with that perseverance peculiar to their character. In this order the Indians remained, following in silence, until they reached Lake Champlain, where all the army had been ordered to rendezvous. This lake was then frozen and less covered by snow than the shores, and was taken as a more convenient route for the army. With their thoughts wrapped up in the single contemplation of the unhappy captivity of their bell, the Indians remained taciturn [118] during this pensive march, exhibiting no symptoms of fatigue or of fear; no regret for their families or homes, and they regarded with equal indifference on the one hand the interminable line of forest, sometimes black from dense evergreens, and in others white from loads of snow; and on the other, the bleak lines of rocks and deserts of snow and ice, which bordered their path. The French soldiers, who suffered dreadfully from fatigue and cold regarded with admiration the agility and cheerfulness with which the Indians seemed to glide over the yielding surface of the snow on their snow shoes.

The quiet endurance of the proselytes of Father Nicolas formed a striking contrast with the irritability and impatience of the French soldiers.

When they arrived at the point where now stands the city of Burlington, the order was given for a general halt, to make more efficient arrangements for penetrating through the forests to Massachusetts. In leaving this point, de Rouville gave to Father Nicolas the command of his Indian warriors, and took the lead of his own himself, with compass in hand, to make the most direct course for Deerfield. Nothing which the troops had thus far suffered could compare with what they now endured on this march through a wild country, in the midst of deep snow, and with no supplies beyond what they could carry.

The French soldiers became impatient, and wasted their breath in curses and complaints at the hardships they suffered, but the Indians animated by a zeal which sustained them above the sense of hardships, remained steadfast in the midst of fatigue, which increased with the severity of their sufferings.

Their custom of travelling in the forest had qualified them for these hardships which elicited the curses and execrations of their not less brave, but more irritable companions.

Some time before the expedition arrived at its destination, the priest Nicolas, fell sick from over exertion. His feet were worn by the labor of traveling, and his face torn by the branches which he neglected to watch in his eagerness to follow the troops.

He felt that he was engaged in a holy expedition, and recalling to mind the martyrdom of the saints, and the persecutions which they endured, he looked forward to the glory reserved for his reward for the sufferings which he might encounter in recovering the bell.

On the evening of February 20th, 1704, the expedition arrived within two miles of Deerfield without being discovered.

De Rouville here ordered his men to rest, and refresh themselves a short time, and he here issued his orders for attacking the town.

The surface of the snow was frozen, and crushed under the feet, but De Rouville with a remarkable sagacity, adopted a stratagem to deceive the inhabitants and the garrison.

He gave orders that in advancing to the assault, his troops should make frequent pauses, and then rush forward with rapidity: thus imitating the noise made in the forest by the irregular blowing of the wind among branches laden with ice.

The alarm was at length given, and a seven, combat ensued, which resulted in the capture of the town, and the slaughter or dispersion of the inhabitants, and the garrison.

This attack occurred in the night, and at daybreak the Indians who had been exhausted by the labors of the night, presented themselves before Father Nicolas in a body, and begged to be led to the bell, that they might by their homage prove their veneration for it. Their priest was greatly affected by this earnest request, and De Rouville and others [119] of the French laughed immoderately at it, but the priest wished not to discourage them in their wishes, and he obtained of the French chief permission to send one of his soldiers to ring it in the hearing of the Indians.

The sound of the bell in the stillness of it cold morning, and in the midst of the calmness of the forest, echoed clear and far, and fell upon the ears of the simple Indians, like the voice of an oracle. They trembled, and were filled with fear and wonder.

The bell was taken from the belfry, and attached to a pole in such a manner that four men could carry it, and in this way it was borne off with their plunder in triumph, the Indians glorying in the deliverance of this miraculous wonder.

But they shortly perceived it was too heavy a burden for the rugged route they pursued, and the yielding nature of the snows over which they traveled. Accordingly upon arriving at the point on the lake, where they had left it, they buried their cherished treasure, with many benedictions of Father Nicolas, until the period should arrive when they could transport it with more convenience.

As soon as the ice had disappeared, and the bland air of spring had returned, giving foliage to the trees, and the fragrance and beauty of flowers to the forests, lather Nicolas again assembled at the church, his Indian converts, to select a certain number of the tribe, who with the assistance of a yoke of oxen, should go and bring in the dearly prized bell.

During this interval, all the women and children of the Indian village, having been informed of the wonderful qualities of the bell, awaited its arrival with eagerness and impatience, and regarded its advent, as one of those events which but rarely mark the progress of ages. As the time approached, when the curious object should arrive, they were assembled on the hank of the river, and discoursing upon the subject, when far off in the stillness of the twilight, there was heard from the depths of the forest, a sound, which from being feeble and scarcely audible, became every moment louder. Every one listened, when presently the cry arose, *it is the bell! it is the bell!!* and in a moment after, the oxen were seen emerging from the wood, surrounded by a group of Indians, and bearing the precious burden on a pole between them. They had hung upon the beam and around the bell, clusters of wild flowers and leaves, and the oxen were adorned with garlands of flowers. Thus marching in triumph, Father Nicolas entered his village, more proud of his success, and received with more heartfelt joy, than a Roman general returning in triumph from the conquest of nations.

From this triumphal march in the midst of the quiet of the evening, which was broken only by the murmur of the rapid, softened by the distance arose the shouts of rejoicing, us the cortege entered the village, and the idol bell was deposited in the church. Every one gratified his eager curiosity by examining the strange and musical metal, and the crusade had been crowned with unqualified success.

In due time it was raised to its place in the belfry, and has ever since, at the accustomed hours, sent its clear tones over the broad bosom of the St. Lawrence, to announce the hour of prayer and lapse of time, and although its tones are shrill and feeble beside its modern companion, they possess a music, and call up an association, which will long give an interest to the church of the Saut St. Louis, at the Indian village of Caughnawaga."

Mrs. Sigourney, whose chaste and elegant poetry, is justly admired for [120] the melody of its versification, as well as its delicacy of sentiment, has written a poetical account of this legend, which we will here take the liberty of quoting. It will he seen that it is in accordance with the erroneous belief of its being carried to the St. Regis, the inconsistency of which has been above stated.

THE BELL OF ST. REGIS.

The red men came in their pride and wrath,
Deep vengeance fired their eye,
And the blood of the white was in their path,
And the flame from his roof rose high.
Then down from the burning church they tore
The bell of tuneful sound,
And on with their captive train they bore,
That wonderful thing toward their native shore,
The rude Canadian bound.
But now and then with a fearful tone,
It struck on their startled ear—
And sad it was 'mid the mountains lone,
Or the ruined tempest's muttered moan,
That terrible voice to hear.
It seemed like the question that stirs the soul,
Of its secret good or ill;
And they quaked as its stern and solemn toll,
Reechoed from rock to hill.
And they started up in their broken dream,
Mid the lonely forest shade,
And thought that they heard the dying scream,
And saw the blood of slaughter stream
Afresh through the village glade.
Then they sat in council, those chieftains old,
And a mighty pit was made,
Where the lake with its silver waters rolled,
They buried the bell 'neath the verdant mould,
And crossed themselves and prayed.
And there till a stately powow came,
It slept in its tomb forgot,
With a mantle of fur, and a brow of flame,
He stood on that burial spot.
They wheeled the dunce with its mystic round
At the stormy midnight hour,
And a dead man's hand on his breast he hound,
And invoked, ere he broke that awful ground,
The demons of pride and power.
Then he raised the bell with a nameless rite,
Which none but himself might tell,

> In blanket and bear-skin he bound it tight,
> And it journeyed in silence both day and night,
> So strong was that magic spell.
> It spake no more, till St. Regis's tower
> In northern skies appeared,
> And their legends extol that powow's power
> Which lulled that knell like the poppy flower,
> As conscience now slumbereth a little hour
> In the cell of a heart that's seared."

The act of 1802, which will be hereafter given, empowered the trustees then created, to purchase a bell, and it is very probable that this may have been the one that was broken up, and recast a few years since. The earliest settlers of the country agree in this statement that a bell was in the church at a very early period, and that the village presents now very nearly the same aspect that it did half a century since; with the difference that it now is more decayed and neglected than then.

The capture of Deerfield, divested of romance and tradition, occurred under the following circumstances.

"In the evening of the 39th of February, 1704, Major Hertel de Rouville, with 200 French, and 142 Indians, after a tedious march of between 2 and 300 miles through deep snows, arrived at an elevated pine forest about two miles north of the village, (now called Petty's plain,) bordering Deerfield meadow, where they lay concealed till after midnight. Finding all quiet, and the snow being covered with a crust sufficient to support the men, Rouville left his snow shoes and packs at the foot of the elevation, and, crossing Deerfield river, began his march through an open meadow before daylight, with the utmost caution, which however, was unnecessary, for the guard had retired to rest, a little before daylight. Arriving at the north west quarter of the fort, where the snow had drifted in many places nearly to the top of the palisades, the enemy entered the place, and found all in a profound sleep. Parties detached in various directions, broke into the houses, and dragged the astonished people from their beds, and whenever resistance was made they were generally killed. A party forced the door of the house of the Rev. Mr. John Williams, who awakened by the noise, seized a pistol from his bed tester and snapped it at one of the Indians who were entering the room. He was seized, bound, and kept standing in his shirt for nearly an hour. His house in the meantime was plundered, and two of his children, with a black female servant, were murdered before the door. They then permitted him and Mrs. Williams, with five other children to put on their clothes.

The house of Capt. John Sheldon was attacked, but as the door at which the Indians attempted to enter was firmly bolted, they found it difficult to penetrate. They then perforated it with their tomahawks, and thrusting through a musket, fired and killed the captain's wife, as she was rising from a bed in an adjoining room. The captain's son and wife, awakened by the assault, leaped from a chamber window at the [122] east end of the house, by which the latter strained her ancle, and was seized by the Indians, but the husband escaped to the woods and reached Hatfield. After gaining possession of the house, which was one of the largest in the place, the enemy reserved it as the depot for the prisoners, as they were collected from other parts of the village. The whole number made prisoners was 112, and the number of killed was 47. Having collected the prisoners, plundered and set fire to the buildings, Rouville left the place when the sun was about an hour high. Every building within the fort was reduced to ashes, except the meeting house, and that of Captain Sheldon, which was the last one fired, and saved by the English, who assembled immediately after the enemy left the place. The night following the attack, the enemy encamped in the meadow, in what is now Greenfield, about four miles from Deerfield village, where by clearing away the snow, and constructing slight cabins of brush, the prisoners were as comfortably lodged as circumstances would admit. The second day of the journey, Mrs. Williams, who had been confined but a few weeks previous, became exhausted through fatigue, and proving burdensome, her Indian master sank his tomahawk into her head, and left her dead at the foot of a hill near Green river. The march of the captives, on the Connecticut river continued several days without any incident of note, except now and then murdering an exhausted captive, and taking off his scalp.

  At the mouth of White river, Rouville divided his force into several parties; that which Mr. Williams accompanied proceeded down Onion river to Lake Champlain, and from thence into Canada. After his arrival there he was treated with civility and even humanity. In 1706, a flag ship was sent to Quebec, and Mr. Williams and fifty seven other captives was redeemed and brought to Boston. All the surviving children of Mr. Williams were redeemed with the exception of his daughter Eunice, who was left behind, being about ten years old."[3]

She adopted the language, dress and religion of the Indians, and married one of the Caughnawagua tribe. She subsequently visited her New England relatives, but could not be induced to abandon her adopted people. Capt. Thomas Williams, at St. Regis, of whom we give a biographical notice, in this work, and whose name occurs on most of the treaties which the St. Regis Indians have held with the state, was a descendant of this daughter of the Rev. John Williams.

  During the revolutionary war a considerable portion of the St Regis and a part of the Caughnawaga Indians joined the British; others led by Colonel Louis Cook, of whom we shall give a particular account in the following pages, joined the American cause.

Concerning the history of the village during this period we have been unable to obtain any knowledge.

At the opening of the revolutionary war, the continental cause received much injury from the influence of the Johnson families, in Tryon county, and especially from Sir John Johnson, a baronet, and son of Sir [123] William, who secretly instigated the Indians to hostilities, and created much mischief on the frontier.

To prevent this calamity it was thought advisable by Gen. Schuyler, to arrest Sir John, and thus put it out of his power to do further mischief.

Accordingly in May, 1776, Col. Dayton, with a part of his regiment then on its way to Canada, was sent to prosecute this enterprise.[4]

Receiving timely notice of this, from his tory friends in Albany, he hastily assembled a large number of his tenants, and others, and prepared for retreat, which he successfully accomplished, taking to the woods and avoiding the route of lake Champlain, from fear of falling into the hands of the Continentals, supposed to be assembled in that direction, he struck deeper into the woods, by way of the head waters of the Hudson, and descended the Raquette to Canada. Their provisions were soon gone, their feet became sore from traveling, and numbers were left to be picked up by the Indians, sent back for their relief. After nineteen days of hardships, which have had few parallels in our history, they reached Montreal. So hasty was their flight, that the family papers were buried in the garden, and nothing was taken, but such articles as were of prime necessity. His extensive family estates were confiscated, and he thenceforth became a most active loyalist, and the scourge of the Mohawk settlement during the remainder of the war.

Some historians have supposed that an expedition of Mohawk Indians was despatched from Montreal to meet Sir John; and Brant long after, in rehearsing the exploits of his tribe, during the Revolution, says: "We then went in a body to a town, then in possession of the enemy, and rescued Sir John Johnson, bringing him fearlessly through the streets."[5]

When on a visit of historical inquiry, at the Indian village of St Regis, in June 1852, the author obtained a tradition, that that people sent numbers of their warriors to meet the fugitives, carrying parched corn and sugar to preserve them from perishing, until they could reach the Canadian settlements.

We will return to the history of Gordon, and briefly trace the progress of the catholic mission, and then present the series of events which have marked the history of the village.

There is a tradition that a tract of land on the east side of the river, and extending up two miles, was granted to the priest as a support, [124] but this claim has not been asserted, nor is it known that there is any written evidence of the fact.

Father Gordon's health failing, he went back to Caughnawaga, in 1775, where he died in 1777. The mission was then without a priest, five or six years. Father Denaut,

Oct. 1784, from the Cedars, and Lebrun, a Jesuit from Caughnawaga, in January and September 1785, appear from the parish records, to have visited the place, to administer religious rites.

Denaut subsequently became Bishop of Quebec, and the mission at the Cedars was supplied by L'Archambault, who also occasionally visited St. Regis, in the absence of an established priest.

In December, 1785, Roderick McDonnell, a Scotch Priest, succeeded, and remained till 1806, when he died. He is interred under the choir of the church. Being a part of the time sick, he was assisted by A. Van Felsen, of Quebec, who was here from May 5, 1800, till September 30, 1802.

During McDonnell's residence, the present church was erected in 1791 and 1792, at first without a belfry.

The frame church was then standing, but soon after demolished. The present church is a massive stone building, of ancient and venerable appearance, the walls nearly four feet thick, the windows high, and a door in the middle of the sash, for ventilation, after a custom prevalent in Canada. Across the end of the church opposite the door is a railing, and beyond and elevated above the floor of the church, is an ample space for the altar, and the various fixtures of the catholic worship. The altar is unusually decorated with gilding and ornaments, and the interior of the church is adorned with paintings and prints of religious subjects. The history of two of these paintings will be given elsewhere.

A gallery extends across the end of the church over the door, for the accommodation of strangers and others, and in the body of the church near the wall, are a few seats for the singers. The greater part of the Indians, during worship, kneel or sit upon the floor, and the appearance presented to a stranger by the striking uniformity of dress and attitude, which he notices on first visiting the church during service, is very impressive.

Preaching is performed in the Mohawk dialect of the Iroquois language every sabbath, and all the ritual of the catholic church is observed with scrupulous care.

McDonnell was immediately succeeded by Father Rinfret, a Canadian, who remained a year, when he removed to Caughnawaga, where he died a few years later. He was followed by Jean Baptiste Roupe, who arrived in the fall of 1807, and remained till the last of July, 1812. He was taken a prisoner in his house, at the affair which happened at St. Regis, in the fall [125] of 1812. He was succeeded by Joseph Marcoux, of Caughnawaga, who left in March, 1819, when Nicholas Dufresne, held office of priest till 1825. He then removed to the Sulpician Seminary, at Montreal, and has been for ten or twelve years a missionary at Two Mountains, 36 miles northward from Montreal.

In 1825, Joseph Valle arrived, and continued in the office till the fall of 1832, when he was succeeded by the Rev. Francis Marcoux, the present missionary. Father Valle died in 1850, below Quebec.

The sovereignty of the soil of the northern part of the state, was anciently vested in the Mohawks, who, from the earliest period of authentic history, exercised jurisdiction over it. Upon the emigration of a part of this people to Canada, they claimed to carry with them the title from whence the villagers of St. Regis, asserted their claim to the northern part of the state, in common with the other Mohawk Nations of Canada.

The Mohawks it is well known, espoused the royal cause in the revolution, through the influence of the Johnson family, and emigrated to Grand river in Upper Canada, where they still reside on lands given them by government. Whatever title to the land remained with them, was surrendered by the following treaty, held at Albany, March 29, 1795.[6]

"At a treaty, held under the authority of the United States, with the Mohawk nation of Indians, residing in the province of Upper Canada, within the dominions of the King of Great Britain. Present, the Hon. Isaac Smith, Commissioner appointed by the United States, to hold this treaty, Abram Ten Broeck, Egbert Benson and Ezra L'Hommedieu, agents for the State of New York, Captain Joseph Brant and Capt. John Deserontyon, two of the said Indians, and deputies to represent the said nation at this treaty.

The said agents having in the presence, and with the approbation of the said commissioners, proposed to, and adjusted with the said deputies, the compensation as hereinafter mentioned, to be made to the said nation for their claim to be extinguished by this treaty, to all lands within the said state. It is thereupon finally agreed and done, between the said nations and the said deputies, as follows, that is to say: The said agents do agree to pay to the said deputies, the sum of one thousand dollars for the use of the said nation, to be by the said deputies paid over to, and distributed among the persons and families of the said nation, according to their usages, the sum of five hundred dollars, for the expenses of the said deputies, during the time they have attended this treaty, and the sum of one hundred dollars for their expenses in returning, and for carrying the said sum of one thousand dollars to where the said nation resides. And the said agents do accordingly for, and in the name of the People of the State of New York, pay the said three several sums to the deputies, in the presence of the said commissioners. And the said deputies do agree to cede and release, and these present witness that they accordingly do, for and in the name of the said nation, in consideration of the said compensation, cede and release to the people of the state of New York, forever, all the right or title of the said nation, to lands within the said state, and the claim of the said nation to lands within the said state, is hereby wholly and finally extinguished.[126]

In testimony whereof, the said commissioner, the said agents, and the said deputies, have hereunto, and to two other acts of the same tenor and date, one to remain with the United States, one to remain with the said State, and one delivered to the said deputies, to remain with the said nation, set their hands and seals at the city of Albany, in the said State, the twenty-ninth

day of March, in the year one thousand seven hundred and ninety-five."
    Signed, sealed, and acknowledged.
    (*Copied from a MSS. volume entitled "Indian Deeds, and Treaties,* 1712—1810," *in the office of Secretary of Slate, at Albany. Page* 187.)

Treaties with the Indians for their lands, were by a provision of the first constitution of the state, adopted April 20, 1777, reserved to the legislature. It was therein ordained,

"That no purchases or contracts for the sale of lands, made since the fourteenth day of October, 1775, or which may hereafter be made, with or of the said Indians, within the limits of this state, shall be binding on the said Indians, or deemed valid, unless made under the authority, and with the consent of the Legislature of the state." (*Laws of New York. vol. i, p.* 16, 1813.)

By an act passed April 4, 1801, it was provided:

"That if any person should without the authority and consent of the Legislature, in any manner or form, or on any terms whatsoever, purchase any lands within this state, of any Indian or Indians residing therein, or make any contract with any Indian or Indians, for the sale of any lands within this state, or shall in any manner, give, sell, demise, convey or otherwise dispose of any such lands or any interest therein, or offer to do so, or shall enter on, or take possession of, or to settle on any such lands by pretext or color of any right, or interest, in the same, in consequence of any such purchase, or contract, made since the 14th day of October, 1775, and not with the authority, and consent of the Legislature of this state, every such person shall in every such case, he deemed guilty of a public offence, and shall on conviction thereof, before any court having cognizance of the same, forfeit and pay to the people of this stole, two hundred and fifty dollars, and be further punished by fine and imprisonment, at the discretion of the court."

The state being accordingly the only party whom the Indians could recognize, to them they applied for the settlement of their claims, to lands in the northern part of the state.
    These claims were based upon ancient and primitive occupation, and especially upon the rights which they conceived they had, for compensation for services which some of them, particularly Colonel Louis Cook, their head chief had rendered in the war. The nature and amount of these services we will give in our notice of that chief.
    In 1780, he applied for a confirmation of a tract of land, in the present town of Massena, which he claimed was his own individual right, and this was subsequently confirmed to him by the Legislature.
    In 1792, the Caughnawaga and St. Regis tribes, claiming to represent the Seven

Nations of Canada, sent a deputation to the governor of the [127] state of New York, to assert their claims, but this embassy produced no action in their favor.

As we shall have frequent occasion to allude to these Seven Nations, it would be well to understand who and what they were, but here our knowledge is less definite than might be desired, especially in relation to the origin of the term, and of the league or combination of tribes of which it consisted.

They appear to have been made up of several of the detached settlements of Iroquois emigrants from New York, and of Algonquins, &c., whom the catholic missionaries had domiciliated and settled in villages.

The St. Regis branch did not originally form, it is said, one of the seven, which consisted according to the Rev. F. Marcoux, of an Iroquois, an Algonquin, and a Nipessing nation at the Lake of Two Mountains, an Iroquois tribe at Caughnawaga, the Oswegatchie tribe of Iroquois at La Presentation, a colony of Hurons at Lorett, nine miles north of Quebec, and a settlement of Abenekis at St. François, below Montreal, near the Sorel.

After the breaking up of the French at La Presentation, and the partial dispersion of the Oswegatchies, tradition relates, that a grand council was held, and it was therein resolved, that the St. Regis, who had formed a part of the Caughnawagas, at the formation of the league, should take the place of the scattered tribe, and they thenceforth represented them in the assemblies.

According to the gentlemen above mentioned, the tribes which represented the Seven Nations, have at present the following numbers, (June, 1852).

At the Lake of Two Mountains, of Iroquois, ... 250
At the Lake of Two Mountains, Algonquins and Nipessing, together, 250
At Caughnawaga, of Iroquois,...1300
At St. Regis,... 1100
At Lorett, of Hurons, a very few.

At St. François of Abenakis, a few only. The numbers of the two latter were not known.

Failing in their first negotiation with the state, the St. Regis people prosecuted their claims, and in 1793 again appeared, by their deputies, at Albany, and laid their case before the governor, but without success. The following credentials are without date, but are believed to have been those furnished these Indians on this occasion:

"The Chiefs at Cak-ne-wa-ge, head of the Seven Nations.
To our brother, Commander and Governor, *Ni-haron-ta-go-wa,*
George Clinton, at the State of New York. Brother, this is what we [128] agreed upon, that we should have councils and conversations together, of peace and unity.

Now brother, we beg that you will pay attention that you can take the matter into good consideration betwixt yon and us. We have sent the bearers, which will give you to understand our real minds and meaning, which is:

Thomas Aragrente,
Thomas Tharagwanegen,
Lumen Tiatoharongiven,
William Gray,
Atthi naton.

All the chiefs' compliments to you, and beg you will not let the bearers want for victuals or drink, as much as may be for their good.

Te gan ni ta sen,	On sa te gen,
O na tri tsia wa ne,	On wa ni en te ni,
Sga na wa te,	Tha na ha,
Te ha sen,	Sga hen to wa ro ne,
Tha ia iak ge,	Si no he se,
Tha hen the tha,	Sa ie gi sa ge ne,
Ga ron ia ra gon.	Ga ron ia tsi go wa."

(Signed by their marks.)

This negotiation also failed in its object, and the deputies returned home in disappointment.

In the winter of 1793-4, Colonel Louis, with three other warriors, again repaired to Albany, to get, if possible, some specific time designated, when the state would meet with them for their claim. They held an interview with the governor, but he declined at that time any negotiations with them on the subject, without referring their case to the legislature.

The journal of the assembly, for 1794 (page 106), contains the following record in relation to the St. Regis Indians:

"Mr. Havens, in behalf of Mr. Foote, from the committee appointed to take into consideration the communication made to this house by His Excellency the Governor, relative to the St. Regis Indians, reported that they have enquired into the several circumstances connected with the claim of the said Indians to certain lands within the jurisdiction of this state, and are of the opinion that it will be necessary to appoint commissioners to treat with the said Indians, and to authorize them, by law, to extinguish the said claim, or to take such measures relative to the said business, as shall be most beneficial to this state, and to the United States."

The following was the message of the governor, above alluded to. It was reported on the 21st of February of that year:

"GENTLEMEN,
You will receive with this message the conclusion of my conference with the Oneida Indians, and a copy of an additional speech of the Cayugas,

and my answer thereto.

  I also transmit to you a speech made to me by Colonel Lewis, of St. Regis, who, with three other warriors, arrived here some days ago, as a [129] deputation from the chiefs of the seven nations, of Lower Canada. You will perceive by my answer to them, that I have, for the reasons therein mentioned, declined entering into conference with them on the subject of their deputation, other than that of receiving their communication, which is now submitted to the consideration of the Legislature.

GEO. CLINTON.

So far as we have been able to learn, the course advised by the committee was not adopted, and no encouragement was given the deputies further than the indefinite and unsatisfactory assurance that their claim should be examined at as early a day as might be consistent.

What the probable result would be, might perhaps be surmised, when we consider, that the state had already patented to Macomb and his associates the territory claimed by these Indians, reserving only a tract equal to six miles square, near the Indian village. It is very probable, that the Indians did not know of the sale, and still honestly believed themselves entitled to a large tract in the north part of the state.

In December, 1794, they again appeared at Albany to urge their claim. The governor appears to have been absent, and a communication intended for him was delivered to John Taylor, of Albany, who addressed the governor the following letter, inclosing that which he had received from the Indians:

ALBANY, 10th January, 1795.

"SIR:

  The enclosed message was delivered me by one of the men who came down last winter, Col. Louis, and attended the Legislature at this place, on the subject of their lands. He says he was deputed by the Seven Nations for that purpose, and had directions to proceed to New York, if I could not do the business. As a journey to New York would have been attended by expense to the state, and trouble to you, I promised to transmit the message, and recommended him to return home.

    I am your Excellency's
      most obedient servant,
        JOHN TAYLOR."

The letter referred to in the foregoing, was as follows:

"ALBANY, December, 1794.

NEWATAGHSA LEWEY:

Brother: The Seven Nations of Upper Canada are still of the same mind as they were when you spoke with them last winter; but they expected you would have met them this summer on the business that they came about to your great council last winter. They suppose that the business of the war, which was expected, prevented your meeting of them. They hope you will attend to the business, and meet them, as you promised, as early as possible next summer, as they are still of the same mind they were when they spoke to you, and expect you are so likewise."

The governor accordingly appointed Samuel Jones, Ezra L'Hommedieu, N. Lawrence, Richard Varick, Egbert Benson, John Lansing, Jr., and James Watson, commissioners, to hold an interview with the Indians [130] to settle some preliminaries with them, but without the power to treat definitely with them on the subject.

The following is the result of their negotiations, which was addressed to Governor Clinton:

"NEW YORK, 6 March, 1795.

SIR:

In consequence of your Excellency's appointment of us to that trust, we have this morning had an interview with the eleven Indians now in the city, from the nation or tribe, distinguished as the St. Regis Indians, or the Indians of the Seven Nations of Canada, and Colonel Lewis, one of their number, as their speaker, made a speech to us, purporting that during the last winter, they had come to Albany while the Legislature was sitting there, and made known their desire that a future meeting might be appointed, in order to treat, and finally conclude and settle with them respecting their right and claim to lands within the limits of this state; that they had returned home with what they received, as assurances that such future meeting would have been appointed; that they had waited in expectation of it during the whole of the last season; that they are not authorized to treat or conclude therefor; that the only object of their present journey is again to propose such meeting, when all the chiefs will attend, so that whatever may then be agreed upon, should be binding on all the tribes.

To this speech we have deferred giving an answer, supposing it most fit that we should previously be informed of the sense of the Legislature on the subject; it being most probably the interest of both houses, that the act of the 5th instant should be limited to an agreement or an arrangement to be made at this time, and with the Indians who are now present.

We have the honor to be, sir, with due respect, your most obedient, humble servants.

SAMUEL JONES,   RICHARD VARICK,
EZRA L'HOMMEDIEU,   EGBERT BENSON,

      N. Lawrence,   John Lansing, Jun.,
        James Watson.
        His Excellency, Governor Clinton."

The following were the speeches exchanged on this occasion:

"*Brothers:*

Since that parchment was delivered us, which you will remember, as well us some of our chiefs now present, for it was during the Indian war when we were employed to make peace, and we made known to the other Indians the promises therein contained, and they made peace, we have claimed payment for those lands by means of that parchment, and he has promised to do us justice.

Brothers:

With respect to our affairs with you, we rest upon your word; you have promised to do us justice, and we depend upon it.

We have requested justice with the king, and he has promised to have a meeting, and to do us justice in the summer, and therefore we wish a settlement of our matter with you sooner. For if we should be engaged in settling that affair, and you should call upon us at the same time, we should have our hands full. Therefore, we wish a settlement with you first.

Brothers:

When we have made this settlement with you, we shall live with you like brothers, and not say that you have wronged us." [131]

To the foregoing speech, the agents made the following reply:

"*Brothers:*

We have listened to what you have now told us.

Brothers:

The king and we are friends and neighbors, but he can not take a part in any business between you and us, nor can we take a part in any business between him and you.

Brothers:

You may rely on our promise, that the proposed meeting between you and us shall take place, but we can not now fix the time more precisely than we have done, for we do not know when we shall be ready, and if we should now fix a time, and should not then be ready, you would come to the place, and not finding us there, you would think we meant to deceive you.

Brothers:

We will certainly meet you as soon as we can, and we will give you seasonable notice.

NEW YORK, 11th March, 1795.
RICHARD VARICK,   EGBERT BENSON,
JAMES WATSON,   EZRA L'HOMMEDIEU.
SAMUEL JONES.

The foregoing communication of the agents was transmitted to the Legislature on the 7th of March, 1795, by the governor, in the following message.

"Gentlemen:
With this message you will receive a communication from the agents appointed to confer with the representatives of the St. Regis Indians, which will necessarily require your immediate attention.

The concurrent resolution of the 3d instant, only refers to the accommodation of the Indians while in the city, and neither provides for the customary gratuities, nor the expenses arising from their journey here and their return.

It must readily occur to you that no legislative direction exists with respect to the greater part of the expense incident to this occasion. I also transmit a letter from some of the chiefs of the Onondaga nation, respecting the agreement made with them in 1793, by the commissioners appointed for the purpose."

GEO. CLINTON.

Greenwich, 7 March, 1795.

In pursuance of this advice the following resolution was introduced in the senate and passed.

"*Resolved.* That his Excellency the Governor, be requested to direct that suitable accommodations be provided for twelve St. Regis Indians, who are expected in town this afternoon, on business relative to the claims on the State, and that the Legislature will make provision for defraying the expense."

On the 9th of March, 1795, the resolution of the senate was referred to the assembly, and the following record appears on their journal.

"*Resolved.* As the sense of both houses of the Legislature, that it is advisable a future meeting should be appointed by his Excellency the [132] Governor, to be held with the Indians, generally known and distinguished as the Indians of St. Regis, in order to treat, and finally to agree with the said Indians touching any right or claim which they may have, to any lands within the limits of this state; and further, that his Excellency the Governor, in addition to the request contained in the concurrent resolution of both houses, of the third instant, be also requested to cause the twelve Indians mentioned in said concurrent resolution, to be furnished with such sum of money as may be requisite to defray the expenses of their journey to this city, and on their return home, and also that his Excellency the Governor, be requested to cause such presents or gratuities he shall deem proper to be given to the said Indians, in behalf of this state, and that the Legislature will make the requisite provision for carrying these resolutions into effect."

Ordered. That the consideration of the said resolutions be postponed until to-morrow.

The agents appointed by the Governor, held another interview with the Indians, and the speeches that were exchanged on the occasion are preserved, and were as follows:

Speech of the Agents for the State of New York to Colonel Louis, and other St. Regis Indians.

"Brothers:

When we met you, a few days ago, on your arrival in this city, we told you our chief the Governor, was sick, and that he had appointed us to meet you in his stead.

Brothers:

We then also bid you welcome, and which we now repeat to you.

Brothers:

You then told us that you had come to see us, and only to propose that there should be another meeting between us and you, when all your chiefs would attend, and treat and settle with us about land, which is within our state, and which you say belongs to you.

Brothers:

This was the substance of what you then told us, and we have told it to our chief the Governor, and our council the Legislature, and they have listened to it, and have directed us to tell you that they very willingly assent to what you have proposed, and that a message will be sent to you during the next summer, to inform you of the time and place, when, and where, we will meet you on the business, and we can now only promise, that the place will be as near where you live as conveniently may be, so as to save you the trouble of a long journey, and that the time will not he later in the next fall than when the travelling is good.

Brothers:

We wish you in the mean time to possess your minds in peace, for it is as much our wish as it is yours, that the business should be talked over and settled between you and us, in friendship and integrity, as between brothers, for as we do not desire any land which belongs to you without paying you

for it, so we hope you do not desire we should pay you for that which does not belong to you.
Brothers:
    We now bid you farewell, for the present, and wish you a safe journey home, and that we may meet each other again in peace and in health, at the intended future meeting."[133]

To this speech of the commissioners the St. Regis Indians through Colonel Louis, their speaker, replied as follows:

"*Brothers:*
    It is usual when brothers meet, if it is even the next day, to thank Providence for preserving each of them, so as to meet again.
Brothers:
    We are very thankful that you have taken so much pity on your brothers, who have come so great a distance to see you, that they were almost barefooted and uncovered, and you at our first arrival in the city, gave us a pair of shoes and hat each, for which we are thankful.
Brothers:
    When we first arrived here, we told you the business we had come upon, and which we had come upon several seasons before, and particularly last winter. You then promised that you would meet us, but you have not done it.
    We have business at home as well as you, brothers, and for that reason we request you to consider about the matter deliberately.
Brothers:
    We think it is a long time hence that you have fixed upon. We told you when we came, that we had other business with the king, who also is on our lands. All the other nations to the westward are concerned in that business, and I expect I have that to see to, as they depend on my council. If that should take place at the same time as yours, it will be inconvenient, we therefore wish to have our business with you first settled, before we settle with the king.
Brothers:
    We were at Albany when you received the speech of the king; I then told you the minds of our chiefs upon that subject, for I know it. You told us then your minds were to do us justice, and that made our breasts cool. We returned home and told the king to perform the promise he had made to us.

{Here Colonel Louis produced a printed proclamation in parchment, by the late Sir William Johnson.}

For this reason we expect our matters with you first settled. For the king told us, that about midsummer he would come and settle with us for the lands of ours which he had possessed and improved.

Then, brothers, we shall be able to come and inform you how we have settled with him."

The Legislature by an act passed March 5, 1795, provided,

"That it shall and may be lawful, for the person administering the government of this State, either by himself, or by such agent or agents as he shall thereunto appoint, to make such agreement and arrangements with the Indians of St. Regis, or with the representatives of the said Indians, respecting their claims to any lands within this State, or any part or parts thereof, as shall tend to ensure their good will and friendship to the people of the United States, and to extinguish any, and every such claim, and in such manner as he or such agents so to be appointed may think proper, but no such agreement or arrangement by such agents shall be valid, unless ratified and confirmed by the person administering the government of this State, any thing in the ' act relative to Indians resident within the State' passed the 27th of March, 1794, to the contrary hereof notwithstanding." [134]

The act here referred to, was a law relative to the Indians resident within the state, which appointed the Governor, with William North, John Taylor, Abraham Van Vechten, Abraham Ten Broek, Peter Gansevoort, Jr., and Simeon Dewitt, trustees for the Indians within the state, and for each and every tribe of them, with full power to make such agreements and arrangements with the tribes of central New York, respecting their lands, as shall tend to produce an annual income to the said Indians, and to insure their good will and friendship to the people of the United States.

No grants were to be made by the Indians, except to the state.

They were further empowered to treat with any other Indians, for any other lands within the state, and the consideration paid for the extinguishment of these claims, was to be paid at the time of making the contract, or within one year thereafter.

Commissioners were again appointed, who met the deputies at Fort George, at the south end of Lake George, in September, 1795, where an interview was held, but without arriving at satisfactory results, or an agreement between the parties. We have not been able to procure the speeches that were made on this occasion, or what transpired between them, further than the intimations contained in the following pages.

The results were communicated by the agents of the state to Governor Jay, who in the month of January, transmitted the following message to the legislature.

GENTLEMEN:
"I have now the honor of laying before you the proceedings at a treaty

with the Indians, denominated the Seven Nations of Canada, comprising those usually denominated the St. Regis Indians, held at the south end of Lake George, in this State, on the 26th day of September last, with a letter of the 2d instant, from the agents who were appointed to attend it on the part of the State.

It appears from the above mentioned letter, that the expenses incident to the said treaty have been paid, and the accounts duly audited and passed, except the allowance usually made by the United States to the commissioners whom they employ for holding treaties with Indians.

The compensation due to the said agents for their services, still remain to be ascertained and ordered by the Legislature.

NEW YORK, 23d January, 1796.

JOHN JAY."

On the 26th of March, 1796, the governor transmitted to the legislature a message, accompanying a letter from the department of war, dated the 19th inst., together with the report of the secretary of state, on the subject of claims made by the Indians called the Seven Nations of Canada, to lands within the state.

This message with the accompanying papers, was referred to the committee of the whole. [135]

This was subsequently referred to a joint committee of the two houses, who reported on the 1st of April, as follows:

"That although the several matters stated by the agents of this State to the said Indians, at the late treaty held with them at Lake George, are to be relied on as true, and to be considered as sufficient to prevent the supposition that the said Indians have a right to lands claimed by them; and that although these matters both in respect to fact and inference, remain unanswered by the said Indians, yet that it will be proper whenever a treaty shall be held for the purpose by the United States with the said Indians, that agents for this State should again attend, in order further to examine and discuss the said claim, and if they shall deem it eligible, then also further to propose and adjust with the said Indians, the compensation to be made by this State for the said claim."

This resolution met with the concurrence of the house.

In pursuance of this concurrent resolution of the senate and assembly, the governor appointed Egbert Benson, Richard Varick and Jas. Watson, agents on the part of the state, to meet the deputies of the St. Regis and Caughnawaga tribes, who then claimed, and have since been recognized by the state, to be the representatives of the Seven Nations of Canada, to negotiate in the presence of a commissioner appointed by the government of the United States, for the extinguishment of the Indian title to lands in the northern part of the state. The following is an account of the proceedings at this treaty, which we derive from the original manuscript in the office of the secretary of state, at Albany:

"At a treaty held at the city of New York, by the United States, with the nations of Indians denominating themselves the seven nations of Canada; Abraham Ogden, commissioner for the United States, appointed to hold the treaty, Ohnawiio, alias Good Stream, a chief of the Caughnawagas, Oteatohatongwan, alias Colonel Louis Cook, a chief of the St. Regis Indians; Teholagwanegen, alias Thomas Williams, a chief of the Caughnawagas, and William Gray, deputies authorized to represent these nations or tribes at the treaty, and Mr. Gray also serving as interpreter.

Egbert Bensen, Richard Varrick, and James Watson, agents for the state of New York.

MAY 23, 1796.

The deputy, Thomas Williams, being confined to his lodging in this city by sickness, was unable to be present; the other three deputies proposed, nevertheless, to proceed to the business of the treaty. The commissioner thereupon, informed them generally, that he was appointed to hold the treaty; that the sole object of it was, to enable the state of New York, to extinguish by purchase, the claim or right of these nations or tribes of Indians, to lands within the limits of the state, and that agreeably to his instructions from the president, he would take care the negotiation for that purpose, between the agents for the state and the Indians, should be conducted with candor and fairness.

Mr. Gray, then read and delivered the following speech, as from the deputies, written in English. [136]

A [talk] from the seven nations of Indians residing in the state of New York, and Upper and Lower Canada, to the commissioner of the United States and state of New York, concerning a claim of lands in the state of New York.

Brothers:

We are sent from our nations to you, and fully empowered by them to treat with you respecting our lands, or on any other occasion that may be attended with a good meaning, or cause to brighten and strengthen the chain of friendship betwixt you and us. This power now given us, present, Colonel Louis Cook, Ohnawiio, Good Stream, Teholagwanegan, Thomas Williams, and William Gray, our interpreter at Caughnawaga, the place where our Great Council Fire is held, and where our nations were all assembled and in full council, and there to convince you, brothers, and in order that your business might be attended to with care, and speed, they gave us their full power, to act in behalf of our nations, and that whatsoever should be agreed upon betwixt you and us, the same should ever hereafter be indisputable, and stand for just, to us, or any of us. This power was given to us on paper, and signed by all our principal chiefs, and the same paper, lodged in the hands of our great brother, George Washington, the President, one who we had too much confidence in, to believe that he would have misplaced a paper, of that consequence, however it does not alter our power, as we have before mentioned. We are sent to you for the purpose of having a final settlement with you before we return to them, and brothers, our chief's last charge, when we parted with them at the great council at Caughnawaga, was to reason the case with our brothers, and to act with judgment; for that whatsoever was agreed on at this meeting, thro' us, should stand for just to the whole of our nations.

Brothers:

At our meeting last fall, at Fort George, you, after some conversations, desired us to point out the laud we claimed in this state, and accordingly we did.

Brothers:

You then brought in several objections against our claim, but we could not find either of them to be reasonable, or in any way sufficiently weighty, if we had ever sold any of our lands, either to the king of France or Great Britain, or either of the United States, we should have of course signed our names to the agreement, which if that were the case, we are sensible that such papers would be brought forward against us, and that too with great justice, but so far from anything of the kind, that we bid defiance to the world, to produce any deed, or sale, or gift, or lease, of any of the lands in question, or any part of them, from us, to either the king of France, or Britain, or to either of the United States, or to any individual, excepting those we have adopted into our nation, and who reside with us.

Brothers:

You produced to us a copy of a deed from several Mohawks, for eight hundred thousand acres of land, which these Mohawks had as good a right to sell, as they have to come and dispose of the city of New York, notwithstanding this, you at the treaty of last fall, pointed those people out to us, to be too just a people, you thought to do a thing of the kind; but what makes them just in your eyes, we expect is because they stole from us, and sold to you. This is what makes them a just people. [137]

Brothers:

Had we several years ago, done as those have, whom you call a just people, that is; had we sold off all our lands, then; underhandedly sold our

brothers, and then fled our country; took up arms and come and killed men, women, and children, indiscriminately: burnt houses and committed every other act of devastation, and in short, done everything we could, against our once nearest friends, then according to what you say of these Mohawks, you would have esteemed us a just people, and therefore would not have disputed our claim.
Brothers:

From what we have seen, within a few years, we have reason to believe that a people as those, are most esteemed in your eyes; we need not mention to you the conduct of the western Indians, nor of their friends, you can judge who we mean, but it seems those who injure you the most, you are the readiest to serve.
Brothers:

It seems that before a nation can get justice of another, they must first go to war, and spill one another's blood, but brothers, we do not like this mode of settling differences; we wish justice to be done without, and it so far from the conduct of a Christian people, that we are fully determined we never will resort to such means, unless driven to it by necessity.
Brothers:

It is our earnest wish, to live in friendship and unity with you, and we have always endeavored to persuade our brother Indians to take pattern by us, and live peaceably with you, and to think that our brothers of the United States were a just people, and never would wrong them of any of their hinds that justly belonged to them.
Brothers:

This we did on the strength of your former promises to us, which we think you remember too well to need them to be repeated. You who depend on ink and paper, which ought never to fade, must recollect better than we, who can not write, and who depend only on memory, yet your promises are fresh in our minds.
Brothers:

We ask for nothing but what is our just due, and that we ever shall expect to get, until such time as you deny your own words, not only by breaking your promises, but making false speakers of us in all that ever we said to our brother Indians, in your behalf, and encouraging those who always have been endeavoring to injure both you and us, all that ever lay in their power.
Brothers:

We entreat you only to look back, and consider the privileges your brother Indians formerly enjoyed, before we were interrupted by other nations of white people, who feign themselves to us as brothers, and let justice take place betwixt you and us, in place of arbitrary power, for that brothers, you very well know, is a thing that never gave contentment to any people, or nation whatsoever.

Brothers:

Formerly we enjoyed the privilege we expect is now called freedom; and liberty becomes an entire stranger to us, and in place of that, comes in flattery and deceit, to deprive poor ignorant people of their property, and bring them to poverty, and at last to become beggars and laughingstocks to the world. [138]

Brothers:

This is what we have already seen, but, however, we wish never to reflect on what is past, but trust in the Great Spirit who made us all, to so order it that justice may take place, and that better is to come.

Brothers:

We pray you to take this matter into good consideration, and do by us as you would wish to be done by brothers, that is what we wish for, that every brother might have their rights, throughout this continent, and all to be of one mind, and to live together in peace and love, as becometh brothers; and to have a chain of friendship made betwixt you and us, too strong ever to be broke, and polished and brightened so pure, as never to rust: This is our sincere wishes.

Brothers:

We wish likewise to enjoy our own laws and you yours, so far, that is, if any of our people, Indians, should commit a crime to any of their brothers, the white people of the United States, that he may be punished by his own nation, and his chiefs to make good all damages; and likewise on the other part, if any white person shall commit a crime to any Indian, that we the Indians, are not to take revenge on the person, but resign him up to justice, and there let him be punished according to the laws of his nation.

Brothers:

This we think will be one great step towards strengthening the chain of friendship, and to prevent all differences and disputes hereafter, and that is what we could wish that after this settlement with you brothers, that there never may hereafter arise differences or disputes betwixt you and us, but rather, if any nation, people or individual, should attempt to cause any difference or dispute betwixt you and us, or to intrude, or wish to injure either of us, that we may be all agreed as one, to drive such ill-minded people from off our continent, that does not wish to live amongst us in time of peace.

Brothers:

These are our sincere wishes, and we hope that you will consider this matter well, and let us make a good path for your children and ours to walk in after us; this brothers, is our greatest desire, and to live in peace and love

with you.
Brothers:

As to our lands, we wish our children after us to share their part of the lands as well as us that are now living, and we are sensible, brothers, that if you do by us as you wish to be done, were it your case, as it is ours, and let justice speak, and make us an offer for our lands, yearly, exclusive of a small piece we wish to reserve for our own use, we are satisfied that as you know the value of lands so much better than we do, that your offer will prevent any further contention on the business.

Brothers:

We with patience wait your answer.

May 24, 1796.

Speech from the Agents of the State to the Deputies for the Indians.

Brothers:

We have considered your speech to us of yesterday, and we find the question respecting your claim, remains as it was at the conferences betwixt [139] you and us, at the treaty held at Lake George, last fall, were closed. Without some further evidence, it appears to be scarcely reasonable in you to expect we should admit your claim, and the only inducement with us to have it released or extinguished is, as we have before stated to you, because we desire to live in peace and good neighborhood with you, and to avoid all controversy in future, and consequently not any supposed merit or justice in the claim itself, but merely contentment and satisfaction to you, are the considerations in determining as to the amount of the compensation to be allowed you. We have therefore offered you three thousand dollars, which you declined accepting, without any offer or proposal in return from you; and although it was then intended as a definite offer from us, we are still willing to add to it or to vary it to an annuity, in order to which, however, you must now inform us what your wishes or expectations are. This will be necessary, otherwise the negotiations will not be conducted on terms duly fair and equal between us."

May 25, 1796.

Mr. Gray read and delivered to the agents the following speech, as from the deputies, written in English.

A speech from the Seven Nations of Canada and the State of New York, to their Brothers of the State of New York.

"Brothers:

We have considered your answer of yesterday, to our speech to you on the day before, wherein you say, you find the question respecting our claim remaining as it was when we parted last fall from the treaty at Lake George. Very true, so it does; for if we remember right, you told us you would give us three thousand dollars for a release or quit claim for all the lands in our claim, exclusive of six miles square, to be reserved for the use of the village of St. Regis; and that was all you could offer, as you was sent there by them that was greater than you. We told you we was not able to comply with your offer, as we did not wish to bring our children to poverty by an action of that kind. Neither did you ask us what we did expect to have for our land; if you had we should immediately have told you.

Brothers:

Now you say, without some further evidence, you can not see fit to admit our claim.

We want our brothers to tell us what further proof you wish us to shew than what we already have shown? We have told you, time past, and we tell you now, that our claim is just, and as to finding any other nation or people that say that our claim is not just, or that there is a better title can be procured than ours, as we told you before, we are sensible that can not be done, in justice; however, for your satisfaction, brothers, as we have mentioned several times before, that if you was not convinced that our claim was just, to be at the expense of calling the different nations whose boundaries join our claim, and let them be evidences for and against us. We likewise tell you, that if we ever had sold any part of the lands we now claim to bring forward the papers signed by our chiefs, and they will end the business betwixt you and us, and for further evidence, we think it, brothers, unnecessary.

Brothers:

We will now tell you what we expect to have, and do justice to you, [140] and ourselves. That is, to reserve for our own use, in land, to begin at the village of St. Regis, and to run east ten miles on the line of the latitude of forty-five, then up the River St. Lawrence, from the village of St. Regis to a place called the Presque Isle, which we think is about thirty-five or forty miles from the village, and that distance to continue twenty miles in breadth. This piece we wish to reserve for our own use, which is but a very small piece. And the principal do we offer for your settlements, or any other use you may see fit to put it to. We should think it no ways out of reason or justice, to allow us the sum of three thousand pound's yearly, which will come to a trifle over one dollar for each person that is now living, and has a right in this claim, which is but a small sum towards clothing a person yearly, when before your clearing up our hunting grounds, we supported ourselves both in victuals and clothing, from what nature provided for us from off those lands.

Brothers:

Your compliances to these terms, will give contentment to the minds of your brethren, the Indians of the Seven Nations.

26th May, 1796.

Speech from the Agents to the Deputies.

Brothers:

We had intended to have avoided all further examination of the merits of your claim, and that the conferences between you and us should have been confined only to adjusting the compensation to be allowed to you for the extinguishment of it; but there are some parts of your speech of yesterday which we suppose ought not to remain wholly [unnoticed] by us.

Brothers:

You say there is no other people can be found, who can say your claim is not just, and if we are not convinced your claim is just, that we should be at the expense of calling the different nations whose boundaries join your claim, to be evidences for, and against your claim.

Brothers:

It would be sufficient for us merely to say, that considering the objections we have made to your claim, and the very unsatisfactory manner in which you have endeavored to answer them, that it is not reasonable in you to propose that we should be at the expense of procuring the attendance of the Indians, to whom you refer as witnesses. We will however, state a fact, to convince you that if they did attend, such is the probability that their testimony would be against your claim, as to render it unavailable even for you to call them.

Brothers:

The Six Nations of Indians, by a deed dated the 30th day of November, 1787, and in consideration of an annuity of two thousand dollars, sold to John Livingston, and his associates, for the term of nine hundred and ninety-nine years, lands described in the said deed as follows:

"All that certain tractor parcel of land, commonly called and known by the name of the Lands of the Six Nations of Indians situate, lying, and being, in the state of New York, and now in the actual possession of the said chiefs, and sachems of the Six Nations. Beginning at a place commonly known and culled by the name of Canada Creek, about seven miles west of Fort Stanwix, now Fort Schuyler, thence north easterly, to the line of the province of Quebec, thence along the said line to the Pennsylvania line, thence east on the said line, or Pennsylvania [141] line, to the line of Property, so called, by the state of New York, thence along said line of Property to 'Canada Creek' aforesaid."

These boundaries, you perceive, include nearly, if not all the lands you claim within this state, and the deed is signed by forty-five Indian chiefs, and among the witnesses to it is Colonel Louis, the deputy here present.

This deed was confirmed by another, bearing date the 9th day of July, 1788. Signed by sixty-six chiefs, and among the witnesses were Colonel John Butler, and Captain Joseph Brant. These deeds having been given up to the state, by the persons to whom they were made, have been lodged in the Secretary's office, and they are now produced to you, in order that you may see them. This purchase by Mr. Livingston, and his associates, without the consent of the Legislature, was contrary to the constitution of the state, and therefore void.

It is, notwithstanding, sufficient for the purpose for which we principally mention it, as it is not to be presumed, that these Indians would ever declare that lands which they intended to sell, and be paid for, as belonging to themselves, did belong to others. Not only so, but the persons who have subscribed the deeds, as witnesses, and having a knowledge of Indian affairs, and some of whom, even Colonel Louis himself, if we are not much misinformed, assisted Mr. Livingston, and his associates, in making the purchase, were called on as witnesses, between you and us, they must declare, that they never had heard or believed, that any part of the lands described in these deeds, belonged to any other nations than the Six Nations, otherwise they must declare that they were witnesses to a transaction, which they knew to be intended fraudulent, and injurious to you; so that it must evidently be fruitless in you to depend on the testimony of the neighboring nations, to establish your claim.

Brothers:

When we first came together, at the treaty held lost fall, and before any formal speeches had passed between you and us, you mentioned, that you claimed the lands also on the east side of the line between this state, and the state of Vermont; but the intent of that treaty, being only for the extinguishment of your claim to lands within this state, the lands in Vermont were omitted out of the boundaries of your claim, an you afterwards described it to us.

This you again affirmed to us verbally, yesterday, and you declared the lands claimed by you, within the limits of Vermont, as running from Ticonderoga to the Great Falls on Otter Creek, thence easterly to the heights of land, dividing the waters which run eastwardly, from the waters which run into Lake Champlain, thence along these heights, and the heads of the waters running into Lake Champlain, to the forty-fifth degree of latitude, and we take it for granted, you mean your claim is the same as well with respect to the lands in Vermont as to the lands in this state.

The king of Great Britain, however, when the territory was under the jurisdiction of this state, as the colony of New York, made grants of land, within the boundaries of your claim, as extending into Vermont, without requiring a previous purchase from you, or any other nation, or tribes of Indians, which is a further proof against the existence of any title, in you, to the lands you claim.

Brothers:

In 1782 and 1788, we purchased from the Oneidas, Cayugas, and Onondagos, the whole of their lands, except some tracts which were reserved [142] for their own use, and the land which we purchased from each of these nations, and exclusive of the reservations, are certainly not less in value, than the lands you claim, as comprehended within this state.

Their title was not disputed—your title is not only disputed, but utterly denied by us. We are still willing however, but from motives of prudence and good will, only, to place you in respect to the amount of compensation, on an equal footing with them, and therefore will allow you, the average of what was then allowed them, which will be an immediate payment of one thousand pounds, six shillings and eight pence, an annuity, of two hundred and thirteen pounds, six shillings and eight pence. The tract equal to six miles square, near the village of St. Regis, still to be applied to your use, as reserved in the sale to Alexander Macomb. If this offer is accepted by you, it will then remain to be adjusted between you and us, as to the time, place and manner, in which the payments are to be made.

Brothers:

We shall now await for your answer.

28th May, 1796.
Speech from the Deputies to the Agents.

Brothers:

We have considered your offers to our last speech, and we think that we understand the greater part of them, and we are happy to think that after so long a time, you have thought fit to take some part of our speeches into good consideration.

Brothers:

We did say there was no people could with justice say your claim is not just, and we still repeat to you, brothers, that these deeds, you have shewn to us, are unjust, that is, we mean according to all information we can get from Colonel Louis, who was present when such purchase should have been made, and according to all the conversations we have had with the different nations, that should have sold this tract of land, belonging to us, and we never understood by these nations, that they had disposed of any lands within our boundaries.

We have strictly examined Colonel [Louis] that was present when these purchases were made, of those nations, and he solemnly declares that he did not know of their selling any part of our lands, or any other, only [the] lands that belonged to them, and we take him to be a man of better principles, than to be a witness to so great a piece of misconduct against his own tribe, and then not to inform us of it before this time; we therefore must needs tell you, that we think there is a great deception in those deeds, as there has been in many other former purchases from our brother Indians, and to convince you, brothers, that we do not make an unjust demand; was it not for our poverty, we should not have requested you to have been at the expense of calling the different nations for witnesses between you and us, as we wish to convince you that we are a people that always have acted on honest principles, and mean to continue in doing the same. However, it seems you are indifferent about having these nations to come forward, and for our parts, brothers, we think it a great honor to settle matters that concern you and us among ourselves, and not to trouble our neighbors with our business. We therefore are willing to comply with any thing in reason and justice, rather than it should be said by those ill-minded people that are always trying to invent mischief between us, that we could not agree. But there is one question we wish to ask you brothers;—have you not known us to be the right owners of these [143] lands, why did you direct your good advice to us at the beginning of the trouble between you and the king of England?

We are sensible that a nation or people without lands, are like rogues without friends; of neither, is notice taken, or confidence put on them. But we received your council, heard your advice and your promises to us, and took them to be sincere, and we ever since have endeavored to live up to them with you as near us as possibly was in our power, and we believe we can with safety say, that since we have been neighbors, that we never have injured you or your properties, even to the value of a fowl. Neither have we made any demands from you while we could support ourselves by hunting, and always thought it to be a favor to our brothers in the new settlements, rather than to think or have the least mistrust that it would be a detriment to your justifying our claim when made. No brothers, we put too much confidence in your good and fair promises, to have the least mistrust of a thing of the kind.

Brothers:

Respecting our lands in Vermont, our claim in that state is as our claim in this state, which is just; and as to the king of Great Britain giving grants for settlements without requiring a purchase of us, that was not much for him to do at that time. If that had been the only mis-step he had taken towards the welfare of his children, we dare say you would not have rebelled against the government and laws of Great Britain, for the sake of obtaining liberty.

So we think that but a very small part of the reason why we should be deprived of our rights. And we have mentioned to you in a speech at the treaty last fall, at Fort George, that he did request us to sell those lands to him, and our answer was to him that we could not sell our lands, and that we had reserved them for the maintenance of our children, after us, and that has always been the advice of our forefathers, never to sell any part of our lands, but to lease them for an annuity, if it was ever so small, and we shall never forget their advice to us. And on these principles our lands were settled, and that was when we could not support ourselves by hunting, that those who resided on our lands must expect to give us some assistance for the use of our lands.

Brothers:

And in respect to your last offer to us for our lands in this State, we must beg you to have a little patience, and consider this matter once more, and we will now make an offer, which we are sure you will not think unreasonable, that is, brothers, we are not able to bring our reserve into as small a compass as possible, without interfering with our plantations, which will be resigning up to you about two thirds of the reserve, which we never did intend to dispose of on any consideration whatever. Still, as we have before mentioned, that we are willing to comply on any terms in reason, for the sake of good neighborhood and friendship with you, you will allow us to reserve to our own use, as follows:

Beginning at the head of the second [island] above Long Saut, on the river St. Lawrence, and run down the stream of the said river, ten miles below the village of St. Regis; then back into the woods [twenty-one] miles, then westwardly in rear the same distance as in front, and from thence to the river, opposite to said island, to the place of beginning. This reserve, brothers, we will not be able to make any less, brothers, without interfering with the plantations of our people, which is out of our power, so to do; and an annuity of four hundred and eighty pounds, with all expenses free, to the place where we may agree for the delivery of said payments; if so be you may see fit to agree to this offer, [144] which we are sure you can not think unreasonable, for we are sensible it will not be more than half a cent per acre yearly; and the payment to be as you propose.

Brothers:

We hope you will not request us to vary from this offer, which we beg you rightly to consider, find let us live as well as yourselves. We will wait your answer.

28TH MAY, 1796.

[Speech] from the Agents to the Deputies.

Brothers:

The offer which we made you the day before yesterday, was upon mature consideration, and appeared to us to be as liberal as you could possibly expect, and it is now to be considered, as definite between you and us, so that it only remains for you to give us your final answer, whether you are willing to accept it or not, in order that the [negotiations] at the present treaty may be brought to a close. We would however, explain to you, that a reasonable allowance to you as deputies, for your services and expenses in attending this treaty, and such presents as are usual on these occasions, will be made to you, exclusive of the compensations which we have proposed, should be for the nations or tribes whom you represent.

30TH MAY, 1796.

Speech from the Agents to the Deputies.

Brothers:

After we had made our speech to you the day before yesterday, you verbally suggested to us, that the Indians of St. Regis had built a mill on a river, which you call Salmon river, and another on a river which you call Grass river, and that they had always supplied themselves with hay from the meadows on Grass river. You describe these rivers generally, only as emptying into the river St. Lawrence and being in the vicinity of St. Regis; and it is uncertain, whether they, and especially the places on them, where the mills are built, will be included in the tract equal to the six miles square, reserved in the sale to Mr. Macomb.

If you had seasonably informed the state of your claim, they might have reserved lands for your use, to any extent which might have been judged proper, but they have now sold all the lands on that quarter, to Mr. Macomb, and as reservations can not be made without the consent of the persons who have purchased from him, we have spoken to them on the subject, and they have consented, that we should further offer to you, that a convenient tract at each place where the mills are built, and the meadows on both sides of the Grass river, although they may hereafter be discovered to be not within the tract, equal to six miles square, shall be reserved to the use of the St. Regis Indians.

31st May, 1796.

The deputies having declared their acceptance of the compensation, as proposed to them by the agents; three acts of the same tenor and date, one to remain with the United States, another to remain with the said Seven Nations, or tribes, and another to remain with the state, were thereupon this day executed, by the [commissioners] for the United States, the deputies for the Indians, the agents for the state, and Daniel McCormick, and William Constable, for themselves, and their associates, purchase under Alexander Macomb, containing a cession; release, and quit-claim from the Seven Nations or tribes of Indians, of [145] all lands within the state, and a covenant for the state, for the payment of the said compensation, and also certain reservations of land, to he applied to the use of the Indians of the village of St. Regis, as by the said acts, reference being had to either of them, more fully may appear."

Signed,
Abram Ogden.

The following is a copy of this treaty.

"*The People* of the State of New York, by the grace of God, free and independent. To all to whom these presents shall come, greeting. Know ye that we having inspected the records remaining in our Secretary's office, do find there filed a certain instrument in the words following, to wit:

"At a treaty held in the city of New York with the nation or title of Indians, denominating themselves the Seven Nations of Canada, Abraham Ogden, commissioner appointed under the authority of the United States to hold the treaty, Ohnaweio, alias Good Stream, Teharagwanegen, alias [Thos.] Williams, two chiefs of the Caughnawagas, Atiatoharongwan, alias Colonel Louis Cook, a chief of the St. Regis Indians, and William Gray, deputies authorized to represent these Seven Nations or tribes of Indians at the treaty, and Mr. Gray serving also as interpreter, Egbert Benson, Richard Varick and James Watson, agents for the state of New York. Wm. Constable and Daniel McCormick, purchasers under Alex. Macomb.

The agents for the state, having in the presence and with the approbation of the commissioners, proposed to the deputies for the Indians, the compensation hereinafter mentioned for the extinguishment of their claim to all lands within the states, and the said deputies being willing to accept the same, it is thereupon granted, agreed and concluded between the said deputies and the said agents as follows: The said deputies do for, and in the name of the said Seven Nations or tribes of Indians, cede, release and quit claim to the people of the state of New York, forever, all the claim right or title of them, the said Seven Nations or tribes of Indians, to lands within the said state, provided nevertheless, that the tract equal to six miles square reserved in the sale made by the commissioners of the land office of the said state, to Alexander Macomb, to be applied to the use of the Indians of the village of St. Regis, shall still remain so reserved. The said agents do for and in the name of the people of the state of New York, grant to the said Seven Nations or tribes of Indians, that the people of the state of New York shall pay to them at the mouth of the river Chazy, on Lake Champlain, on the third Monday of August next, the sum of one thousand two hundred and thirty pounds, six shillings and eight pence, lawful money of the said state; and on the third Monday in August, yearly, forever thereafter, the like sum of two hundred and thirteen pounds, six shillings and eight pence. Provided nevertheless, that the people of the state of New York shall not be held to pay the said sums, unless in respect to the two sums to be paid on the third Monday in August next, at least twenty, and in respect to the said yearly sum to be paid thereafter, at least five of the principal men of the said Seven Nations or tribes of Indians, shall attend us deputies to receive and to give receipts for the same. The said deputies having suggested that the Indians of St. Regis have built a mill on Salmon river and another on Grass river and that the meadows on Grass river are necessary for hay, in order therefore to secure to the Indians of the said village, the use of the said mills and meadows, in case they should hereafter appear not to be included in the above tract, so as to remain reserved.

It is therefore also agreed and concluded between the said deputies and [146] the said agents and the said William Constable and Daniel McCormick, for themselves and their associates, purchasers under the said Alexander Macomb, of the adjacent lands, that there shall be reserved to be applied to the use of the Indians of the said village of St Regis, in like manner as the said tract is to remain reserved, a tract of one mile square at each of the said mills, and the meadows on both sides of the said Grass river, from the said mills thereon, to its confluence with the river St. Lawrence.

In testimony whereof, the said commissioners, the said deputies, the said agents, and the said William Constable and Daniel McCormick, have hereunto, and to two other acts of the same tenor and date, one to remain with the United States, another to remain with the state of New York, and another to remain with the Seven Nations or tribes of Indians, set their hands and seals in the city of New York, the thirty-first day of May, in the twentieth year of the Independence of the United States, one thousand seven hundred und ninety-six. Abraham Ogden (L. S.), Ohnaweio, alias Good Stream (mark L. S.), Otiatoharongwan, alias Colonel Louis Cook (mark L.S.), Wm. Gray (L. S.), Teharagwanegen, alias Thos. Williams (mark L. S.), Egbert Benson

(L. S.), Richard Varick (L. S.), James Watson (L. S.), Wm. Constable (L. S.), Daniel McCormick (L. S.).

Signed, sealed and delivered in the presence of Samuel Jones, Recorder of the city of New York, John Taylor Recorder of the city of Albany, Jo's Ogden Hoffman, Attorney-General of the state of New York.

May 30th, 1797. Acknowledged before John Sloes Hobart, Justice of Supreme Court of Judicature.

Feb. 28, 1800. Exemplified signed and sealed by the Governor, John Jay."

The above treaty is engrossed upon a large size sheet of parchment, to which is affixed a large waxen seal, having on one side the state arms and inscription, "The great seal of the state," and on the other the device of waves beating against a rock, and the word "Frustra," "1798." The back and margins are covered with receipts.[7]

This and the other treaties which have been held between the St. Regis Indians and the state of New York, are carefully preserved by the clerk of the American party at St Regis. The agreements made in the treaty of May 31, 1796, were confirmed by an act which was passed April 4, 1801. It had previously received the sanction of the general government, as appears from the following:

On the 20th of February, 1797, the governor sent to the senate the following message:

Gentlemen:

"I have the honor of laying before you a letter of the 18th ult., from the Secretary of the United States, for the department of war, enclosing a copy of the resolution of the Senate, advising and consenting to the ratification of the treaty concluded on behalf of the state with the Indians, calling themselves the Seven Nations of Canada.

JOHN JAY."

In the negotiations between these Indians and the state, the name of Brant, the celebrated partisan Indian, was used in connection with proceedings, [147] which the Mohawks had held with the state, in the cession of their lands, in such a manner as to awaken a controversy between him and the deputy superintendent, which ultimately became embittered by mutual allegations of pecuniary delinquency. The six nations had bargained with Colonel Livingston, in 1787, as we have previously stated, for a large tract of land which the Caughnawaga and St. Regis Indians insisted was fraudulent.

As Brant was a witness to the treaty, and was one of the most prominent of those by whom it was made, this denial of their right amounted to little else than a charge that those who made it, had pocketed the avails for their own benefit. This charge Brant indignantly repelled, denying that the Caughnawagas had a right to a foot of the lands which had been sold to Livingston, and demanding of them their authority, for their charges against him, and the Grand River Indians. They replied that their information was derived from the representations of the officers of the state of New York, at Albany. To ascertain the ground there might be for this, he addressed a letter to Governor Clinton, which received the following reply.

GREENWICH, 1ST DECEMBER, 1799.

Dear Sir:

"On my return from the country, about a month ago, I was favored with your letter of the 4th of September. I am much gratified by the determination you express, of furnishing Doctor Miller with the information he requested of you, and I hope as the work for which it is wanted is progressing, you will find leisure to do it soon. I am confident he will make a fair and honorable use of it; and, as far as he shall be enabled, correct the erroneous representations of former authors respecting your nations.

I am surprised to find that you have not received my letter the 11th of January, last. It was enclosed and forwarded as requested, to Mr. Peter W. Yates of Albany. Had it reached you; I presume you will find, from the copy I now enclose, it would have been satisfactory; but as a particular detail of what passed between the Caughnawagoes and me, respecting their lands may be more agreable, I will now repeat it to you as far as my recollection will enable me.

In the winter of 1792-1793, our Legislature being in session in Albany, a committee from the Seven Nations or tribes of Lower Canada, attended there, with whom I had several conferences. They complained that some of our people had settled on their lands near Lake Champlain, and on the River St. Lawrence, and requested that commissioners might be appointed to enquire into the matter, and treat with them on the subject. In my answer to their speeches, I answered that it was difficult to define their rights and their boundaries; and that it was to be presumed that the Indian rights to a considerable part of the lands on the borders of the lake, had been extinguished by the French Government, before the conquest of Canada, as those lands, or a greater part of them, had been granted to individuals by that government before that period. In their reply they described their southern boundary, as commencing at a creek or run of water between Fort Edward and George, which empties into [148] South Bay, mid from thence extending on a direct line to a large meadow or swamp where the Canada Creek, which empties into the Mohawk opposite Fort Hendrick, the Black and Oswegatchee Rivers have their sources. Upon which I observed to them that this line would interfere with lands patented by the British Government previous to the Revolution, and particularly mentioned Totten and Crossfield's purchase and Jessup's patent; but I mentioned at the same time that I was never authorized or disposed to controvert their claims, that I would submit to the Legislature, who I could not doubt would pay due attention to them and adopt proper measures to effect a settlement with them upon fair and liberal terms. This I accordingly did, and some time after commissioners were appointed to treat with them in the presence of an agent of the United States, the result of which, I find you are informed of.

I believe you will readily agree that no inference could be drawn from any thing that passed on the above occasion to countenance the charge made against your nations. The mentioning and interference of their boundaries, as above stated, with tracts patented under the British Government, could certainly have no allusion to the cessions made by the Six Nations, or either of them to the state, especially as (if I recollect right) those cession are of the territory of the respective notions by whom they were made without defining them by any particular boundaries, and subject only to the reservations described in the deed.

I wish it was in my power to transmit to you copies of their speeches and my answer at full length; but it is not for the reasons mentioned in my former letter, should they, however, be deemed necessary to you, I will endeavor to procure and forward them; in the mean time you may rest assured that what I have related is the substance of them.

I am with great regard and esteem,

Col. Joseph Brant.   Your most obedient servant,
                                             GEO. CLINTON.

This correspondence, and that which ensued with Governor Jay, did not satisfy Brant, and he accordingly caused a deputation of his tribe to repair to Albany, at the head of which was his adopted nephew, John Norton, to meet a similar deputation of the Caughnawagas, face to face, and require his accusers connected with the government of the state of New York, either to substantiate their charges or acquit him in the presence of both delegations.

The result of this double mission is not known, save that the chiefs were not satisfied with it.

In July of the same year (1799,) Brant proceeded to the Caughnawaga country in person, accompanied by a body of chiefs of several of the tribes, for the purpose of a through investigation in general council. Such a council was convened; and the difficulties from the reports of speeches preserved in writing by Captain Brant, were fully discussed; and that too in a most amicable manner. From several intimations in these speeches, it appears that the whole of these difficulties had been caused by "chattering birds," and by the machinations against Captain [149] Brant, of the old Oneida sachem, Colonel Louis.[8] The council fire was kindled on the 8th of July, on the 9th Captain Brant was satisfied by the explanations given, and remarked, "that he had pulled up a pine, and planted down beneath it the small bird that tells stories."

On the 10th, the Caughnawaga chief replied:—"Brothers, we return you thanks;

we also join with you to put the chattering bird under ground, from where the pine was taken up, there being a swift stream into which it will fall beneath, that will take it to the big sea, from whence it never can return." *(See Stone's Life of Brant, vol. ii, p. 410, 414.)*

The evident partiality of the writer of the life of Brant, has perhaps prevented him from giving to the Canada Indians their due in discussing their claims to the lands in the northern part of the state.

The St. Regis people having decided the question of the amount of land they were to receive, were desirous of having the boundaries known.

To settle definitely however their rights, they addressed the following letter to the governor.

To our Great Brother, John Jay, Governor of the State of New York.

Brother:

We the chiefs and chief warriors at St Regis, have sent the Bearers, Louis Cook, Sag Shaketlay, Loren Tarlelon, and William Gray, our interpreters, to enquire of you Brother, how we are to know the distance of our reserve, equal to six miles square, reserved to us by a treaty held at the city of New York, the 30th of May, 1796, with our deputies Louis Cook, Ohnaweio, Good Stream, Thomas Williams, and William Gray, and another reserve of one mile square on Salmon Creek, twelve miles below St. Regis, at a saw mill belonging to us chiefs.

Brother:

The reason of our sending the Bearers to you, is, that some time the latter part of last fall, some of your children, our brothers of this state, was marking and running lines within what we expect is our reserved lands, and we know no other way, but to come and inform you that we might know what to do, and we beg that you will inform the Bearers that they, as soon as is convenient to you may return home and inform us what to do.

We hope you will not let thy Bearers want for victuals and drink, what will he for their good, we wish you health and happiness with your family. From your Brothers the chiefs of St. Regis."

Chiefs.

For the Chiefs at
St. Regis, WILLIAM GRAY.

TIO-NA-TO-GEN-A,
THA-RON-IA-HE-NE,
TA-TE-GA-IEN-TON,
TO-TA-RO-WAN-NE

[150]
This petition led to the passage on the 30th of March, 1799, of the following act:

"The surveyor general be, and he is hereby directed in his proper person, to lay out and survey, in such manner as the chiefs of the St. Regis Indians shall deem satisfactory, all the lands reserved to the said Indians, by the treaty held at the city of New York, and conformable thereto, the twenty-third day of May, in the year one thousand seven hundred and ninety six; and the treasurer is hereby required to pay to him, out of any money in the treasury, four hundred dollars to defray the expense thereof, which sum the surveyor general shall account for with the comptroller."

The surveyor general performed this duty and reported as follows:

"*Sir:*—Pursuant to the act of the legislature, directing the surveyor general to lay out and purvey the lands reserved to the Indians residing at St. Regis. I have surveyed in a manner satisfactory to the chiefs of that tribe the tract equal to six miles square, reserved to them at their village; as also the two tracts of one mile square each, at the mills on Salmon river, and Grass river, maps descriptive of the boundaries of these I have the honor herewith to deliver.

When I was about to commence the survey of the meadows, reserved to the use of these Indians on Grass river, they informed me in council that they considered themselves entitled to a tract of a half a mile on each side of the river, from its mouth up to the mill, and that they had caused it to be run out in that manner, for their meadow reservation, and intimated a desire that my survey should be made in a corresponding manner. I was obliged to inform them that I had no guide but their treaty, and consequently could regard no survey made without authority, and that nothing but the meadows barely, along that river, was pointed out as their property. They then pointedly desired me to make no marks on that ground, observing at the same time that as a deputation from their nation would have to repair to Albany on other business, during the sitting of the legislature, they wished by that opportunity to obtain an explanation of what they considered to be a misapprehension between the parties of the treaty.

Not being permitted to make a survey of the meadows, I availed myself of the opportunity of going up and down the river, of making an estimate of them, with a view to report the same as an article of information that might be serviceable in case a compromise respecting them should he contemplated.

These meadows consist of narrow strips along the margin of the river, where inundations have prevented the growth of limiter. They lie in a number of patches, of from half a chain to three or four chains in width, making in the whole extent which is about six miles, not exceeding sixty acres altogether, as nearly as I could judge.

The grass on them with small exceptions, is all wild grass.

Their value, though of no very great consideration, as an appendage to the adjoining lands, is however esteemed as almost inestimable by Indians, who consider the clearing of land as a matter entirely beyond their power to accomplish. It will be impossible moreover, that the Indians should ever enclose the meadows with fences, so us to prevent their destruction by the cattle of the while inhabitants, who soon will settle thick in their neighborhood, and this will inevitably become the cause of disagreeable differences.

It is proper for me to observe that the ground on which these meadows [151] are situated, as well as the mile square, at the mill on Grass river, has been patented in tracts distinct from Macomb's purchase; and therefore the sanction which the proprietors of that purchase pave to the treaty, will not exonerate the state from the duty of compensating the owners of the lands from which these parts of the reservation are taken."

{The remainder of the report relates to other subjects.}

Signed,

SIMEON DE WITT.

ALBANY JAN. 14, 1800.

The troubles from trespass anticipated in the above, were soon realized; for the particulars of these the reader is referred to our account of Massena.

On February 20, 1800, there was received in Assembly from the Senate, a resolution:

"That the commissioners of the land office be directed to settle with the St. Regis Indians, for such tracts of land, included in the lands confirmed to them by the late treaty, and before located by individuals, and granted by this state, by making compensation for the lands so granted, or by satisfying the individuals owning such lands in such manner us they shall judge most advantageous to the state, and the legislature, will make provision for carrying into effect any agreement which may be made by the commissioners for extinguishing the claims of the said Indians, or of the individual proprietors aforesaid."

This resolution was postponed by the assembly, nor is it known what was the final action of the legislature upon it.

On the 9th of April, 1801, a law was passed making it lawful for the governor to cause a treaty to be holden with the St. Regis Indians, for the purpose of extinguishing their right to a tract of a mile square at the mill on Grass river, and for that purpose to appoint an agent on the part of the state, and procure the appointment if a commissioner, on the part of she United States, to attend the holding as such treaty. *Provided* that the consideration to be paid the said Indians for the said tract, shall not exceed a permanent annuity of two hundred dollars. A sum not exceeding $500 was appropriated to defray the expense of holding this treaty.

The surveyor general was directed to cause the meadows reserved to the use of the said Indians, upon Grass river, and which had been disposed of by the state, to be surveyed, and the quantity ascertained, and to report the same to the legislature at the next session. It was further made lawful for the agent to extinguish the right of ferriage, belonging to the said Indians over the River St. Lawrence, adjoining their reservation, for such reasonable annuity as they may deem proper.

The future payments of the annuity stipulated with the said Indians, was directed to he made at the town of Plattsburgh, in the county of [152] Clinton. The act referred to makes a provision for the patenting by the state to William Gray, of two hundred and fifty-seven acres of land, including the mill on the Salmon river.

The president of the United States, by a message making sundry nominations, and addressed to the senate, February 2, 1802, recommended the nomination of John Taylor of New York, to be a commissioner to hold a treaty between the state of New York, and the St. Regis Indians.

He was led to this, from having received a communication from the governor of New York, purporting that the St. Regis Indians had proposed ceding one mile square, including the ferry, to the state of New York, and requesting a commissioner to be appointed on the part of the United States, to sanction the business, which it was proposed should be accomplished during the ensuing winter at Albany.

(American State Papers, Indian Affairs, vol. i, p. 565.)

In 1802, agents were appointed to treat with the St. Regis Indians for the sale of their mile square, and meadows. The following communication made to the Assembly by Governor Clinton, March 15, 1802, contains the results of their negotiations. It was first reported to the senate.

Gentlemen:
"I now submit to the Legislature, the report of the agents appointed to treat with the St. Regis Indians, for the extinguishment of the mile square, and the meadows on Grass river. I also present to you a petition from those Indians, praying among other things, for legislative provisions, to enable them to lease a part of their lands, to establish a ferry across the St. Regis river, and to apply the income to the support of a school for the instruction of their children. It may be proper to observe, that as the petitioners have uniformly evinced a warm attachment, to the state, and have made uncommon advances towards civilization, they have a claim to the attention of the Legislature, arising as well from principles of policy, as benevolence. They discover an anxiety to return home as soon as possible, but at the same time are unwilling to leave this city, until the result of their application to the Legislature is known."

GEO. CLINTON.

The report of the agents referred to, in his excellency's said message, and the petition of the St. Regis Indians, were also severally read, and together with the message, referred to the committee of thee house. The petition was as follows:

"To our great and Honorable Brother, John Jay, Governor of the State of New York:

Brothers:

We, the chiefs and warriors of the village of St. Regis, have sent the bearers, Colonel Louis Cook, Jacob Francis, Peter Tarbell, as deputies, and William Gray as interpreter, to act and settle all business for us that [153] may concern this state, or us, the above mentioned village, or any individual belonging to this state.

Firstly, we beg you brother, to order means to have our meadows on Grass river, surveyed, and the number of acres contained there, to have as many acres cleared near our village, within the reservation made to us by this state, and then to have the use of the meadows on Grass river, till such time as those lands will be fit to mow grass on.

Secondly, brother, we wish to inform you, that at the west end of our meadows, on Grass river, we have one square mile of land, likewise reserved to us by the state, with a saw mill in the centre of mile square, for which Amable Foshee is bound to pay us the sum of two hundred dollars per year, as long as he keeps it in his custody, and we are not satisfied with his usage to us.

Thirdly, brother; there is a route that leads from Plattsburgh on Lake Champlain, crosses the Chateaugay river, and comes straight to the village of St. Regis, where there ought to be a ferry kept for the accommodation of the public, and the use of this ferry is like to create quarrels and disputes:

Now brothers in order to prevent all these disagreeable contentions, we wish to propose to you, for to take one hundred acres, and the privilege of the ferry, and where there may be a good potash works erected for those people who wish to give us two hundred and fifty dollars, as a yearly rent.

Fourthly, brother, we wish to inform you, that there are nine miles between houses, however the route runs through our reservation, and we mean to rent a part of our lands, in order to make it convenient for travelers, and as some benefit to ourselves and children, who may follow us, and we began to inform all our brothers who may see fit to rent the lands of us, that we expect they will pay their rents according to contract, as you have law and justice in your power, and we are not acquainted with our brother white people's laws.

Fifthly, brother, there is a request from your sisters of the village of St.

Regis, the women of families, which is, that you pity them, and send them a school master, to learn their children to read and write.

Brother, your compliance to these requests will cause us ever to pray your welfare and happiness, who remain your brothers, chiefs, and their wives in the St. Regis."

        Te-ha-ton-wen-heon-gatha,
        Ti-e-hen-ne,
        Te-ga-ri-a-ta-ro-gen,
        On-wa-ri-en-te,
        Ori-wa-ge-te,
        To-ta-to-wa-ne,
        At-ti-ax-to-tie.

  Witness, William Gray.

Accordingly, two laws were enacted, relating to these people, at the ensuing session of the Legislature. The first was passed March 8, 1802. which provided,

"that it shall be and may be lawful for his Excellency the Governor, and the Surveyor general, to treat with the St. Regis Indians for the extinguishment of their claim to the mile square, and the meadows on Grass river, ceded to them in the year 1796, on such terms as they shall deem most condusive to the interests of the state, or to purchase the same from the individuals to whom it has been granted by the state before it was ceded to the said Indians, in case the latter purchase can be made on more favorable terms than the extinguishment of the Indian claim.
[154]
  That in case the said lands can not be purchased of the said Indians, or of the said patentees at a reasonable price, his Excellency, the Governor, shall represent the same to the Legislature that further provisions may be made respecting those claims."

The meadows were subsequently purchased of the patentees for the Indians:
During the same session, an act was passed, relating to the St. Regis Indians, March 26, 1802, as follows.

"Be it enacted by the people of the state of New York, in Senate and Assembly, That William Gray, Louis Cook and Loren Tarbell, belonging to the tribe of the St. Regis Indians, be and they are hereby appointed trustees for the said tribe, for the purpose of leasing the ferry over St. Regis river, with one hundred acres of land adjoining, and also one mile square of land on Grass river, within their reservation within this state, for such term of time as they shall judge proper, not exceeding ten years, and it shall and may

be lawful for the said trustees, to apply the rents and profits of the said ferry and lands for a support of a school for the instruction of children of the said tribe, (of which the said trustees shall have the superintendence,) and for such other purposes as the said trustees shall judge most conducive to the interests of the said tribe, and the powers hereafter invested in the said trustees, may be exercised by them or any two of them.

And be it further enacted, That it shall be and may be lawful for the said St. Regis Indians, on the first Tuesday of May next, and on the first Tuesday of May in every year thereafter, to hold a town meeting on their said reservation, within the state, and by a majority of male Indians above, twenty-one years of age, to choose a clerk, who shall keep order in such meeting, and enter in a book to be provided by him for that purpose, the proceedings of the said meetings.

And be it further enacted, That it shall and may be lawful for the said tribe, at any such meeting aforesaid, to make such rules, orders and regulations, respecting the improvement of any other of their lands in the said reservation, as they shall judge necessary, and to choose trustees for carrying the same into execution, if they shall judge such trustees to be necessary.

And be it further enacted, That it shall and may be lawful for the said William Gray, Louis Cook, and Loren Tarbell, to procure a bell for the church belonging to the said tribe, to be paid for out of their annuity.

And be it further enacted, That it shall and may be lawful for the person administering the government of this state, to cause to be sent to the said tribe at the place where their annuity is paid, two suits of silk colors, one with the arms of the United States, and the arms of this state as a gratuity, and to draw a warrant on the treasury for the expense of the same."

On the approach of war, the situation of St. Regis, on the national boundary, placed these people in a peculiar and delicate position. Up to this period, although residing in both governments, they had been as one, and in their internal affairs, were governed by twelve chiefs, who were elected by the tribe, and held their offices for life.

The annuities and presents of both governments were equally divided among them, and the cultivation of their lands, and the division of [155] the rents and profits arising from leases, they knew no distinction, of party.

The war operated with peculiar severity against them, from the terror of Indian massacre, which the recollections and traditions of former wars, had generally inspired the inhabitants.

So great was the terror which these poor people excited, that they could not travel, even where acquainted, without procuring *a pass*, which they were accustomed to obtain from any of the principal inhabitants, whose names were publicly known. A paper, stating that the bearer was a quiet and peaceable Indian, with or without a signature, they were accustomed to solicit, and this they would hold up in sight, when still at a distance, that those who might meet them should not be alarmed. They were likewise accustomed to require persons traveling across their reservation, to have, if strangers, a paper, purporting the peaceable nature of their business. The chiefs, it is said, appointed certain persons to grant these passes, among whom was Captain Polley, of Massena Springs. As few of them could read it became necessary to agree upon some emblem by which the signification could be known, and the following device was adopted: If a person were going through to French Mills, a bow was drawn on the paper, but if its bearer was designing to visit St. Regis village, an arrow was added thus.

Thus cut off from their usual means of subsistence, they were reduced to a wretched extremity, to obtain relief from which, Col. Louis repaired to Ogdensburgh, and sent the following letter to Gov. Tompkins:

"I address you these lines, for the purpose of expressing the situation of my nation, and of giving you assurances of our constantly cherishing good will and friendship towards the United States, and of our determination not to intermeddle with the war which has broken out between them and the English, and which has placed us in so critical a situation. Our young men being prevented from hunting, and obtaining a subsistence for their families, are in want of provisions, and I address myself in their behalf to the justice and liberality of the governor of this state, to obtain a supply of beef, pork and flour, to be delivered to us at St. Regis, during the time that we are compelled to give up our accustomed pursuits, which it seems, if continued, would give alarm to our white brethren. I have come myself to this place, to communicate the distressed situation of our nation to Col. Benedict, who has promised to submit the same to you, and in hopes of soon receiving a favorable answer to my request, I subscribe myself with much attachment, your affectionate brother and friend."

(Signed,)   his
Louis X Cook,
mark.

One of the chiefs of the nation of the St. Regis Indians, and a Lt. Col. in the service of the United States of America.

[156]

In consequence of the foregoing letter, orders were issued that the St. Regis Indians should be supplied with rations during the war at French Mills. They accordingly received during the war, about 500 rations daily, at the hands of Wareham Hastings, the agent for the government.

The Indians, while drawing their rations, begged some for their priest, from the best of motives, which the latter received as a kindness from them; but this circumstance gave him more trouble than it conferred benefit, for it was with the greatest difficulty, that he was able to justify or explain this course, with the British and ecclesiastical authorities. He narrowly escaped imprisonment on suspicion of receiving bribes from the American government. It will be remembered that the priest's house was on the Canadian side of the boundary.

In 1812, it was agreed between a British and an American commissioner, that the natives should remain neutral in the approaching contest.

It is said that in the month of June, Isaac Le Clare, a Frenchman, then and still living at St. Regis, being down at Montreal with a raft of wood, was met by an uncle, who suggested an interview with the governor, which resulted in his receiving a lieutenant's commission, on the recommendation of Col. De Salaberry.

Before his return, the British company stationed at St. Regis, was captured as below stated, and Lieut. Le Clare succeeded to the pay, but not to the rank, of captain, in place of Montigney. He raised a company of about 80 Indian warriors, and crossed to Cornwall. These Indians participated in several engagements during the ensuing war. At the taking of Little York, they were posted at Kingston. At the attack upon Sackett's Harbor, twenty British St. Regis Indians were present under Lieut. St. Germain; and at Ogdensburgh, in Feb., 1813, about thirty of the same, under Capt. Le Clare, crossed to the town. At the battle of Chrysler's field, they were at Cornwall, and prevented by Col. McLean, of the British army, from engaging in the battle.

Chevalier Lorimier, an agent of the British government, in 1813, came up from Montreal with the customary presents to the Indians, and offered them, on condition of their crossing the river and taking up arms against the Americans. They would not do this, and he returned with his presents. This was after Capt. Le Clare had raised his company, or about the time.

During the fall of 1812, Capt. Montigney, with a small company of British troops, in violation to the previous agreement, arrived, and took post at St. Regis. Maj. Guilford Dudley Young, of the Troy militia, stationed at French Mills, receiving an account of this, resolved to surprise, and if possible capture this party; considering himself justified in [157] entering upon neutral ground, as the enemy had first broken their agreement. He accordingly, about the 1st of October, 1812, proceeded quietly through the woods by an obscure path, guided by Wm. Gray, the Indian interpreter; but on arriving opposite the village of St. Regis, he found it impossible to cross, and was compelled to return.

Having allowed the alarm which his attempt had excited to subside, he resolved to make another descent, before the enemy should be reinforced, and for this purpose he marched a detachment at 11 o'clock at night, on the 21st of October, crossed the St.

Regis river at Gray's Mills, (now Hogansburgh,) on a raft of boards, and arrived about 5 o'clock in the morning, within half a mile of the village, without attracting the notice of the enemy. Here the Major made such a judicious disposition of his men, that the enemy were entirely surrounded, and after a few discharges surrendered themselves prisoners, with the loss of five killed, among whom was Captain Rothalte. The fruits of this capture were forty prisoners, with their arms and equipments, and one stand of colors, two bateaux, &c. They returned to French Mills by 11 o'clock the next morning, without the loss of a man, and the prisoners were sent forward to Plattsburgh. Ex-Governor Wm. L. Marcy held a subordinate office in this affair.

This was the first stand of colors taken by the Americans during the war, and these were received at Albany with great ceremony. An account of the reception of the colors is taken from the *Albany Gazette* of Jan. 1813.

> "On Thursday the 5th inst, at one o'clock, a detachment of the volunteer militia of Troy, entered this city, with the British colors, taken at St. Regis. The detachment, with two superb eagles in the centre, and the British colors in the rear, paraded to the music of Yankee Doodle and York Fusileers, through Market and State streets to the Capitol, the officers and colors in the centre. The remainder of the vestibule and the grand staircase leading to the hall of justice, and the galleries of the senate and assembly chambers were crowded with spectators. His excellency, the Governor, from illness being absent, his aids, Cols. Lamb and Lush, advanced from the council chamber to receive the standards. Upon which Major Young, in a truly military and gallant style, and with an appropriate address, presented it to the people of New York; to which Col. Lush, on the part of the state, replied in a highly complimentary speech, and the standard was deposited in the council room, amid the loud huzzas of the citizens and military salutes. Subsequently to this achievement Maj. Young was appointed a Colonel in the U. S. army."

This officer was a native of Lebanon, Ct.

> "After the war, he entered the patriot service under Gen. Mina, and lost his life in the struggle for Mexican independence, in 1817. The patriots, 269 in number, had possession of a small fort which was invested by a royalist force of 3,500 men. The supplies of provisions and water being cut off, the sufferings of the garrison and women and children in [158] the fort became intolerable; many of the soldiers deserted, so that not more than 150 effective men remained. Col. Young, however, knowing the perfidy of the enemy, determined to defend the fort to the last. After having bravely defeated the enemy in a number of endeavors to carry the fort by storm, Col. Young was killed by a cannon shot from the battery raised against the fort. On the enemy's last retreat, the Colonel, anxious to observe all their

movements, fearlessly exposed his person by stepping on a large stone on the ramparts; and while conversing with Dr. Hennessay on the successes of the day and on the dastardly conduct of the enemy, the last shot that was fired from their battery, carried off his head. Col. Young was an officer whom next to Mina, the American part of the division had been accustomed to respect and admire. In every action he had been conspicuous for his daring courage and skill. Mina reposed unbounded confidence in him. In the hour of danger he was collected, gave his orders with precision, and sword in hand, was always in the hottest of the combat. Honor and firmness marked all his actions. He was generous in the extreme, and endured privations with a cheerfulness superior to that of any other officer of the division. He has been in the U. S. service as Lieut. Col. of the 20th regiment of infantry. His body was interred by the few Americans who could be spared from duty, with every possible mark of honor and respect, and the general gloom which pervaded the division on this occasion, was the sincerest tribute that could be offered by them to the memory of their brave chief."

(See Barber's Hist. Coll. and Antiquities of Ct.)

In the affair at St. Regis, the catholic priest was made prisoner, and this surprisal and attack soon after led to a retaliatory visit from the enemy, who captured the company of militia under Capt. Tilden, stationed at French Mills, a short time after. Those who were taken in this affair were mostly the identical troops who had been the aggressors at St. Regis, and for these they were subsequently exchanged.

During the war, considerable quantities of pork, flour and cattle, from the state of New York, it is said, were brought by night to St. Regis, and secretly conveyed across the river for the subsistence of the British array. These supplies were purchased by emmisaries under a variety of pretexts, and by offering the highest prices.

An Indian of the British party at St. Regis, was lately living, who was employed as a secret messenger to carry intelligence, and was very successful in avoiding suspicions and in accomplishing his errands.

It is a well known fact that there were American citizens who secretly countenanced these movements, and who openly denounced the war and its abettors; who hailed a British victory as a national blessing, and who mourned over the success of the American arms, with a pathos that proved their sincerity.

Impartial TRUTH would require their names to be held up to the execration of honest men, through all coming time, but CHARITY bids us pass them unnoticed, that they may perish with their memories.

By virtue of powers supposed to be vested in them by the law of [1802] [159] the trustees of these Indians had leased considerable tracts of the reservation in the vicinity of Salmon river, which had thus become settled and cleared up; but this measure was found to produce jars and discords which led to the passage of a general enactment, passed June 19, 1812:

> "That it shall be unlawful for any person or persons other than Indians, to settle or reside upon any lands belonging to any nation or tribe of Indians within this state; and if any person shall settle or reside upon any such lands, contrary to this act, he or she shall be deemed guilty of a misdemeanor, and shall on conviction, be punished by fine not less than twenty-five dollars, nor more than five hundred dollars, or be imprisoned not less than one month, nor more than six months, in the discretion of the court having cognizance thereof; and it shall he the duty of the courts of oyer and terminer, and general sessions of the peace in the several counties of this state, in which any part of said lands are or may be situated, to charge the grand juries of their respective counties, specially to indict all offenders against the provisions of this section."

Meanwhile many persons had in good faith expended considerable sums in improvements, which it was desirable should be secured to them by a more reliable tenure than Indian leases, which led in 1816, to the passage of a law:

> "That in case the St. Regis Indians may be desirous of selling the mile square of land reserved by them at or near the village of French Mills, in the town of Constable, in the county of Franklin, or any other lands lying within this state, to which the St. Regis Indians have any title or claim, the person administering the government of the state shall be and is hereby authorized to purchase the said lands from the said Indians, in behalf of this state, and that the treasurer be and is hereby authorized on the warrant of the comptroller, to pay to the order of the governor such sum of money to defray the expense of completing the said purchase as the governor may think reasonable to give for the said lands."

The following treaty was accordingly held March 15, 1816:

> "A treaty made and executed between Daniel D. Tompkins, governor of the state of New York, in behalf of the people of the said state, of the one part, and Peter Tarbell, Jacob Francis and Thomas Williams, for and in behalf of the nation or tribe of Indians, known and called the St. Regis Indians, of the second part (at the city of Albany, this fifteenth day of March, in the year of our Lord, one thousand eight hundred and sixteen), witnesseth.
>
> *Article* 1. The said tribe or nation of St. Regis Indians do hereby sell and convey to the people of the state of New York, for the consideration hereinafter mentioned, a certain piece or parcel of their reservation, called the one mile square, situated in the county of Franklin, on Salmon river, to

have and to hold the same, to the said people of the state of New York, and their assigns for ever, and also a separate and additional tract of land, of their said reservation, situate in the county aforesaid, containing five thousand acres of the easterly part of their said reservation, adjoining their aforesaid mile square of land, within the territorial limits of the state of New York, to be measured from the east boundary line of said reservation, so as to make the said west boundary line of said five thousand acres to run due north and south; to have and [160] to hold the said five thousand acres of land, to the said people of the state of New York, and their assigns forever.

Article 2. The said Daniel D. Tompkins, governor, as aforesaid, for and in behalf of the people of the state of New York, covenants and agrees, with the St. Regis nation of Indians, that the said people, for the said several tracts of one mile square of land, and of five thousand acres of land hereinbefore granted and conveyed, shall pay to the said nation annually for ever hereafter, the sum of one thousand three hundred dollars, at French Mills, on said premises, the first payment of the said annuity to be paid on the first Tuesday of August next, and the whole annuity to he paid on the first Tuesday of August, in each year thereafter.

Article 3. The said St. Regis tribe or nation of Indians also covenant and agree to depute and authorize three of the chiefs or principal men of their tribe to attend at the times and places aforesaid, to receive the said annuity. And that the receipt of the said chiefs or principal men, so deputed, shall be considered a full and satisfactory discharge of the people of the state of New York, from the annuities which may be so received."

Signed, sealed, witnessed, acknowledged and recorded.

In consequence of the great distress among the St. Regis and other Indian tribes of the state, from the short crops in the cold summer of 1816, the legislature, at the recommendation of the governor, by an act passed February 12, 1817, authorized the payment of annuities to be anticipated for that year, for the purchase of the necessaries of life.

The concessions of the last treaty being found not to cover the territory that had been leased, another treaty was held on the 20th of February, 1818, as follows:

"At a treaty held at the city of Albany, the 20th day of February, in the year of our Lord one thousand eight hundred and eighteen, between his excellency Dewitt Clinton, governor of the state of New York, on behalf of the people of the said state, and Loran Tarbell, Peter Tarbell, Jacob Francis and Thomas Williams, on behalf of the nation or tribe of Indians, known and called the St. Regis Indians, it is covenanted, agreed and concluded as follows, to wit:

The said St. Regis Indians sell and convey to the people of the state of

New York, two thousand acres out of the lands reserved by the said Indians, to be bounded as follows, to wit: On the north and south by the north and south bounds of said reservation; on the east by the lands ceded by said Indians to the people of the said state, by a treaty dated 16th March, 1816, and on the west by a line running parallel thereto, and at such a distance therefrom as to contain the said two thousand acres; also, four rods wide of land through the whole length of their reservation, for a public road, to the west bounds thereof, together with four rods wide of land, for the same purpose, commencing at the boundary line near the village of St. Regis, to run in a direction so as to intersect the aforementioned road a little westerly of the place where it shall cross the St. Regis river, which will be about one mile and three-quarters in length. On condition that both the said roads be laid out by Michael Hogan, with the assistance of Loran Tarbell, and such other person as his excellency, the governor of the said state, shall appoint; and further, that in case a turnpike gate, or gates, shall be established on said road, [161] all the Indians of the said tribe shall be allowed to pass free of toll, and on the further condition that those on the lands they have now and heretofore sold, shall he compelled before the state gives them or any other person title thereto, to pay up the arrearages of rent due on the hauls occupied by the said settlers.

  In consideration of which cession or grant, it is hereby covenanted, on the part of the said people, to pay to the said Indians, annually, for ever hereafter, on the first Tuesday of August, at Plattsburgh, an annuity of two hundred dollars. And it is further covenanted by and between the said parties, that the annuities parable to the said Indians, in consequence of the former treaties between them and the said suite, shall hereafter be paid them on the said first Tuesday of August, at Plattsburgh, instead of the places where they are made payable by such treaties. In testimony whereof, the said governor, on the part of the people of the said state, and the said Loran Tarbell, Peter Turbell, Jacob Francis, and Thomas Williams have hereunto set their hands and seals, the day and year first above mentioned."

Signed, sealed, acknowledged and recorded.
  The lands ceded by the treaty of 1818 were by an act of April 20th, of that year directed to be laid out into lots and farms and sold.
  The report of the commissioners appointed by the governor to perform this duty, will be given in our account of Fort Covington.
  The commissioners were to receive $4 per day for their services.
  The following memorial explains itself, and indicates the necessity of the course which was subsequently to be pursued.

ALBANY 16, February, 1818.
"To his Excellency, Governor Clinton, of the state of New York:

The chiefs of the St. Regis Indians, by their petition, most respectfully approach your excellency, to shew, that in March 1802, a law was passed for the benefit of our tribe, appointing the trustees, namely: William Gray, Louis Cook, and Loren Tarbell, to manage and improve their affairs. From that period until the late war, they continued happy amongst themselves, but the war having produced a feeling of opposite interests in the tribe, they became divided almost equally in number, of young men, having your old chiefs with their adherents steady in the cause and interests of the United States. In course of the war, their trustee, William Gray, was taken prisoner at St. Regis, and carried to Quebec, where he died a prisoner of war. Their other trustee, Colonel Louis Cook, after being actively engaged with General Brown, near Buffalo, died at that place. Since his death, your excellency's petitioner, Loren Tarbell, the surviving trustee, taking to his private council Peter Tarbell, and Jacob Francis, old chiefs, in whom the tribe have full faith, has continued to act as for the whole, and has the satisfaction of assuring your excellency, that the trust reposed in him, has been discharged conscientiously, and with full regard to justice.

Now your excellency's petitioner, growing old, and desirous to be relieved in part from the responsibility which he has felt in the discharge of his duties, humbly prays your excellency to get a law passed, appointing the above mentioned Peter Tarbell and Jacob Francis, to his aid, to fill the vacancies occasioned by the death of the former trustees, and confirming the acts of your petitioner done in conjunction with the latter, since the death of the former trustees. [162]

And your petitioner will as in duty bound ever pray &c."

LOREN TARBELL, (signed by his mark.)

WILLIAM L. GRAY, Interpreter.

In consequence of the foregoing petition and memorial, an act was passed on the 3d of April, 1818, appointing Peter Tarbell and Jacob Francis, chiefs of the said tribe, to be trustees in place of Colonel Louis and William Gray, deceased, and to act with the surviving trustee Loren Tarbell.

Much difficulty arose between the Indians and their former tenants, in relation to their arrearges of rent, concerning which they memorialized the legislature, and on the 10th of March 1824, procured an act directing the Comptroller, to draw his warrant on the treasury, for the payment of any sum not exceeding $735.07 in favor of Asa Hascall, district attorney, for the county of Franklin, upon his certificate or certificates of the amount of rents due to the said St. Regis Indians, from settlers on certain lands ceded to them, by the people of this state, by treaty dated Feb 29, 1818, and it was made the duty of the said district attorney, on receiving the said money, to pay it over to the Indians as a full satisfaction and discharge of their claims.

On the 10th of April 1824, the foregoing act was extended to include the lands ceded March 15, 1816.

The mill on Grass river, and one mile square reservation, continued to be the property of these people, until March 16, 1824, when at a treaty held at Albany between Joseph C. Yates, Governor, and Thomas Williams, Michael Cook, Lewis Doublehouse and Peter Tarbell, at which they sold and conveyed for the sum of $1,920, this property.

The following is a copy of the power of attorney, under which the deputies of the foregoing treaty acted:

"Know all men by these presents, that we, the undersigned, chief warriors of the tribe called St. Regis Indians, constitute and appoint Thomas Williams, Lewis Doublehouse, and Peter Tarbell, as our true and lawful attorneys, to go to Albany, and sell such a quantity of our lands, to the people of this state, as they may think proper, and to transact all other business which shall be thought best for the welfare of our nation, and whatsoever our attornies shall lawfully act or do, we will ratify and confirm. Done at St. Regis in general council, this eighth day of March 1821."

Eleazer Skarestogowa,	Charles Sagahawita,
Peter Trewesti,	Ignace Gareweas,
Loran Cook,	Joseph Bern,
Charles Williams,	Evrer Gagagen
Thomas Turble,	Baptiste Satchweies,
Lewey Sabonrani.	

(signed mostly by their marks.)

[163]
The appointment made by the legislature in 1818 of trustees to fill the vacancy made by the death of Cook and Gray, appears to have been unsatisfactory to the tribe, as is seen from the following petition that was signed by the same parties as those who furnished the credentials of the deputies at the previous treaty.

"To the honorable the Legislature of the state of New York, in senate and assembly convened.

We the undersigned, chiefs and warriors of the St. Regis tribe of Indians, humbly represent to your honorable body, that our old chiefs that were appointed as trustees are all dead, except one, who is old and unable to transact public business. We therefore earnestly pray that your honorable body, will appoint Thomas Williams, Mitchel Cook, Lewis Doublehouse, and Peter Tarbell, as trustees to oversee and control the affairs of the St. Regis Indians.

Done in general council at St. Regis, this ninth day of March, 1824.

The following memorial was also prepared to be forwarded to the legislature:

"At a public council or town meeting, of the chiefs, head men, and warriors, of that part of the St. Regis nation, or tribe of Indians, which claim the protection and countenance of the state of New York, and which receive annuities from, and held lands under the authority of the said state; assembled on this 31st day of May, 1824, on their reservation lands, in the said state, it is unanimously resolved, that in order to put an end to all quarrels for power, we will not henceforth encourage any other individuals to be chiefs, or trustees, except Thomas Williams, Mitchel Cook, Lewis Doublehouse, Peter Tarbell, and Charles Cook; and we do hereby fully authorize, and empower them to transact for, and on behalf of our said tribe of American St. Regis Indians, all manner of business which they may deem for the general good.

 We authorize them, especially, to receive all annuities, payable to us by virtue of any bargains or treaties, made, or to be made, by the state of New York, or of individuals under the sanction of law, and others, and to distribute all money or property, as received amongst the said tribe of American St. Regis Indians, according to our claims. We also authorize and require them, to execute to the governor of the said state, or other proper authority, all necessary grants, conveyances, releases, or receipts, which may be required, in consequence of any bargain or treaty heretofore made, or hereafter in their discretion to be made on our behalf, and for our benefit, with the governor of the said state.

 We do further authorize and require them, to endeavor to make such a bargain with the governor, as that all the moneys which we are now, or shall be entitled unto, shall in future be paid on our reservation lands, to our said chiefs, and trustees, and not elsewhere. We also authorize them to make such arrangements with the governor, that some individual in whom the governor, as well as our said chiefs, can place confidence, may hereafter be considered the only proper channel of mutual communication between the governor and our said chiefs, on behalf of our said tribe, excepting all occasions in which our said chiefs may be at Albany. We fully approve all that was done by our deputies, and chiefs, Thomas Williams, Michael Cook, Louis Doublehouse, and Peter Tarbell, in the bargain or treaty made at Albany, on the 16th March last. We earnestly request that the governor will bear in mind, these resolutions [164] of the American St. Regis Indians, and that our minds may be known, we have each of us caused our several names and seals to be affixed to this paper, and another like it , and ordered one copy to he delivered to the governor, and one to be kept by our said chiefs."

 {Signed by about sixty Indians.}

Copied from the duplicate at St. Regis.

As a further evidence of authenticity, the foregoing was accompanied by a declaration of allegiance, a copy of which is here given:

> "Know all whom it may concern, that we, whose names are hereto annexed, do solemnly declare ourselves, to belong to the American Tribe of St. Regis Indians, that we owe no fealty to the British government, nor receive any annuities or benefits from the same; that we were friendly to the United States during the late war, and have continued to be so since, and that it is our fixed determination, to establish and continue our residence within the limits of the said United States, the protection and countenance, and especially of the state of New York, we hereby claim for said tribe. In witness of all which we have hereto caused our names and seals to be affixed this 31st day of May, in the year 1824, within our reservation lands, in the state of New York, done in duplicate one copy to be kept by our chiefs, and one copy to be delivered to the governor of the state of New York."
> {Signed by about sixty Indians.}

The author has been unable to ascertain what action, if any, was taken on this subject by the legislature, further than in a treaty, held on the 29th of June, 1824, between Governor Yates, and Thomas Williams, Mitchel Cook, Louis Doublehouse, Peter Tarbell, and Charles Cook, the latter are recognized as trustees.

By this treaty, they ceded in consideration of $1,750 down, and an annuity of $60, payable on the 1st Tuesday in August, at the village of Plattsburgh, to the said chiefs and trustees, a tract of 1000 acres of land bounded as follows:

> "On the northeast, by a line commencing on the easterly side of St. Regis river, at the termination of the roll way, so called, about four or five chains northerly from the mast road, and running thence southeast to the south bounds of the said reserved lands; on the south by the said south bounds; on the northwest by the said St. Regis river, and the land leased by the said Indians, to Michael Hogan, and on the southwest by a line to be run southeast, from the said St. Regis river, to the south bounds of said reserved lands."

On the 14th of December, 1824, the same Indians, who are styled, "Principal Chiefs and head men," confirmed to the people of the state of New York, for a payment of $1, and an annuity of $305, a certain tract of land which their predecessors had "in two certain indentures of lease, or instruments in writing, under seal, bearing date respectively, on the 20th and 23d days of October, in the year of our Lord 1817, and made and executed by and between their predecessors in office, and Michael Hogan, and subsequently confirmed by an act of the legislature." [165]

On the 20th of April, 1825, the legislature confirmed this cession by an act, the preamble and body of which set forth the causes that led to the measure.

> "Whereas the Indians of the St. Regis tribe did, by two certain indentures of lease bearing date the 20th of October, and the 23d of October respectively, in the year 1817, (which leases were sanctioned and confirmed by the Legislature of this state,) convey certain premises therein described in consideration of a certain annuity or rent annually to be paid for a term of years, with the condition for the renewal of the said leases as often as the same might expire, and upon the same terms; And whereas, by the subdivision of said premises among a number of occupants, or by the removal of the said Indians from their present possessions, they may experience difficulty and loss in collecting and receiving the rents, reserved and annually due, by virtue of the conveyances aforesaid; Therefore,
>
> *Be it enacted by the People of the State of New York,* That it shall and may be lawful for the grantee, in the said conveyances named, or his assigns, to convey the premises therein described to the people of this state; and whenever the said grantee or his assigns shall have paid or secured to be paid into the treasury of the state a sum equal to the principal of the annuity yearly payable to the said Indians by virtue of the conveyances aforesaid, at the rate of six per cent, per annum, it shall be the duty of the commissioners of the land office, to reconvey by letters patent to the said grantee or his assigns so paying or securing the payment of the sum above mentioned, and forever thereafter the annuity reserved in the conveyances aforesaid, shall annually be paid to the said Indians, in like manner as their other annuities from the state are now payable."

A treaty was held Sept. 23, 1825, between Governor De Witt Clinton and Thomas Williams, Mitchel Cook, Louis Doublehouse, Peter Tarbell, Charles Cook, Thomas Tarbell, Mitchel Tarbell, Louis Tarbell, Battice Tarbell, Jarvis Williams and William L. Gray, by which the latter as chiefs and trustees for the tribe, sold a tract of land, of 840 acres, on the east side of the St. Regis river, which is now the site of a part of the village of Hogansburgh. For this they received $1100 down, in full of all demands.

This tract was bounded as follows:

> "Beginning on the easterly side of the St. Regis river, at the most westerly corner of the lands ceded by said Indians to the people of said state, on the 12th day of June, in the year 1824, and running thence along the last mention lands, S. 45° E., to the south bounds of the said reserved lands; then

along the same, westerly to the said St. Regis river, and then along the same to the place of beginning."

The foregoing are believed to be all the negotiations that have taken place between these people and the state in relation to their lands. There remains to be mentioned some notices on the personal history and present condition and habits of these Indians. [166]

In 1826, a young Frenchman, by the name of Fovel, who had been for some time at Montreal, visited St. Regis, and induced one *Joseph Torakaron*, (sometimes known by his English name of Tarbell,) to consent to accompany him to Europe. Torakaron was to travel in the character of an Indian chief, (which office he then held at St. Regis,) and his companion in that of interpreter, solicitor, treasurer and agent. The motives held out to the chief were, that they should be able to obtain donations for the endowment of their church, and doubtless large sums as presents to themselves. Having made all necessary arrangements, and being furnished with letters from St. Regis, Montreal and Quebec, certifying the standing of Torakaron at home, the two proceeded by way of New York and Havre, to Paris. The conductor here obtained an interview with Charles X, and so favorable an impression was made upon the mind of the king, that he presented them with three fine paintings, and a large sum in money, and other valuable articles.

Thence they proceeded by way of Marseilles, to Rome, and obtained an interview with the pope.

During a conversation, the pope asked the Indian if he could converse in another language than his own, and finding him able to use the English and French to some degree, he invited him to a second interview alone. The result was, that a set of books and silver plate, for the service of the church, a rosary of jewels and gold, worth it is said $1400, and other articles of value, were given him. They thence returned to Marseilles, where they spent the winter, and in 1828 returned by way of Paris and Havre to New York. Here the treasurer, or interpreter, or whatever else he might be called, evinced his true character by absconding with every article of value, except the rosary and paintings, leaving Torakaron without means even to return home. He was enabled to do so through the charity of friends, and the paintings were soon alter deposited in their destined place. Two are now at St. Regis, and the third at the church in Caughnawaga. Of the former, those who visit the church will [recognize] in a painting over the altar, the portrait of St. Regis, and in the one to the left, near the pulpit, that of St. François Xavier.

They are both evidently by the same hand, of the size of life, and very well executed. The third is the portrait of St. Louis, and is in the church dedicated to that saint in the Indian village near Montreal.

St. Regis is represented in the attitude of preaching; St. Francois as reclining on a bank, with a book before him and pointing to a cross, and St. Louis as a king, in royal robes, bowed in the attitude of the deepest humility, in prayer.

Fovel subsequently visited the Iroquois settlements of New York, as a [167] priest, and occasioned much trouble, which rendered it necessary for Bishop Dubois to visit those places.

He afterwards went to Detroit, and appeared as a priest among the French at that city.

In the spring of 1829, the small pox appeared at the village of St. Regis, and swept off great numbers. All the tribe were then vaccinated, by direction of the British government.

In 1832, the Asiatic cholera broke out at this place, on the 20th of June, at first appearing in a mild form, for which the priest prescribed successfully for a short time, by administering large doses of laudanum and hot brandy. Of the first sixty cases thus dealt with, there are said to have been but two that were fatal.

Dr. McAuley, of Cornwall, was sent over by government, to attend the sick, and Dr. Bates, of Fort Covington, was also employed. The latter has remarked, that two in fifteen of those remaining in the village, died of this pestilence, and that when the east wind blowed, there were sure to be new cases. In one instance, a family of eleven were attacked, and but one survived. About 340 persons had the disease, some two or three times, making in all perhaps 500 cases. Friends became frightened, and fled away, leaving the sick, in some instances, to die unattended, and all mourning for the dead ceased.

This alarming pestilence was attended by the typhus fever, but it was observed that the two diseases did not attack the same persons, although they raged with equal severity. The cholera raged but eleven days, in which time 78 died, and the number of those who died in the year 1832, of this and other diseases, was 134.

As a natural consequence, this fearful visitation caused the greatest terror throughout the whole country, and exaggerated reports of its ravages at St. Regis spread rapidly to the neighboring villages, and led to the issuing of an order from the brigadier general of militia in the county, to the subordinate officers under his command, to take measures for preventing all intercourse with the infected village. Several persons volunteered to guard the road leading to Hogansburgh, and this vigilance was maintained about a week. It appeared to be unnecessary, because the epidemic limited itself to the vicinity of the river, and the village of Hogansburgh, two miles distant, was but very slightly affected.

In 1849, the cholera again appeared, taking off 29, and in the same year, the small pox broke out, with 500 cases, of which 30 were fatal. Bergen, of Cornwall, was employed by the British government on this occasion.

In 1850, the typhus raged the whole summer.

A remark was made by the Rev. Mr. Marcoux, which is worthy of the [168] attention of the medical profession, that the cholera and the typhus were associated in both cases, although they did not attack the same persons; and that they admitted and required alike a sustaining and stimulating course of treatment.

The filthy and negligent habits of these people appear to have rendered them fit subjects for any pestilence that might chance to make its appearance; and the observation so often made has been here confirmed, that rigid cleanliness and suitable regard for neatness, are the best preventives of contagion, and more efficient than cordons of troops, or quarantine regulations.

The annuities of the St. Regis Indians continued to be paid at Plattsburgh, until 1832, when, by a law passed April 24, the place of payment was transferred to the town of Fort Covington.

By this act the comptroller was directed to appoint an agent, who was to receive a sum not exceeding two percentum on all such disbursements.

He was directed to pay each of the heads of families under the direction of the trustees of the tribe, their equal shares of the annuities, taking the necessary receipts from the legal trustees of said tribes, for the annuities received.

As the village of St. Regis was then in the town of Fort Covington, these annuities have since been generally paid at that place.

The agents appointed by the comptroller, to pay these annuities, since this office was created, in 1832, have been, James B. Spencer, Amherst K. Williams, John S. Eldridge, Phineas Attwater, Wm. A. Wheeler, J. J. Seaver, and James C. Spencer.

During the summer of 1834, these Indians remonstrated against the payment of any part of the annuity of 1796, to the Caughnawagas, urging that previous to the war, a release was executed by the latter to them. During the war, the latter had not received their share. A few years after the war, through the agency and interference of Peter Sailly, of Plattsburgh, that moiety of the annuity was restored to them, with the express understanding, that $50 annually of that portion should be paid to Thomas Williams, who had left that tribe, with his family, during the war, at a great sacrifice, and joined the Americans. Williams was paid without objection, till 1833, when the Caughnawagas entered a protest, and he was not paid.

Before the war, the St. Regis Indians were allowed to hold, in common with their brethren in Canada, all the Indian lands, and also to receive the rents and profits of them. Since the war, the British government refused them the privilege of even occupying the lands on the St. Lawrence river, in common with their brethren in Canada. [169]

For this reason, they conceived that they had an exclusive right to the state annuities. They accordingly applied to the legislature, in 1835, for the payment to them of the annuity which had been previously shared by the Caughnawagas.

They also asked that the payment of their annuities might be made at a more convenient season of the year, and to those who reside in the suite of New York, or within the United States only. They also applied for a change of the existing law for the election of trustees, and desired that the governor might be empowered to appoint not less than three nor more than six principal Indians, who should be called chiefs, and hold their office during pleasure, a majority of whom were to act for the tribe.

This memorial was referred to A. C. Flagg, the comptroller, who made a report to the legislature, in which he reviewed the history of the Indian title, and from which we will take the liberty of making a few extracts.

After briefly enumerating the several treaties made, by whom and for what consideration he gives the following summary of the compensation and annuities received for their lands.

	Sum paid at the treaty.	Amount of annuities.
Treaty of 1796 with the Seven Nations,	$3,179.96	$533.33
" 1816 " St. Regis		1,300.00
" 1818 " "		200.00
" 1824 " "	1,920.00	
" 1824 " "	1,750.00	60.00
" 1824 and act of 1825		305.00
" 1825 with the St. Regis,	2,100.00	
	$8,949.96	$2,398.33

In relation to the claims of these Indians, the comptroller said:

"It should be borne in mind, that the treaty was originally made with British as well as American Indians, which treaty is in the nature of a contract, on the part of the state, to pay annually a certain sum of money in consideration of the relinquishment, by the Seven Nations, of Canada, of certain lands belonging to them. When the treaty was made, the Caughnawagas were British Indians, as much as they are now; the state did not refuse to treat with them, and purchase their lands, because they resided in Canada; and having made the treaty with them, shall the state refuse to fulfill it?

If the annuity is to be confiscated because the Caughnawagas, or some of them, may have taken up arms against the United States during the late war, then the question would arise, whether the confiscation should be made for the benefit of the state treasury or the St. Regis tribe; and if the Caughnawagas are to be cut off, because some of their warriors [170] aided the enemy, the same rule would deprive the St. Regis Indians of their annuities, since some of their warriors were understood to have joined the British army during the war. It should be recollected, however, that the Caughnawaga Indians did not promise allegiance, by the treaty of 1796, nor did they owe allegiance to the United States, or this state, when the war of 1812 was declared.

A request is made in the memorial, that the annuity of $533.33 may hereafter be paid only to such of the St. Regis tribe as reside in this state, or the United States. By the treaty of 1796, it was agreed, that if the Seven Nations of Canada, would relinquish their lands to the people of this state, they should receive forever an annuity of $533.33. After the Indians, in pursuance of this agreement, have relinquished their lands, and after the state has taken possession of and sold them, can the government of this state refuse to fulfil the stipulations of the treaty, because the Indians do not reside on the American side of the national line?

The St. Regis Indians represent that Thomas Williams left the Caughnawagas during the war, with his family, at a great sacrifice. It is true that he joined the American side during the war, and for doing this, his property may have been confiscated. But it will be seen by referring to the treaties, that Thomas Williams, who in 1796 was a Caughnawaga chief, in 1816, had become one of the chiefs and head men of the St. Regis tribe, and assisted in securing to the latter tribe an annuity of $1,300 for the sale of lands, reserved in the treaty with the Seven Nations of Canada. By joining the St. Regis Indians and aiding in the subsequent sale for the sole benefit of this tribe, of the lands reserved by the treaty of 1796, Williams would of course lose all favor with the tribe to which he had originally belonged.

The exclusion of the Caughnawagas from a participation in the annuity secured by the treaty of 1796, is only one of the disturbing questions with which the St. Regis Indians are agitated. There are two parties in the tribe, one denominated the American party, and the other the British party; and as they elect trustees under the authority of the laws of this state, the British Indians, it is alleged, join in and in some cases control these elections.

The strife in relation to the choice of trustees may have been increased and aggravated, from the circumstance that these trustees have been in the habit of issuing due bills, which are circulated and form a kind of paper currency. These due bills are made payable on the first Tuesday in August succeeding the date thereof, and are based of course on the money in the treasury and which is payable to the Indians on that day."

The comptroller advised against changing the time or mode of paying the annuities.

In 1834, there had been paid to one hundred and three families, comprising three hundred and thirty-six individuals, $2,131.66 to the St. Regis, and $260.67 to the Caughnawaga tribe.

It is stated that when the government, after the war, decided to restore one half of the annuity of 1796, to the latter, that Mr. Denniston, the agent, told their deputies, that Williams having been a party to the treaty, ought to have a share of the money, and accordingly $50 had been paid to him annually. [171]

Those who wish to pursue this examination, will find by referring to the assembly documents of 1835, a further statement, with a copy of the paper purporting to confer upon the St. Regis Indians, authority to receive the annuities of 1796, which the comptroller decided to be spurious; and also a correspondence of James B. Spencer, at that time the agent, and documents showing that the St. Regis were deprived of certain rights previously enjoyed, in consequence of the course adopted in the war. Our space does not admit of further reference to this question.

The Caughnawagas being decided to be entitled to a portion of the annuity above mentioned, continued to receive it until 1841, (May 25,) when the commissioners of the land office were authorized,

> "To direct the payment, in their discretion, to the Caughnawaga and St. Regis tribes, representing the Seven Nations of Canada, or any part or portion of them, of the principal of the annuities, or such portion thereof as they, the said commissioners, may from time to time deem proper, remaining under the control of this state, for the benefit of said Indians, or any portion of them. They were authorized also, to treat with any remaining tribes of Indians in the state for their lands, or the payment of moneys belonging to them, or in relation to roads running through their lands.
>
> The acts of these commissioners were to be submitted to the governor for his approval, before they could have effect. Actions for trespass were to be prosecuted by the district attorney of the counties where they were committed, and the excess recovered, after paying the expense of prosecution, was to be distributed among the Indians. Three of the chiefs of the tribe might in like manner bring a suit for its benefit, with the written approbation of the supervisor of the town where the land was situated, or of any judge of the county courts, and security for costs in the latter case being given, approved by the supervisor or judge, at any time before or on the return of the first process in the suit."

The Caughnawagas have accordingly been paid the principal of their share of the annuity.

By an act passed April 27, 1841, the trustees of the St. Regis tribe duly elected, at a regular meeting, were authorized with the advice and consent of the agent for the payment of their annuities, to execute leases to white persons for any part of their unoccupied lands, for any term not exceeding twenty-one years, for such rents as may be agreed upon. The income of these leases was to be divided for the general benefit of the tribe. The district attorney of Franklin county, was to prepare the form of the lease, and none were to take effect unless with the written consent of the district attorney, or Indian agent, endorsed thereon. The fee for preparing the lease, attending to its execution, and endorsing it, was fixed at three dollars.

In pursuance with powers thus granted, considerable portions of the reservation have been leased, mostly to Canadian Frenchmen. [172]

The question of the propriety of this measure, has ever been a subject of contention and party strife among them, at their annual election of trustees. For several years, the party opposed to leasing land, has been in the ascendancy, and the measure has been discontinued.

The grass meadows on Grass river, in the town of Massena, were purchased from the St. Regis Indians, by the commissioners of the land office, in pursuance of powers vested in them by the legislature, on the 21st of February, 1845.

The amount purchased was, according to Lay's Map of 1801, two hundred and ten acres, at three dollars per acre. It was stipulated that if the amount of land should be found to overrun, the excess should be paid for at the same rates.

The Indian meadows on Grass river were surveyed by John W. Tate, in 1845, and patented in small lots in the years 1846, '7, '8, '9, and 1851.

By an act making provision for the education of the different Indian tribes of the state, passed April 30, 1846, it was enacted: That the sum of two hundred and fifty dollars should be appropriated for the building and furnishing of a school house, on the lands of the St. Regis Indians; and the further sum of two hundred dollars a year, for the term of five years, for the payment of the wages of a teacher and other expenses of the said school.

These moneys were to be paid from time to time, by the agent, who was to give his usual official bond, and report annually to the superintendent of common schools.

This appropriation was very judiciously expended by Phineas Attwater, Esq., the agent, in the erection of a school house, on the reservation, and between the village and Hogansburgh.

In addition to the amount named in the previous act, a further sum of $75 was appropriated May 7, 1847, out of the United States deposite fund, to be expended by the agent paying annuities, in completing the school house on the St. Regis reservation, and in improving the school lot.

The act of 1846 was so amended as to give $300 per annum for the years 1847, 1848, for the payment of a teacher.

The novelty of the measure, with other causes, made it at first very popular, and the school was very fully attended. The parents evinced an interest in the measure that was surprising, and often visited the school, and took a deep interest in its success; but it became necessary to discharge the teacher, and those who have since been employed have failed to awaken the interest which was at first felt.

The British government have also maintained a school here for several years, hut with no better success. [173]

The natives have often expressed their sense of the degrading influences which the use of ardent spirits have exerted to their injury. The following memorial from the Oneidas, more than fifty years ago, addressed to the legislature as coming from the different Indian tribes, possesses a melancholy interest, and engages our sympathy as expressive of a refined sentiment of the heart, and a feeling that would do honor to man's nature, if expressed, not by the illiterate savage, but by one who had enjoyed all the advantages which civilization has conferred upon him.

"To the Legislature of the State of New York:
Brothers:
We, the sachems and chiefs of the different nations, desire your attention. You have often manifested a respect to our welfare, by way of good council. You have told us, that we should love one another, and to live

in peace. You also exhorted us, to abandon our savage life, to adopt your mode of life in cultivating our laud; to raise grain; to be sober and many other good things. We have made attempts to follow the good path you have pointed out for us, but find ourselves still deficient. And you seem to blame us for our backwardness, and we are to be blamed.
Brothers:

We have been often consulting upon our welfare, and to promote it—we made but slow progress. For we find our great obstacle which we look upon as our enemy, by whose means our nations are almost reduced to the ground. Our young men seem to be willing to become slaves to this tyrant, who goes in the name of SPIRITUOUS LIQUOR. To us he is a servant of evil spirit. When we found that our own endeavors and powers were too weak to prevent such an enraging tyrant, we united our voices, two years ago, to you for your assistance, that you might bind this tyrant But you refused to give your assistance, which one brother bad right to expect from another.
Brothers:

If such of your color, as sell us this article, were obliged to keep us in their houses while we are distracted with it, and suffer us in the desolation it makes, we then believe they would willingly call out as loud as we do for help, and existence. Therefore we can not but hope and firmly believe, that you will at this time, give all possible relief.
Brothers:

Remember, that we were willing to assist you to fight against your enemy. We were willing to let you have our lands when you needed. We were willing to maintain the chain of friendship with you, and we desire to live in peace, and to enjoy all your privileges. But how can we come to this, so long as you as it were willing to see us destroyed by this tyrant In consequence of which, numberless audiences have taken place amongst us. And besides that you often told us, that the Great Spirit will send all drunkards to everlasting fire after death.
Brothers:

You are wise people, and you know the mind of the Great Spirit. But we are ignorant people, and you often call us savages. We know but little, and can do but little. And as you are our brothers, we would again look to you for help to lessen abundantly, that distracting article [174] by some law of yours that we may have fair trial to walk in that path which you so highly recommended to us.

And in compliance with this our request, we shall ever acknowledge your friendship, and we leave it to your wisdom and humanity."

By a general act passed April 10, 1813, it was enacted:

> "That no pawn taken of any Indian within this state for any spirituous liquor, shall be retained by the person to whom such pawn shall be delivered, but the thing so pawned may be sued for, and recovered, with costs of suit, by the Indian who may have deposited the same, before any court having cognizance thereof."

It was made a penal offence to sell liquors to certain tribes by this act. By a law passed April 11, 1820, the provisions of a previous general act restricting the sale of ardent spirit, was extended to the Seneca and St. Regis tribe; and in this was prohibited the selling to any Indians of said tribes, or residing or visiting with them, any rum, brandy, gin, or other ardent spirits.

The traffic and use of ardent spirits with these people, was still further restricted by an act of April 20, 1835, which provides:

> "That if any person shall knowingly sell or furnish to any Indians, belonging to or residing with the St. Regis tribe, any rum, brandy, gin, or other spirituous liquor, within the counties of Franklin or St. Lawrence, such person shall be deemed guilty of a misdemeanor, and on conviction thereof shall be fined at the discretion of the court, not exceeding twenty-five dollars for one offence, or may be imprisoned not exceeding thirty days, and shall also forfeit for every such offence the sum of five dollars, to be recovered with costs in an action of debt by any person who will sue for the same, one half of which forfeiture to be paid to the prosecutor and the residue to the commissioners of common schools in each town; and that on the recovery of such forfeiture, the offender shall not be liable for any other or further prosecution for the same offence."

The act of 1826 was by this repealed. A still more stringent law was passed April 16, 1849, which forbade the sale or gift of ardent spirits to the Indians, or receiving pawns from them, under a penalty of not less than twenty-five dollars for the former, and a forfeiture of ten times the value of the latter for each offence.

Notwithstanding the most stringent and explicit laws prohibiting the sale or gift of ardent spirits to the Indians, it has been found hitherto impossible to restrain many from habits of intemperence, although there is far less of this now, than formerly. The influence of the present priest appears to be decidedly in favor of temperance.

The state, in its negotiations with the Indian tribes within its borders, has regarded them as a foreign power, so far as the cession of their lands is concerned, and as wards or minors as relates to their internal affairs, and their intercourse with individuals. [175]

A clause in an act passed April 11, 1808, directed that the district attorney in the county of Washington, should advise and direct the St. Regis Indians, in the controversy among themselves and with any other persons, and defend all actions brought against any of them by any white person, and commence and prosecute all such actions for them or any of them as he might find proper and necessary.

On the 11th of April, 1811, the substance of the foregoing act was repassed, with the following preamble and provision:

> "And whereas, by the rules and customs of the said Indians, (many of whom are infants,) they are all tenants in common of their property, and all suits brought by them, or in their behalf, must be brought in the name of all of the individuals of the said tribe. Therefore;
> Be it enacted, that it shall and may be lawful for the said district attorney, in all suits which he may find proper and necessary to commence and prosecute on behalf of the said Indians, to bring it in the name of the St. Regis Indians, without naming any of the individuals of the said tribe, any law, custom or usage to the contrary notwithstanding."

The district attorney of Washington county, continued to be charged with the trusts reposed in him by the foregoing acts, until April 21, 1818, when a law was passed directing the governor to appoint district attorneys in each of the counties of the state, and making it the especial duty of the one in Franklin county to perform all the duties previously required of the district attorney of the fifth judicial district relative to the St. Regis Indians.

It has since continued the duty of this officer to act in their behalf, but it is said that he is seldom called upon to settle the internal difficulties of the tribe, although upon several occasions individuals have become amenable to the laws and have been dealt with accordingly.

In their internal affairs, they have seldom troubled their neighbors, and have been at little or no expense to their town or county as paupers.

The St. Regis are at present nominally divided into five bands:

1st. OKAWAHO, *the wolf.* At present the most numerous.
2d. RATINIATEN, *the big turtle.*   Second in numbers to the former.
3d. OKWARI, the bear.   Third   "   "
4th. ROTINESIIO, *the plover.*   Fourth   "   "
5th. ROTISENNAKEHTE, *the little turtle*, the least numerous.

This division is a traditionary one, the purport and meaning of which are entirely lost.

It anciently related to war parties, and rude pictures of these several objects were used as distinctive marks in designating or recording events. A satisfactory account of these and other bands, will be seen in the first volume of the Documentary History of New York.

These distinctions descend in a line by hereditary succession, from mother to son.
[176]
The female succession is common among all Indian tribes, and is accounted for

by them in a characteristic manner, by saying that the mother of a person may be known with certainty, but not the father.

This classification is somewhat similar to that of the clans of Scotland, and probably had its origin under similar circumstances, namely, petty wars, led by small parties and extending not far from the locality where they originated.

The marks became distinctive symbols by which they were known, and constituted a kind of heraldic designation, when painted on their garments and weapons, or marked upon the bark of trees to indicate the class or band to which the wearer or maker of the device belonged.

The St. Regis Indians observe none of the festivals or ceremonies of their ancestors, and no public demonstrations are made, except those imposed by the canons of the catholic church. The principal rites of that sect are here observed, and none with more pomp and parade than *corpus christi,* which is depended upon easter, and falls generally in the first half of June. Preparations for this often occupy weeks; the streets are lined with green boughs and garlands of flowers, a military company from among their number, joins in the processions, and the ceremony usually attracts hundreds of curious spectators from the neighboring towns.

St. Regis day is not observed, but by a regulation of the bishops of Quebec, made several years since, the anniversary of patron saints of churches, is observed on the first Sunday of November. This day is observed with ceremonies in all the catholic churches in Canada.

The only national pastime which these Indians appear to possess, is that of *ball-playing,* in which they engage with much zeal, and for which they evince a strong passion.

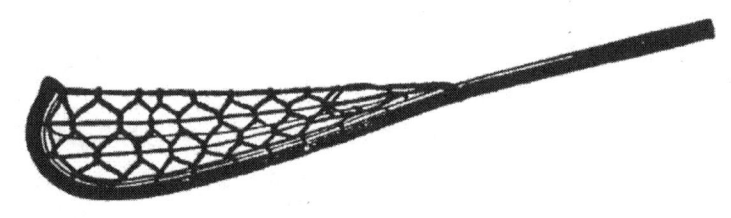

The instrument which is used for this purpose, is formed of a rod about four feet in length, bent as in the following figure, and having drawn across its curvature a net of deerskin thongs. The manner in which the game is conducted is as follows:

About a dozen Indians divided between two parties, and having no clothing but a girdle around the middle, and each with a bat like that [177] above represented, repair to some spacious plain, in the middle of which is laid a ball. The game consists in seizing the ball on the net and tossing it from one to another till it arrives at the side of the field. Each party has its goal, to which it endeavors to toss the ball, and the rivalry which it excites, leads them to the most active efforts. The ball is seldom allowed to touch the ground, and it rebounds from side to side, alternately favoring one and the other party. As a natural consequence, it often results in personal injuries, from blows aimed at the ball, but received by the ball players.

A company of these has lately held public exhibitions in our large towns and villages.

The exact number of the St. Regis tribe at the time of the [author's] visit in June 1852, was 1120, of whom 632 souls belonged to the British, and 488 to the American party. Of this number there is said to be *not one individual of pure Indian blood,* being all more or less mixed with the French and other white races.

The war created a division which has since continued, and the British party still adhere to the election of their twelve chiefs, who hold their office for life.

Their affairs with government are transacted though an agent or clerk who resides in Cornwall, on the opposite shore of the St. Lawrence.

The American party elect three trustees annually, for the transaction of business, on the first Tuesday of May, in pursuance of statute.

The British party of the St. Regis tribe, at present, receive $1,000 as interest for a tract of land sold to that government. It will hereafter be somewhat greater. Besides, they receive rents for lands in Dundee, amounting to $1,000 annually, and blankets and clothing at certain rates, depending upon the age of the individual.

From five to nine, a child receives the value of $1-50. From nine to fourteen, about $2-50, and after that period, the worth of $4 or $5; besides, 1 pound of powder, and 4 pounds of shot and balls, for hunting. A woman receives the value of $4 in blankets and cloth.

Several of the British islands in the St. Lawrence, above and opposite St. Regis, belong to these Indians, and they cultivate or rent all that are valuable.

No section of the country possesses greater fertility or value for agricultural purposes, than most of these islands in the St. Lawrence.

The American party receive their annuity, amounting now to $2,131.67 equally divided between men, women and children, to the amount of $4 per head. Besides this, they receive rent for a tract of land near Hogansburgh, on the Indian reservation, amounting to about $700.

The money now paid by the state, is disbursed by an agent who is appointed [178] by the comptroller, and holds his office at the will of the appointing power. He receives at present a salary of $70. The money is paid to heads of families in specie, in proportion to the number of members in each. It is equally divided among all.

A methodist mission has for some time existed at St. Regis, and they have a chapel in the village of Hogansburgh, on the line of the reservation, and as near the Indian village as a title for land on which to build a church could be procured. In the year 1847-8, the Rev. Ebenezer Arnold, of the Black River Conference, who was laboring in an adjoining charge, was led among them, and after preaching to them a few times succeeded in exciting that interest which resulted in the formation of a small and flourishing society, to which on the following conference the Rev. J. P. Jennings, was appointed missionary.

Through the indefatigable exertions of this gentleman, assisted by others who participated in his interest for the mission, and especially by Bishop James, who has the charge of the Indian mission for the time being, the present elegant chapel was erected at an expense of over $1,500, furnished with a fine toned bell, and having a convenient parsonage, pasture, and garden, the whole costing from $2,000, to $2,500. At the end of the second year of his labors, Mr. Jennings was succeeded by the Rev. R. E. King, the present incumbent.

The author is indebted to a work entitled Episcopal Methodism as it Was and Is, by the Rev. P. D. Gorrie, for most of the above data in relation to the methodist mission at St Regis.

Indian Names of Places.

It is scarcely two centuries since the territory now the United States, was an unbroken wild, traversed only by the rude natives, who pursued the bear, and the moose, and set his simple snares for such wild game as served to feed or clothe him. The advent of the European, was his misfortune; and step by step he has retreated before the march of civilization, leaving nothing, but here and there, his names of rivers and lakes, and even these, in too many instances, have been with a most singular injustice, and bad taste, exchanged for those of foreign origin, or of no signification of themselves.

The sonorous, and peculiarly appropriate names of the aborigines, have often been made the subject of commendation by foreigners, and should in most instances take the preference of those of modern origin.

In some cases this would be difficult, but in a new and growing country like ours, in which new sources of industry are daily being developed, and new places springing up, might we not with peculiar propriety adopt the euphonious and often elegant names of the Indians [179] instead of the common place appellation of "_____'s Mills," or "_____'s Corners;" words which convey no association, but those of the most common and indifferent character, and which usually lose all their application after the first generation.

Let any one compare the splendid names of Saratoga, Niagara, and Ontario, with Sackett's Harbor, German Flats, or Lake George, and he will see the contrast between them, and can not fail to approve the taste that would restore the aboriginal names of places, where it may be found practicable.

In making his inquiries into the history of the mission at St. Regis, in June, 1852, the author took special pains to obtain, not only the Indian names of places in the northern part of the state, and immediately within the territory embraced in the work, but also of whatever other localities he might chance to be able, not doubting but that the subject would be regarded as one of general interest.

At the Indian village of Caughnawaga, near the Saut St. Louis, the author met an intelligent half breed, Mr. A. Geo. De Lorimier, alias Oronhiatekha, who is well acquainted with the Mohawk and other Indian languages, from whom he also derived some assistance, especially relating to distant and well known localities. The names derived from this source, will be designated by a † prefixed to the word.

Acknowledgements are especially clue to the Rev. F. Marcoux, of St. Regis, for essential assistance in this and other inquiries. Those names received from this source will be thus marked, ‡.

River and Streams.

Black River.—(‡ Ni-ka-hi-on-ha-ko-wa) "big river." Mr. Squier, in a work entitled The Aboriginal Monuments of New York, has given the name of this river as Ka-mar-go. His authority is not cited.

In a map accompanying L. H. Morgan's work entitled The League of the Iroquois, the name given is Ka-hu-a-go, which is a Seneca word.

Chateaugay.—This by some is supposed to be an Indian name, but it is French, meaning, gay castle. The St. Regis call it ‡O-sar-he-hon, "a place so close or difficult that the more one tries to extricate himself the worse he is off." This probably relates to the narrow gorge in the river near the village.

Chippewa Creek.—In Hammond, (‡Tsi-o-he-ri-sen), This name also applies to Indian Hut Island.

Deer River—(‡Oie-ka-ront-ne) "trout river." The name also applies to the village of Helena, at its mouth.

French Creek.—(‡A-ten-ha-ra-kweh-ta-re) "the place where the fence or wall fell down." The same name applies to the adjoining island.

Gananoqui.— Not Iroquois, supposed to be Huron, and said to mean "wild potatoes," *Apios tuberosa*, (‡Kah-non-no-kwen) "a meadow rising out of the water."

Grass River.—(‡Ni-kent-si-a-ke,) "full of large fishes," or, "where the fishes live." In former times this name was peculiarly applicable. Before [180] dams and saw mills were erected, salmon and other fish not now caught were taken in the greatest abundance, as far up as Russell. Its English name was suggested by the grass meadows near its month. On an old map in the clerk's office it is marked, Ey-en-saw-ye. The letter *y*, does not occur in the Iroquois language.

Indian River.—On Morgan's map, (O-je-quack). The St. Regis name it by the same appellation, as Black Lake, which see.

Oswegatchie, and the village of Ogdensburgh. (‡Swe-kat-si), supposed to be a corrupted Huron word meaning "black water." This river in early times was sometimes called *Black river.*

Ohio.—(O-hi-on-hi-o,) "handsome river." The French designation of La Belle Riviere, was a translation of the original name.

Raquette River.—A French word meaning a "snow shoe." It is said to have been first so called, by a Frenchman named Parisein, long before settlements were begun in this quarter, and that the name was suggested by the shape of a marsh, near its mouth. The Iroquois name ‡ Ni-ha-na-wa-te, or "rapid river," is peculiarly applicable. It is said that Colonel Louis, the Indian chief, told Benjamin Raymond, when surveying, that its Indian name meant "noisy river," for which reason it has been usually written *Racket.*

As rapids are always noisy, this name would have an application, but we shall retain in the map the original orthography. The St. Francois name, as obtained by Prof. Emmons, was Mas-le-a-gui. On Morgan's map, above quoted, it is called Ta-na-wä-deh, supposed to be a Seneca word.

St. Lawrence River.—(‡Cat-a-ro-qui,) said to be French or Huron. Signification unknown. On Morgan's map, Ga-na-wa-ge.

St. Regis River and Village.—(‡Ak-wis-sas-ne,) "where the partridge drums."

Schoharie.—(‡Io-hsko-ha-re,) "a natural bridge," as that formed by timber floating down stream, and lodging firmly, so as to form a bridge.

Salmon river.—(‡Kent-si-a-ko-wa-ne,) "big fish river."

†*Tioinata.*—A small river, tributary to the St. Lawrence, above Brockville. Signifies, "beyond the point."

Lakes.

Black Lake.—(‡A-tsi-kwa-ke,) "where the ash tree grows with large knobs for making clubs."

Champlain.—(†Ro-tsi-ich-ni,) "the coward spirit." The Iroquois are said to have originally possessed an obscure mythological notion, of three supreme beings, or spirits, the "good spirit," the "bad spirit," and the "coward spirit." The latter inhabited an island in lake Champlain, where it died, and from this it derived the name above given. How far this fable prevailed, or what was its origin, could not be ascertained from the person of whom it was received.

Grass Lake.—Rossie, (‡O-sa-ken-ta-ke,) "grass lake."

Ontario.—(†O-non-ta-ri-io,) "handsome lake."

Tupper's Lake.—(‡Tsit-kan i-a-ta-res-ko-wa,) "the biggest lake." A small lake below Tupper's lake is called ‡Tsi-kan-i-on-wa-res-ko-wa, "long pond." The name of Tupper's lake, in the dialect of the St. François Indians, as obtained by Professor Emmons, while making the geological survey of the second district, is Pas-kum-ga-meh, "a lake going out from the river," alluding to the peculiar feature, which it presents, of the lake, lying not in the course of, but by the side of, Raquette river, with which it communicates. [181]

Yellow Lake.—In Rossie, (Kat-sen-e-kwa-r,) "a lake covered with yellow lilies."

Islands.

Barnhart's Island.—(‡Ni-ion-en-hi-a-se-ko-wa-ne,) "big stone."

Baxter's Island.—Upper Long Saut Isle, (‡Tsi-io-wen-o-kwa-ka-ra-te,) "high island."

Cornwall Island.—(‡Ka-wen-o-ko-wa-nen-ne,) "big island."

Isle au Gallop, and the rapid beside it, (‡Tsi-ia-ko-ten-nit-ser-ron-ti-e- tha.) "where the canoe must be pushed up stream with poles."

Isle au Rapid Plat.—Opposite Waddington, (‡Tie-hon-wi-ne-tha,) "where a canoe is towed with a rope."

Lower Long Sault Isle.—(‡Ka-ron-kwi.)

Sheik's Island.—(‡O-was-ne,) "feather island."

St. Regis island.—Same name with river and village.

NAMES OF PLACES.

Brasher Falls.—(‡Ti-o-hi-on-ho-ken,) "where the river divides."

Brasher Iron Works.—(‡Tsit-ka-res-ton-ni,) "where they make iron."

Canada.—(†Ka-na-ta,) "village."

Cayuga.—(†Koi-ok-wen,) "from the water to the shore," as the landing of prisoners.

†*Cataroqui.*—Ancient name of Kingston, "a bank of clay rising out of the waters."

Hochelaga.—Former name of Montreal, or its vicinity, (†O-ser-a-ke,) "Beaver dam."

Helena.—The same name as Deer river.

Hogansburgh.—(‡Te-kas-wen-ka-ro-rens,) "where they saw boards."

Kentucky.—(†Ken-ta-ke,) "among the meadows."

Malone.—(‡Te-kan-o-ta-ron-we,) "a village crossing a river."

Massena Springs.—(‡Kan-a-swa-stak-e-ras,) "where the mud smells bad."

Massena Village.—Same name as Grass river.

Moira.—(‡Sa-ko-ron-ta-keh-tas,) "where small trees are carried on the shoulder."

Montreal.—(‡Ti-o-ti-a-ke,) "deep water by the side of shallow."

New York.—(‡Ka no-no) signification not known.

Norfolk Village.—(‡Kan-a-tas-e-ke,) "new village."

Lower Falls in Norfolk on Raquette river, (Tsit-ri-os-ten-ron-we,) "natural dam."

The Oxbow, produced by the bend of the Oswegatchie river, (‡O-non-to-hen,) "a hill with the same river on each side."

Potsdam.—(‡Te-wa-ten-e-ta-ren-ies,) "a place where the gravel settles under the feet in dragging up a canoe."

Quebec.—(‡Te-kia-tan-ta-ri-kon,) "twin or double mountains."

Raymondville.—(‡Tsi-ia-ko-on-tie-ta,) "where they leave the canoe."

Saratoga.—(†Sa-ra-ta-ke.) "a place where the track of the heel may be seen," in allusion to a locality said to be in the neighborhood, where depressions like footsteps may be seen on the rock."

Schenectady.—(‡Ska-na-ta-ti,) "on the other side of the pines."

Ticonderoga.—(†Tia-on-ta-ro-ken,) "a fork or point between two lakes."

Toronto.—(†Tho-ron-to-hen,) "timber on the water."

Waddington.—(‡Ka-na-ta-ra-ken,) "wet village."

We will conclude our account of St. Regis, by a biographical notice of some of the more prominent of those who have flourished there. [182]

TIRENS, an Oswegatchie Indian, known as Peter the orator, was a man of great natural talent ns a speaker. He was drowned about war time in crossing the St. Lawrence. He was an American Indian, and his descendants still lire at St. Regis. On numerous occasions in council, he produced a great effect from his eloquence.

A half breed Indian, who usually was known as PETER THE BIG SPEAK, was a son of Lesor Tarbell, one of the lads who had been stolen away from Groton by the Indians, and who subsequently became one of the first settlers who preceded the founding of St. Regis.

He was a man of much address and ability as a speaker, and was selected as the mouth piece of the tribe on the more important occasions that presented themselves in their councils.

AT-I-ATON-HA-RON-KWEN,[9] better known as *Louis Cook* or *Col. Louis*, was unquestionably the greatest man that has ever flourished at St. Regis, among the native population. His influence with his tribe was very great, and they always relied upon his council, and entrusted him with the performance of their more important business, not only with the other tribes, but also with the two governments.

In all the treaties we have seen, and in all the reports of councils that are preserved, we uniformly find him mentioned, as one of the deputies of the tribe. He had the misfortune of being illiterate. Had he possessed the advantages of education, combined with his great native strength of mind, and soundest judgment, he would have shone with distinguished reputation in his day.

The following narrative of his life we have derived from his daughter, Mary Ka-wen-ni-ta-ke, at St. Regis, through the kindness of the Rev. F. Marcoux, as interpreter, and from a biographical notice written by the Rev. Eleazer Williams, which was obligingly loaned for the purpose. The author has also availed himself of whatever else came in his way, among the public archives at Albany.

Louis Cook was born about 1740, at Saratoga; his father being a colored man, in the service of one of the government officials at Montreal, and his mother, a St. Francois. In his features he strongly indicated his African parentage.

In an attack made upon Saratoga, towards the close of 1755, the parents of young Louis, were among the captives.[10]

It is said that a French officer seized the boy, and would claim him as his property, but his mother incessantly cried out "uh-ni-ho-wa!," that is, "he is my child." No, no, said the officer, he is a negro, and he is mine. The afflicted mother made an appeal to the Iroquois chief warriors, for the [183] restoration of her child, who immediately demanded of the officer, to have him delivered up to them as one of their own people, and he reluctantly gave up his prize. The mother out of gratitude to her Indian friends, would accompany them home on their return, and she repaired to Caughnawaga with them, where she spent the remainder of her life, and where she died. The Jesuit father of the mission persuaded young Louis to live with him as an attendant, and here he acquired the French language, which he spoke with ease.

His youth was not distinguished by any peculiarities differing from those of his age and condition, further, than that he indicated an enquiring mind, and took an interest in what was going on in the councils of the tribe, which was unusual for those of his age.

From these councils, he often said in his old age, he learned his first lessons of wisdom. His religious principles very naturally inclined with his early associations, and he became and continued through life a catholic, but there was nothing of intolerance or illiberality in his deportment towards others.

In the war between the French and English, which began in 1755, and ended by the complete success of the latter in 1760, Louis took up arms for the French, in common with his tribe, and was sent to watch the movements of the English on Lake George. Early in the spring of 1756, being in the vicinity of Ticonderoga, he was one of a scouting party sent out against the English, and encountered a party of the latter, under Major Rogers, and a skirmish ensued, in which he was wounded. The wound which he received, was long a source of annoyance, but his conduct had gained him a character for courage as a warrior, which he ever afterwards maintained. He was with the French troops at the defeat of Braddock, on the Ohio, and was also present at the taking of Oswego. At a later period, he was with the forces against Abercrombie at Ticonderoga, where he first received the command of a small party of Iroquois, for which service he was chosen, on account of his general reputation for consistency, and courage, and his command of the French as well as Indian languages.

In the attempt to retake Quebec which the French made, he was present, but after the conquest of Canada, his war spirit entirely ceased, and he returned to private life, and the gaining of a livelihood by the chase, respected by the Indians and the whites so far as he was known. His predilection, like those of the greater part of his race, were still with their former allies, the French, and although the opportunity for its exhibition did not recur, it prevented him from engaging zealously in the affairs of the English.

The troubles which preceded, and led to the American revolution, attracted [184] his curiosity, as he heard the matters discussed among the whites, and he is said to have made once or twice a journey to Albany, to get information on the subject. From General Schuyler, and others, he derived an account of the difficulty, and news that he carried with him to Caughnawaga, is believed to have interested the chiefs of that tribe in behalf of the American cause.

When the storm which had so long darkened the political horizon at length broke, and the crisis had arrived when every one must choose a part, this independent minded Indian adopted a course, which, under the circumstances, must he considered remarkable, and resolved to identify his interests with those of the revolted colonies.

It is difficult to assign a probable reason for this course, as his residence was remote from the theatre of civil commotion, and his people could scarcely complain of the grievances which arose from the stamp act, or the trammels upon commerce and industry, of which the colonies loudly and justly complained.

It may perhaps be ascribed to a dislike for his old enemy the English, and a willingness to side with any party that would attempt their defeat. Whatever may have been the motive, the result was certain, that he enlisted with ardor in the cause of the revolution; served the interests of the colonies with zeal and ability in his sphere, and rendered essential service to his adopted cause, by the weight and influence which his abilities secured him among his race. He felt and declared that the cause was just, and would succeed; he had witnessed the military character of the provincials in the late war, and knew them to be brave, and he felt that the objects for which they contended were worthy of the trials and the sufferings which it would cost to achieve them.

After General Washington had assumed the command of the American army before Boston, Louis Cook resolved to pay him a visit. In a letter to the president of congress, dated at the camp in Cambridge, August 4, 1775, General Washington says:

> "On the first instant, a chief of the Caughnawaga tribe, who live about six miles from Montreal, came in here, accompanied by a Colonel Bayley, of Coos. His accounts of the temper and disposition of the Indians, are very favorable. He says, they have been strongly solicited, by Governor Carlton, to engage against us, but his nation is totally averse: that threats as well as entreaties have been used, without effect: that the Canadians are well disposed to the English colonies, and if any expedition is meditated against Canada, the Indians in that quarter will give all their assistance. I have endeavored to cherish that favorable disposition, and have recommended him to cultivate them in return. What I have said, I have enforced with a present, which I understood would be agreeable to him; and he is represented as being a man of weight and consequence in his own tribe. I flatter myself, his visit will [185] have a good effect. His account of General Carlton's force and situation of St. Johns, correspond with what we have had from that quarter.
> (*Washington's Life and Writings, by Sparks, vol iii, p.* 53.)

The nature of the present which our Indian chief received at this time, is not known. In after life, he was wont to exhibit to his friends a silver pipe, having neatly carved upon the bowl, the initials, G. W., as the dearly prized gift of a man he adored almost as his maker; and it admits of the conjecture, that this may have been the token which he received at the hands of Washington, on this occasion.

This visit of Louis afforded the general court of Massachusetts, then in session, an opportunity to learn something in relation to the existing condition of the Indians of Canada, and of the internal affairs of that province. There must have been an air of sincerity and intelligence in the Indian chief, to have secured this notice.

The minutes of the Massachusetts house of representatives for the 2d of August, 1775, contain the following memoranda:

"*Ordered*, That Mr. *Winthrop*, Mr. *Foster* and Mr. *White,* with such as the honorable House shall join, be a committee to confer with Louis, a chief of the Caughnawaga tribe of Indians, (who is now in town, being conducted here by Colonel *Bayley* of *Cohoss*,) in order to gain from him all the intelligence they can, respecting the temper and designs of the Canadians and Indians towards these colonies, or any other matter it may be of importance to us to know."

Read and concurred in, and Mr. *Howard*, Mr. *Batchelder*, Dr. *Church* and Colonel *Orne*, are joined to the committee of the honorable board.

On the following day, "Mr. *Chauncey* brought down the report of the committee of both Houses, who were appointed to confer with Louis, a chief of the *Caughnawaga* tribe of *Indians*, viz:

"In council, *August* 3, 1775.

"The committee appointed to confer with *Louis*, a chief of the *Caughnawaga* tribe of *Indians*, (who is now in town, being conducted here by Colonel *Bayley* of *Cohoss*,) concerning the temper and designs of the *Canadians* and *Indians* towards these colonies, have attended to that service, and beg leave to lay before this honorable Court, the several questions proposed by the committee to the said *Louis*, and the answers made by him; which were as follows, viz:

Question. How many are there in the *Caughnawaga* tribe?
Answer. Five hundred men able to bear arms.
Q. How many in *St. Francois?*
A. I do not know. They are a different nation.
Q. How many in *Aronok?*
A. I do not know.
Q. Is there any other nation of *Indians* near your tribe?
A. Yes, *Cannastaug*. The number of them I can not tell.
Q. Has the Governor of *Canada* prevailed on the *St. Francois Indians* to take up arms against these colonies?
A. The Governor sent out Messrs. St. Lue and *Bæpassion*, to invite [186] the several tribes of *Indians* to take up arms against you. At his desire they held a Grand Council, and the French officers gave each man half a pound of powder and a drink of brandy, and an ox among them, for a feast. They answered, nobody had taken arms against them, and they would not take arms against any body to trouble them; and they chose to rest in peace. Upon this answer, the officers told them, ' if you do not take up arms the *Yankees* will come and destroy you all.' The Indians answered again, when these men come here to destroy us, then we will take up arms and defend ourselves; but we will not go to seek people to quarrel with them. The officers then told them, if you will not take up arms, the regulars will come

and destroy you, and take your lands. They answered, they may come as soon as they have a mind to; and whoever comes to attack us, we will take up arms and defend ourselves.

The officers tried to engage their young men to take up arms, by putting two Johannes apiece into their hands; but when the chiefs knew it they took the money from them, and returned it to the officers, and told the young men if they offered to engage, they would put them to death.

Q. Did you hear of any other nations of Indians that consented to take arms?

A. There is another nation, called *Ottawas*, at a greater distance, which the governor endeavored to engage, telling them that the other nations had agreed to do it. Upon which the *Ottawas* sent twenty of their tribe to the General Council before mentioned, to inform them of the governor's message, and enquire whether they had agreed to take arms? They answered they had not; and if they had any thought of it, they would have given them notice. The *French* officers had further told them, that New York, and all the other governments to the southward, were going to take arms against the *Yankees*.

Q. What do you know of the disposition of the French Canadians towards us?

A. Their disposition is the same as that of the *Indians*. The Governor tried last winter to raise two thousand troops, but he could not engage any. They were disposed to remain upon their own land in peace.

Q. What number of regulars is there in Canada?

A. About five hundred in all.

Q. Where are they stationed?

A. A sergeant and five privates at *Quebeck*, twenty at *Montreal*, and the rest are gone to *St. Johns*.

Q. What account did the French officers give of us?

A. When I went for my pass, the governor told me that you were not capable of defending yourselves, and read me a letter purporting that the king's troops had killed two thousand of your people, without reckoning the wounded, and burnt one of your towns.

All of which is humbly submitted.
By order of the committee."
J. WINTHROP.
(*American Archives, fourth series, vol. iii, p.* 301.)

Impressed with the warmest feelings of patriotism, and an earnest desire to serve the cause of the colonies, he returned to his home, and imparted to his fellows the things he had seen and heard.

In a letter from Sir Guy Carlton to General Gage, written in August, 1775, which was intercepted, the Canadian governor says:

> "Many of the Indians have gone over to them (the Americans), and large numbers of the Canadians are with them. [187] I had hopes of holding out for this year, though I seem abandoned by all the world, had the savages remained firm. I can not blame these poor people for securing themselves, as they see multitudes of the enemy at hand, and no succor from any part, though it is now four months since their operations against us first begun."

This occurred in the summer of 1775. The corn harvest having been secured, and some slight preparations for winter being made, he induced a dozen of the Caughnawaga warriors to visit with him the American camp, that they might learn, from actual observation, the condition of the cause which he was urging them to espouse. They first proceeded to the quarters of General Schuyler, and repaired thence to Cambridge. He had been probably advised to this course, by his friend General Schuyler, whom he had repeatedly visited, on his journeys to Albany, to gain intelligence of the approaching struggle. The latter had previously notified the commander-in-chief of the nature of the visit which he might soon expect to receive, but the journey was delayed a little longer than was expected. We find the occurrence mentioned in the correspondence of General Washington, who, in a letter to Major General Schuyler, dated at Cambridge, 16 January, 1776, says:

> "Our Caughnawaga friends are not arrived yet I will try to make suitable provisions for them during their stay, and use every means in my power to confirm their favorable disposition towards us. They will not, I am fearful, have such ideas of our strength, as I could wish.
> This, however, shall be strongly inculcated."
> (*Sparks's Washington, vol. iii, p. 245.*)

Very soon after this letter was written, Louis with his comrades arrived in the American camp, to tender their allegiance to the cause of Liberty, and testify their respect to the character of the commander-in-chief.

In a letter to the president of congress, dated Cambridge, January 24, 1776, General Washington says:

> "On Sunday evening, thirteen of the Caughnawaga Indians arrived here on a visit. I shall take care that they be so entertained during their stay, that they may return impressed with sentiments of friendship for us, and also of our great strength. One of them is Colonel Louis, who honored me with a visit once before."
> (*Sparks's Washington, vol. iii, p. 260.*)

Louis had an ambition for military distinction, and it appears from what follows, that there was a hesitancy on the part of the American generals in granting this.

To entrust responsible posts in the hands of Indians, of whose character or history they knew little, would be unwise. To send them off without notice, would tend to make them dissatisfied, and for aught that could be known, might serve to render them disgusted with the cause.

The perplexity which the commander-in-chief experienced from this cause, is expressed in the following extract from his letter to General Schuyler, dated Cambridge, January 27, 1776: [188]

"I am a little embarrassed to know in what manner to conduct myself with respect to the Caughnawaga Indians now here. They have, notwithstanding the treaty of neutrality which I find they entered into with you the other day, agreeably to what appears to be the sense of congress, signified to me a desire of taking up arms in behalf of the united colonies. The chief of them who, I understand, is now the first man of the nation, intends, as it is intimated, to apply to me for a commission, with the assurance of raising four or five hundred men, when he returns.

My embarrassment does not proceed so much from the impropriety of encouraging these people to depart from their neutrality, or rather accepting their own voluntary offer, as from the expense which probably may follow.

I am sensible that if they do not desire to be idle, they will be for or against us. I am sensible also, that no artifices will be left unessayed to engage them against us. Their proffered services, therefore, ought not to be rejected; but how far, with the little knowledge I have of their real intentions, and your want of their aid, I ought to go, is the question that puzzles me. I will endeavor, however, to please them, by yielding, in appearance, to their demands; reserving, at the same time, the power to you to regulate the number and movements, of which you shall be more fully informed, when any thing is fixed."

In answer to this, General Schuyler wrote:

"It is extremely difficult to determine what should be done, in what you mention, respecting the offer made by the Caughnawaga Indians; but if we can get decently rid of their offer, I would prefer it to employing them. The expense we are at in the Indian department, is amazing; it will be more so, when they consider themselves in our service; nor would their intervention be of much consequence, unless we could procure that of the other nations. The hauteur of the Indians is much diminished since the taking of Montreal: they evidently see that they can not get any supplies, but through us."

(*Sparks's Washington, vol. iii, p.* 262.)

There is preserved a traditionary account of the interview between the Indian delegates, and the American general, at the audience or council which he gave them on this occasion. It was related by the Rev. Samuel Kirkland, the missionary of the Oneidas, who is said to have acted as interpreter to the one from whom we receive it.

One of the Caughnawaga chiefs arose and said:

"He perceived there was a war cloud rising in the east, which may make great trouble, and bring much distress upon the American people on account of which his very soul troubled him. War was a great evil to any nation or people. He knew this by sad experience, in the war between the English and the French, by which the latter were brought to ruin.

He rejoiced to see the Americans had such independent spirits, as to take up arms and defend their rights and liberties, and that they would succeed because he believed that God was on their side, but that this must be gained at the expense of much blood, and great distress, upon the people. That the king of England was a powerful king, or he could not have conquered the French in Canada, but the king of Heaven is stronger than any earthly king and will defend the oppressed; and With a strong voice he added, "brother Bostonians, be [189] strong and courageous; your cause is good, you will assuredly be supported by the Great Spirit above, whose omnipotent arm will defend you, and in the end will give you a victory; a victory that will resound through all the earth, and this shall be a Sabbath day with you, and your children, and it shall be celebrated with joyful hearts, as long as the true American Spirit shall beat in their breasts. Your true Indian friends in the north, will do what they can in your favor. Indians are born free people; they love liberty, yes, they would wish to live as free as the deer in the forest, and the fowls in the air. Brother Bostonians, you are a great people, and able to meet the king of England, in the battlefield. We are feeble compared to what we were once.

You will, I hope, always remember the feeble people who were once the lords of the soil, but who are now much reduced both in members and strength. But the war spirit is still in us, and we will do what we can to aid you, when the opportunity shall offer, even should it result in the destruction of our village by the British your enemies. Remember brother Bostonians, the words of your brothers of Caughnawaga.

Never forget that a portion of them are your friends at heart, and pray to the Great Spirit, that you become a free people, as the Indians your brothers."

Having been civilly treated at the camp the Indians returned to Albany, where they had an interview with General Schuyler, John Bleecker acting as interpreter; and here they again tendered their services to join the American cause.

After a considerable hesitation from the causes above indicated, it was resolved to grant the request, and Louis Cook, received a commission in the American army. From this time his residence at Caughnawaga became unsafe, and he returned thither no more during the war, unless stealthily.

A portion of the party remained with him, and others returned to Caughnawaga, warm in their friendship to the cause, and intending secretly to promote it as they might find themselves able.

These movements attracted the notice of Governor Carlton, of Canada, who endeavored to secure their adherence to the royal cause, but without effect.

In the winter of 1777-8, Colonel Louis repaired to Oneida, to raise a company of warriors among that tribe, and in this he succeeded. This is confirmed by a statement made in a petition of one Edward Johnson, to the legislature, for a grant of land for services rendered, in which he says:

> "That winter I got acquainted with Louis Cook, a French Mohawk, who came to Oneida to get as many men to join him as he could in the American cause against Great Britain, for which he received a Lieutenant Colonel's commission from the first Congress, and said Louis asked me if I was willing to serve the country with him."

We also find a memorandum that the Oneidas entered Schenectady in July, 1780, under Col. Louis. [190]

This tribe as is well known, was the only one that rendered efficient service to the American cause during the revolutionary war. The Mohawks were influenced by the Johnson families to take up the hatchet against the colonies, and it is well known that the western Indians of New York deserved the chastisement they received at the hands of General Sullivan.

In the summer of 1780, Count de Rochambeau, with a French fleet and army, arrived in the United States, as their allies, in their struggle for liberty.

> "It was deemed advisable by General Schuyler, and others, that a deputation of friendly Indians should be encouraged to visit the French army and fleet at Newport. Many of the Iroquois had been strongly attached to the French in early times, particularly during the last war, and they still retained a lively remembrance the amicable intercourse that had then existed. When M. de Vaudreuil surrendered Canada to the British, he gave to the Indians as tokens of recognizance, a golden crucifix and a watch; and it was supposed that a renewal of the impressions which bad in some degree been preserved among the tribes by these emblems of friendship, would have the effect to detach them from the British, and strengthen their union with the Americans and French. For this end their journey to Newport was planned.

General Schuyler who was at Albany, selected eighteen Indians for this deputation. Thirteen of these were Oneidas and Tuscaroras, and the other five Caghnawagas, from the Saut of St. Louis, near Montreal. They were accompanied by Mr. Deane, who was thoroughly acquainted with their language. They arrived at Newport on the 29th of August, 1780, and were received with a great deal of ceremony and attention by the French commanders. Entertainments and military shows were prepared for them, and they expressed much satisfaction at what they saw and heard. Suitable presents were distributed among them; and to the chiefs were given medals, representing the coronation of the French king. When they went away a written address was delivered to them, or rather a kind of proclamation, signed by Count de Rochambeau, copies of which were distributed among the friendly Indians. It was in the following words:

"The king of France, your father, has not forgotten his children. As a token of remembrance, I have presented gifts to your deputies in his name. He learned with concern that many nations deceived by the English who are his enemies, had attacked and lifted up the hatchet against his good and faithful allies, the United States. He has desired me to tell you, that he is a firm and faithful friend to all the friends of America, and a decided enemy to all its foes. He hopes that his children whom he loves sincerely, will take part with their father in this war against the English."

This paper was written both in the French and English languages, and sealed and signed in due form."

(*Sparks's Washington, vol. vii, p.* 183.)

General Washington in a letter to the Count de Rochambeau, of Sept. 3, 1780, says:

"The visit you have had from the Indians, gives me great pleasure. I felicitate you on that which you must have had in the company of such [191] agreeable and respectable guests. I dare say the reception they met with, will have a good effect. It has been the policy of the English in regard to them, to discredit the accounts of an alliance between France and America; a conviction of which on the substantial evidence of your army and fleet, and not less of your presents and good cheer, will not fail to have a happy influence."

(*Ib., p.* 183.)

These Indians were principally useful as scouts, to carry intelligence and get information — a kind of service for which they are peculiarly adapted by nature, from the knowledge which they have of the forests, and the wary look-out they maintain against surprise or detection by their enemy.

On several of these occasions, Col. Louis was employed successfully. Once he was engaged to convey information to Canada, in connection with the expedition that was sent thither under General Montgomery, and at another time was sent to meet a messenger from Canada, at a designated place, near Lake Champlain. This duty he performed successfully, but when he reached the camp of the Americans, he was almost starved, having lost his provision bag, in crossing a river. He could not hunt on the way, as the British had Indian scouts in the woods.

On several of his expeditions as a bearer of despatches, he crossed Lake Champlain and the Green Mountains, to the upper settlements on the Connecticut.

In whatever enterprise he undertook, he uniformly acquitted himself with credit, and in every act of his life he confirmed the esteem which he had acquired among the officers of the army, who not only learned to trust his fidelity, but ask his opinion on subjects connected with Indian warfare, and varied affairs connected with the Indian tribes.

He continued in active service till the peace, and then not daring to return to his former associates at Caughnawaga, from the active partizan course which he had pursued, he repaired to Oneida, where he continued to reside until about the year 1789.

Many of the Caughnawagas had like him, lost their residence and their homes, by joining the Americans, and from some neglect no provision had been made for them, as for the Canada and Nova Scotia refugees, who for a like reason had become exiles; these patriotic Indians wandered here and there homeless, and a part of them finally settled at St. Regis to which as Caughnawagas they had a claim.

There can be little doubt that the claims of these Indians have been overlooked, as one may search in vain the public records for evidences that they have ever been remunerated by grants of land or otherwise, for their services, with the exception of Colonel Louis.

Some time after the revolution he visited Montreal, Caughnawaga, and St. Francois, and from his known influence with the Indian tribes, [192] he was treated with respect by the agents of that government, who it is said, tendered him strong inducements to engage his friendship, but he rejected them all, that he might be free from this species of obligation. His wife, however, who accompanied him, accepted a gift of twenty dollars, with which she purchased a store that is said to be still owned by her descendents at St. Regis.

The western Indians towards the close of the last century, began to show symptoms of hostility to the United States, and endeavored to excite the same feeling among all the Indians in the country, to whom they sent messages, inviting them to meet in general council, to concert measures for promoting their measures, and of urging certain claims against the general government. The Canada Indians were also invited, and attended. The course which they pursued will be inferred from the following extracts.

> "Colonel Louis of the Cougnawagas also came here to inform the government, that the Seven Castles, so called, in Canada, had been invited to

the council, to be held at the Miami River, of Lake Erie. He also being convinced of the justice of the United States, promised to me his influence towards a peace. (*Letter of Gen. Knox, Feb.* 10, 1792. *American State Papers, Indian affairs, vol. i*, 12, 35.)

The deputies of these tribes accordingly attended the Indian council at the rapids of the Miami, on the 13th of August, 1793, and in the reports of the commissioners appointed on the part of the government, it is recorded, that they used their influence in settling the troubles then existing between the western tribes and the United States, which subsequently ripened into open hostilities.

They however with the others insisted that the Ohio river should be the boundary between the whites and the Indians.

His residence on the frontier of St. Regis was at first quite unpleasant as well as unsafe, from the hostility which his former course had created among the zealous loyalists who settled on the St. Lawrence, after the war.

During a portion of his life, before the war, he had resided at St. Regis, and occupied a tract of land afterwards known as the Mile Square, near the present village of Massena. This he endeavored to have secured to him by letters patent. The following is the petition in which he solicited this favor.

To the Honorable the Senate and Assembly of the State of New York, in Legislature convened;

"The petition of the subscriber respectfully showeth: That at the commencement of the late war, he resided near the village of St. Regis, within this state, and adjoining the north bounds thereof. That he occupied there a certain tract of land, lying on the Niconsiaga River, [193] beginning on the first falls on the said river, and extending up the same on both sides thereof, about one mile, which land had descended to him by inheritance, and is his own distinct property.

That at the commencement of the late war, he left his said habitation, and joined the American army, and continued to serve his country in a military capacity, throughout the war, and that from the part he had taken in the American cause, he finds it inexpedient to return to his former residence, although the land so owned by him is still held and rented out by him. That your petitioner is desirous to have the said lands secured to him and his posterity, by a title to the same, under the authority of the state.

Your petitioner therefore most humbly prays, that the legislature will be pleased, in consideration of the premises, to direct letters patent to be issued to him, for the said tract of land.

And your petitioner will as in duty bound ever pray, &c.

LOUIS COOK.

ALBANY, 8th January, 1789.

The Journal of the senate of the state of New York for 1789, contains the following.

January 10, 1789.

"The petition of Louis Cook, alias Hadaguetoghrongwen, praying that his title to a certain piece of land, may be confirmed to him under the authority of the state, was read and committed to Mr. Clinton, Mr. Hawthorn, and Mr. Tredwell." (*p.* 30.)

February 19, 1789.

Mr. Clinton from the committed to whom was referred the petition of Louis Cook, alias Hadaguetoghrongwen, relative to his claim to a tract of land lying on the Niconsiaga River, near the village of St. Regis, within this state, reported that it was the opinion of the committee, that the prayer of the petitioner ought to be granted, and that a provision be made to direct the commissioners of the land office, to grant letters patent to the said Louis Cook, for such tract of land lying on the Niconsiaga river, beginning on the first falls on the said river, and extending up the same on both sides thereof as they shall find to be his distinct property; provided the same has not been otherwise appropriated; which report he read in his place, and delivered the same at the table where it was again read, and agreed to by the senate." (*p.* 68.)

This petition produced the passage of an act in his relief.
The 16th section of an act passed February 28, 1789, directed:

"That it shall and may be lawful for the commissioners of the land office, to grant letters patent, to Louis Cook, alias Hadaguetoghrongwen, for such tract of land lying on the Niconsiaga River, beginning on the first falls on said river, and extending up the same on both sides thereof, as they shall find to be his distinct property; provided the same has not been otherwise appropriated."

It is not known to the author whether this tract was ever confirmed to him as his individual property, or what was the result of the action directed in the act for his relief.
It is probable, that Colonel Louis was induced to return to St. Regis, [194] by those people, who were solicitous of securing his influence in settling the claim which they had against the state of New York, for lands, and in seeing that justice was done them in the matter of running the boundary between the two governments, which passed through their village.

He was not at first safe in his residence at St. Regis, being on several occasions in danger of his life, from the violence of the Mohawks. His friends, however, promptly informed him of the plots laid against him, in time for him to avoid them.

There is said to have been an especial feeling of ill will between Brant and Louis, arising from the active partizan course which they had pursued on opposite sides in the previous contest.

Colonel Louis took a leading part in the negotiations which finally resulted in the treaty of May 31, 1796, at the city of New York, by which the claims of the St. Regis Indians to the lands in the northern part of the state were extinguished, with the exception of the reservations then made. A history of the negotiations which preceded and attended this treaty, we have given in the foregoing pages. It will be seen that the terms offered by the agents of the state, bore no comparison with the demands of the deputies of the Indians, but here, as elsewhere, and ever, the latter found themselves at the mercy of those whose will was law, and were constrained to accept the terms offered, or none at all, having no tribunal of arbitration or appeal, by which to sustain their claims.

In sustaining his claims, Colonel Louis was seconded by Captain Thomas Williams, a chief of the tribe, and a descendant of the Rev. John Williams, of Deerfield, and by William Gray, a chief and interpreter, who, although a white by birth, had in every respect become an Indian in tastes and habits.

After the conclusion of the treaty, Colonel Louis had on opportunity of attending to his own private affairs, and he continued to be occupied with these, and with business connected with the internal management of matters connected with the tribes with whom the St. Regis people were associated, until the breaking out of the war in 1812.

By an act of the legislature, passed in 1802, he was, with Loren Tarbell and William Gray, made the trustee of his tribe, for the purpose of leasing a ferry, and a tract of land, and of establishing a school among the Indians.

Although without education himself, yet he was, for this reason, the more desirous that his people should acquire it; but the prejudices of the tribe were against it, and so far as we can learn, there was none established until a very recent period. [195]

Louis was ever opposed to the leases and sales, by which the Indians, from time to time, alienated their lands in the vicinity of Salmon river, insisting most strenuously, that they belonged not to them, but to their *children*.

It is not our purpose to investigate the motives which were brought to operate in producing a contrary course, or the propriety of it.

On the declaration of war, Colonel Louis, although borne down by the weight of more than seventy years, and passed that time of life, when one would scarcely be expected to encounter the rugged toils of war; yet he felt rising within him the ancient martial spirit which had inspired him in former times, and he felt his age renewed, when he thought on the perils and the victories in which he had participated, and longed again to serve that cause which, in the prime of life, and vigor of youth, he had made his own.

The British early endeavored to secure the St. Regis people in their interests, and their agent, who bad come up from Montreal, with the customary presents, which that government annually distributed in the payment of their annuities, returned without making the distribution, because they would not agree to take up arms for them.

The residence of Colonel Louis, in consequence of his engaging in the American cause, having become unpleasant, if not unsafe, at St. Regis, he repaired to Plattsburgh, where he spent a considerable portion of the summer. We notice the following in Niles's Weekly Register, of that period:

> Oct. 17, 1812. "Gen. Louis, of the St. Regis Indians, a firm and undeviating friend of the United States, and his son, have been in this village (Plattsburgh), for several weeks. The St. Regis Indians are disposed to remain neutral, in the present contest; but what effect the British influence and British success may have upon them, we know not," &c.

We have noticed, in the foregoing pages, the miserable condition to which the St. Regis people were reduced by the war; as they could scarcely go out of sight of their village, without exciting alarm among the whites, and they had nothing to subsist upon at home.

Colonel Louis represented this condition of things to the governor, who directed, in consequence, that five hundred rations should be delivered daily to them, and they were thus enabled to avoid giving alarm to their white brethren.

During the summer of 1812, he visited General Brown, at Ogdensburgh, where he was received with attention: a new commission was presented him, and through the liberality of Mr. David [Parish], of that place, he was furnished with a new and elegant military dress and equipage, corresponding with the rank which his commissions conferred. On his return to his family, his appearance was so changed, that they did not [196] know him, and his children fled from the proffered caresses of their father, as if he had been the spirit of evil.

His age and infirmities prevented him from active duty, but his influence with the Indian tribes, gave him an importance in the army, which was of signal service to the American cause.

On the arrival of General Wilkinson, at French Mills, he joined that army, and accompanied General Brown from thence to Sacketts Harbor, in February, 1814.

In June following, he repaired to Buffalo, with his sons, and several St. Regis warriors, and was present and actively engaged in the several engagements that took place on the Niagara frontier.

In August, 1813, an affair had taken place near Fort George, in which several Caughnawagas and British were taken prisoners; and colonel Louis was induced, from motives of humanity, to undertake a mission to Niagara for their release.

To excite a prejudice against him, some of his enemies wrote to an officer in the American army, that he was on a visit to their camp, on a secret mission, which reaching its destination before his arrival, led to his arrest, and he was held a prisoner eight days, when some officers from Plattsburgh arriving, he was recognized, and set at liberty. A further investigation was desired, and instituted, and he appeared before the commission, and answered, with great modesty, the several questions that were put to him, by the young officers: but the impertinence of some of them aroused his spirit, and he replied: "You see that I am old, and worn out, and you are young, and know little of the service. You seem to doubt what I have been, and what I am now. It is right that you should watch the interests of your country in time of war. My history you can have." He then gave them the names of several prominent officers of the northern frontier, as references, and with a heavy hand, laid a large black pocket book upon the table, and bid them examine its contents. It contained his commissions as lieutenant colonel; general Washington's recommendatory letters, and those of generals Schuyler, Gates, Knox, Mooers, and governor Tompkins, and a parchment certificate of membership, in a military masonic lodge of the revolution.

These abundantly satisfied them, but he further insisted, that they should write to Plattsburgh, which they did, more to gratify him, than to satisfy themselves. The result was, of course, his complete exoneration from any motives but those entirely consistent with honor and principle.

But time was having its work upon the frame of this worthy Indian chief, and an injury which he sustained, by a fall from this horse, at the [197] head of a party of Tuscaroras, in one of the skirmishes of the campaign, was found to have seriously affected him, and he desired to be carried to the Indian settlements, to yield his last advice, and give up his parting breath among the people whose interests he had so long and so faithfully served.

Colonel Biddle, of the 11th regiment, the son of his former old friend, in Coos county, often sent to enquire after his welfare. Louis at length sent for the colonel, who hastened to his wigwam, and found him in a dying condition, but able to speak. He spoke at some length, on the interest he ever felt for the American cause, and the gratification he experienced in being able to die near their camp. He bid him remember him to his family at St. Regis, to colonel Williams, of that place, and to his friends, whom he named, at Plattsburgh.

To his son, he gave his two commissions which he had cherished as a treasure, and bid him carry them to his family at St. Regis, but this worthless fellow on returning pawned them at an inn for grog!

Colonel Louis died in October 1814, and was buried near Buffalo. His death was announced by the discharge of cannon, as was due to his rank in the army.

He was twice married, the first time at Caughnawaga, and the second at Onondaga, where he is said to have lived a short time after the revolution.

He had three sons, of whom one died at Caughnawaga, one at St. Regis, in 1832, and the third near Brasher Falls in 1833, while on a hunting excursion.

He had several daughters, one or two of whom still reside at St. Regis.

Colonel Louis was tall and athletic, broad shouldered and strongly built, with a very dark complexion, and somewhat curly hair, which in old age became gray.

He was very reserved in his speech, and by most people would be called taciturn.

He seldom spoke without having something to say, and what he said was received with deference, for it always had a meaning, and in all his deportment he strongly evinced possession of prudence, discretion and sense, and when once enlisted in any pursuit, he followed it with a constantcy and perseverance seldom equalled in the Indian character. He was prompt and generally correct in arriving at conclusions, and his judgment was relied upon, and his opinions sought by the officers of the army, with whom he was associated, with much confidence, and he possessed in a high degree the control of the affairs of his tribe, by whom he was beloved, respected, and obeyed.

He was illiterate, but spoke several languages with freedom. His [198] portrait was taken while at Albany, but we have been unable to ascertian whether it be still [preserved.]

WILLIAM GRAY.—Probably no white person has had more influence with the Indian tribe of St. Regis, in their negotiations than William Gray, and his name is constantly found as interpreter, or agent on the old treaties and other papers which were executed by these people. He was born at Cambridge, N. Y., joined the revolutionary army, at the age of seventeen. With a few others he was taken by surprise near White Hall, and carried to Quebec, where he remained till the peace. He then repaired to Caughnawaga, and resided for some time, from whence he removed to St. Regis, and married an Indian woman, and raised a family. He adopted the language, and customs of the tribe and become their chief interpreter. While there, returned to Cambridge, and induced a large number of his father's family to remove to St. Regis, where they remained some time, but never inter married with the natives. His parents died on the Indian reservation.

He had acquired the rudiments of an education, which was subsequently of much advantage to him in his capacity of interpreter and chief.

Possessing considerable native enterprise, he acquired an ascendency with the Indians, and his advice was received with attention. At a very early period he erected a saw mill at what is now the village of Hogansburgh, and engaged in mercantile business at the Indian village.

He acted as interpreter at most of the treaties held previous to his death; and his conduct at that which occurred at New York in 1790, was such as secured him the following recommendation from the governor to the legislature.

> *Gentlemen:*
>
> The agents who on the part of this state, concluded the agreement which has been laid before you, with the Indians called the Seven Nations of Canada, at the treaty held at New York in May last, have represented to me, that William Gray, one of the deputies from these Indians at that treaty, was during the late war captivated in this state by the Indians of St. Regis, that they adopted him into that tribe, and on the 21st of March, 1781, gave him the tract of land specified in the copy of the deed from them to him; with which a copy of the proceedings of that treaty, accompanies this message,

and which he left with the said agents for your information.

That they have no reason to suppose otherwise, than that the said transaction was at the time intended, did take place between him, and the said Indians in good faith; that during the negotiations at the treaty, his conduct was fair and proper, and rather than that the treaty should be in the least impeded by his claims, he readily consented to waive the making of any stipulations in his favor, and to rely entirely on the state [199] for such compensation or gratuity as the legislature should think reasonable."

JOHN JAY.

ALBANY, 28th February, 1797.

This however, failed to secure him the justice which he claimed, and he accordingly presented at a subsequent session, the following memorial, in which his claims are set forth.

"To the Honorable, the Legislature of the State of New York.
The petition of William Gray, respectfully sheweth:

That your petitioner was born in the county of Washington, in this state; that when a boy he was taken prisoner in the year eighty, in the late war, by the Indians of the Seven Nations of Canada, among whom he has ever since continued to reside; that by adoption and marriage, he has become entitled to all the rights and privileges of one of that people, and consequently is with them a proprietor of the lands secured to them by treaty with the state; that he now has a family of children whom he wishes to educate in the manner of their civilized ancestors, and leave some property to make them respectable and useful in society; that according to the customs of the tribe at St. Regis, the place where he resides, individuals have lands assigned to them for cultivation in severally, yet the laws of the state can riot take cognizance of it; that the nation of which he is a member, have set apart to him and wish to have confirmed to him a tract, as his exclusive proportion of the lands 257 acres, bounded on the north by the Salmon river mill tract, on the east by the east boundaries of the large reservation, on the west by a line parallel thereto, and on the south by the south bounds of said reservation, now held in common in their reservation, near the village of St. Regis. Your petitioner therefore, in consideration of all these circumstances, prays that it may be lawful for him to receive such a grant from the nation, and that it may receive the sanction of government, and your petitioner as in duty bound, shall ever pray."

WILLIAM GRAY.

ALBANY, the 19th February, 1800.

This petition secured him the advantages which he sought, in the passage of the following act, April 4, 1801, during the session next following:

> "And whereas, William Gray of the village of St. Regis, having been early in life taken prisoner by the Indians calling themselves the Seven Nations of Canada, and since continued to reside among them, and being in consequence of adoption and marriage, considered as entitled to all rights and privileges as one of their nation, whereby he is equally and with others of them interested in the lands secured by the people of this state to the Indians residing at the village of St. Regis;
>
> And whereas, it appears that the said Indians are disposed to give to the said William Gray, his proportion of their common property to be held in severally by him and his heirs: therefore,
>
> *Be it further enacted*, That it shall and may be lawful for the governor to direct the said agent to obtain from the said Indians, their grant to the people of this state, and to issue letters patent under the great seal of this state, to the said William Gray, his heirs and assigns, forever, for two hundred and fifty-seven acres, bounded on the north by the tract reserved [200] and surveyed for the said Indians, and which includes the mill on Salmon river, on the south by the south bounds of the tract equal to six miles square, reserved to the said Indians, on the east by the east bounds of the said reservation, and on the west by a line parellel thereto, run from the eleventh mile mark, made by the surveyor general, in the south bounds of the said reservation, being in length north and south, one hundred and sixty-four chains and seventy links, and in width east and west, fifteen chains and sixty links."

A further history of the tract thus conveyed, will be given in our account of Fort Covington.

His residence during a few years previous to the war, was in what is now the village of Hogansburgh, west of the river; and this place at that period bore the name of Gray's Mills.

In the war of 1812, he took part with the Americans, and was employed by Colonel Young to conduct the party through the woods from French Mills, which surprised and captured a company of British at St. Regis, in the fall of 1812. Being considered a dangerous partizan, he was surprised and taken by a party of the enemy, on the east side of the St. Regis river, near the village, in December, 1813, and taken to Quebec, where he was confined in prison, and where he died in April or May following.

In his death the tribe lost a true friend and faithful servant. His descendants still reside at St. Regis.

TE-HO-RA-GWA-NE-GEN, alias *Thomas Williams*, whose name we have so often had occasion to mention in connection with the St. Regis tribe, was born about 1758 or 1759, at Caughnawaga, and was the third in descent from the Rev. John Williams of

Deerfield. A daughter of this person by the name of Eunice, who was taken prisoner with him in 1704, became assimilated with the Indians, and afterwards married a young chief by the name of *De Roguers*, to whom she bore three children, viz: Catharine, Mary, and John. Mary was the mother of Thomas Williams, the subject of this notice. She died when her son was an infant, and he was reared by his aunt Catharine, whom he ever regarded as his mother. Having no cousin, he was the sole object of affection by his kind protector, and grew up an active and sprightly lad, in every respect of language and habits an Indian.

In 1772, the Rev. Levi Frisbee, was sent into Canada by the Rev. Dr. Wheelock, of Dartmouth College, who visited Caughnawaga, and took especial notice of Thomas, whose New England parentage was known to him and he obtained with some difficulty, the consent of his adopted parents to take him to Hanover, and place him in the Moore Charity School at that place, but sickness prevented him from attending. His adopted father often took him into the forest with him, on hunting excursions, [201] and he became attached to his kind of life, often visiting in his rambles, Crown Point, Lake George, and vicinity of Fort Edward.

On the outbreak of the revolution, he is said to have participated in several of the expeditions against the colonies, but the lessons he had received from his grandmother Eunice, led him to exert his influence in favor of protecting [defenseless] women and children.

In 1777, he became a chief, and gradually acquired the esteem of the British officers. In the same year he was called upon with others of his tribe, to join General Burgoyne, but big feelings had begun to be enlisted in favor of the Americans, and he accompanied rather with the hope of being able to spare the effusion of blood, than of promoting the cause of his army, which he joined at Cumberland Head. On the retreat of the provincials from Ticonderoga, he was directed to pursue them, but under the pretense of falling upon their flanks, he is said to have purposely led his party by a too circuitous route to effect their object.

He was also sent with the detachment of the enemy against Bennington, but did little for the service in which he was engaged, and in the event almost came in collision with some of the British officers engaged on that expedition.

It is said that on the occasion of the death of Miss Jane McCrea, which formed so striking a tragedy in that campaign, that Thomas was solicited to undertake to bring her to the camp, but that he refused.

This service was according to the Rev. E. Williams, our informant, afterwards accepted by some of the Indians of the Western tribes, who in two parties, each ignorant of the designs of the other, started on the expedition.

One of them had persuaded the girl to attend them to the British camp, and they were on their way thither, when they were met by the other: an altercation arose between them, and in the strife that ensued the girl was brutally tomahawked by one party, that the other might not be able draw the reward which had been offered by the young lady's lover, for bringing her in.

Our informant received this from a Winnebago chief, at Green Bay, who acknowledged having a hand in the murder, which some have attributed to St. Regis Indians.

This shocking barbarity, so abhorrent to human nature, led to a rebuke from Burgoyne, which is said to have weakened the attachment of the Indians for his course, and they afterwards left him.

Williams, among the rest of the Indians, abandoned the camp and returned home. In 1778, he joined an expedition to Oswego, with the view of invading some of the frontier settlements, but returned, and in the following [202] year was one of the party who ravaged Royalton in Vermont, and afterwards participated in expeditions to Penobscot, Schoharie, &c.

In 1783 be visited for the first time his relatives in New England, and at Stockbridge met with the Rev. Samuel Kirkland, the Indian missionary, who served him as an interpreter. Among those whom he wished to visit, was the Rev. Dr. Stephen Williams, the brother of his grandmother Eunice, but he found him dead.

He subsequently visited repeatedly the friends of his grandmother, both in Massachusetts and Vermont, and always evinced a commendable regard for their welfare.

After the war, he resumed his hunting, and often visited Albany, and had a friendly intercourse with General Schuyler.

When the question of settlement of claims against the state came to be discussed, Thomas Williams was entrusted, in company with Gray and Cook, with the negotiation, the history of which we have given. In January, 1800, he visited his relatives in New England, and took with him his two boys, whom he left to be educated at Long Meadow, Moss. The names of these lads were John and Eleazer.

In 1801, with a party of Caughnawagas, in the service of the Northwest Company, he made a journey to the remote western prairies, and nearly to the Rocky mountains. In 1805, with his wife, he visited his sons, and the mother insisted on having John return, which he did, much to the regret of the benevolent gentlemen, who on account of their ancestry, felt a peculiar interest in the welfare of the youths.

The other remained some time longer at the school, and acquired a good English education, and subsequently became an episcopal clergyman, and was employed as a missionary for many years among the Oneidas and Onondagas, and also with the St. Regis Indians. For several years he was engaged in the settlements of the Green Bay emigrants, from the New York tribes, and is at present living near St. Regis, engaged in endeavoring to establish a school among the natives.

During the war of 1812, he is said to have held a colonel's commission, and to have been repeatedly engaged on responsible services for the Americans.

On the declaration of war, Williams resolved to take no part with the British, which led him to be reported with Colonel Louis, as refractory.

In August 1812, an agreement was entered into between Gen. Dearborn and Col. Baynes, that neither party should act offensively before the decision of certain measures then pending should be known.

A conference was subsequently held between agents of the two governments, at which it was agreed that the St. Regis tribe should remain neutral, but as afterwards appeared this was subsequently but little regarded. [203] During the war Thomas Williams continued to exert an influence favorable to the Americans, and his two sons took active but opposite sides in the contest. In 1815 he visited Albany, and Washington, to urge certain claims against government, but not being furnished with the necessary papers, he failed in his purpose.

In consideration of the active part which he took in the treaty of 1796, he for several years after the war, till 1833, received $50 annually of the annuity which was paid by virtue of that treaty.

He died at his native village, August 16, 1849. In person he was above the common size, with an intelligent countenance, and with that in his manner and deportment, which bespoke a superiority above his people in general.

The author is indebted to the Rev. Eleazer Williams, of St. Regis, for most of the data from which the above account is written. Our space has not allowed the full use of the voluminous materials furnished.

1 Another and equally consistent explanation of the adoption of the name, is given:

In the winter time, the ice from the rapids above, coming down under the firm ice at this place, often occasions a sort of tremor or earthquake in miniature, and is attended with a noise very much like the drumming of a partridge. A particular account of the singular phenomena of the ice in the rapids, will be given in our account of the town of Massena.

On the occasion of the author's visit to St. Regis in June 1852, the natives desired to give him a name, and proposed among others, that of their village. Objections being made, they decided upon, O-kwa-e-sen, a partridge, they regarding that bird somewhat at a national emblem, like the eagle to the United States. The idea was doubtless suggested by the particular inquiries made about the origin of their village. The custom of naming those who have business with them in common, and in former times when the drinking of rum was more prevalent, the ceremony of christening and adoption was conducted with excessive demonstration of joy. At present it consists in singing and shouting around the candidate, and the shaking of hands. At times a rude dance is performed, but this people have lost every recollection of the national feasts and dances, which are still maintained among the pagan party of the Iroquois at Onondaga and other Indian settlements, in the interior of the state.

They informed the author that they should consider him as belonging to the Ro-tis en-na-keh-te, or little Turtle band, that being the smallest and feeblest one among them.

2 The old church of Caughnawaga, was in 1845 replaced by the present large and substantial stone edifice, erected with funds given the Indians for that purpose in consideration of lands which the government had appropriated to itself, as having belonged to the Jesuits, but for which they awarded the value, on its being proved that this mission had never belonged to that order. In 1830, a large bell was presented by the English government to the church, and hangs by the side of the time honored and venerable relic which forms the subject of the legend. The latter originally bore an inscription in the Latin language, but this has been effaced by the chisel, probably by its New England owners, to prevent any identification by those for whom it was originally intended. Adjoining the church, stands the priest's house, which still presents the same appearance as when Charlevoix the traveler abode in it. The room is still pointed out in which he lived, and the desk on which he wrote a portion of his history which has made his name celebrated as a historian.

3 See Historical Collections of Massachusetts by John W. Barber, p. 250, 252. Also a Biographical Memoir of the Rev. John Williams by Stephen Williams, Deerfield 1837.

4 Life of Brant, by William L. Stone, vol. i. p. 143, 144, and Sparke's Life and Writings of Washington, note in vol. iv. p. 409, 410.

5 Stone's Life of Brant, vol. i., p. 144, note.

6 NEW NOTE: Year of this treaty was 1797, not 1795, according to other sources

7 NEW NOTE: Hough's transcript of the treaty differs from other copies of the treaty in the terms of the payout. Hough has it as "…the sum of one thousand two hundred and thirty pounds, six shillings and eight pence, lawful money of the said state." The actual treaty says, "…the sum of one thousand two hundred and thirty-*three* pounds, six shillings and eight-pence, *and the further sum of two hundred and thirteen pounds six shillings and eight-pence,* lawful money of said state…"

8 We quote the language of Stone in his Life of Brant. This author was mistaken in supposing Colonel Louis was an Oneida Indian.

9 This word signifies "one who pulls down the people."

10 NEW NOTE: The attack on Saratoga took place in 1745, not 1755.

Further References to Akwesasne

It is important for the reader to appreciate that the chapter about Akwesasne is not the only place where the community is mentioned in *A History of St. Lawrence and Franklin Counties*. References to Akwesasne and its leaders are scattered throughout, and most are worth noting here. Readers may wish to consult the original book for the full context.

The first mention is found in the first chapter, in its discussion of the archaeology of the region:

> On St. Regis Island, directly opposite the Indian village of that name, and at a point where the boundary of 1818 crossed the river, there still exists a barrow or sepulchral mound. "It was excavated by Colonel Hawkins of the United States boundary commission, in 1818, and found to contain near the surface human bones in considerable numbers, and in a good state of preservation, but at the base were found traces of fire, charcoal, burned bones, and fragments of pottery, together with stone implements and ornaments."
>
> Directly opposite to the church, on the east bank of St. Regis river, in the same neighborhood as the preceding, is another barrow or mound of somewhat similar character, which has at some period apparently been explored with the view of ascertaining the nature of its contents. There is no tradition in the village relating to either of them, and no probability that they were made by the existing race of Indians.
>
> They doubtless date back to the era of the other earth-works above described, and belong to a remote period of our history, which has been lost. In making a canal around the rapids on the Canada shore of the St. Lawrence, many years since, a singular mound was dug through, which disclosed relics of copper and various ornaments, and among others a mask of the human face, in terra-cotta or earthen ware, which seemed to have belonged to some image.[1]

The same chapter has a second reference to St. Regis Island. We find it in a quote from the journal kept by Isaac Weld, Jr., of his exploration of North America from 1795 to

1797:

> The Indians not only retain possession of the different islands, but likewise of the whole of the south-east shore of the St. Lawrence, situated within the bounds of the United States; they likewise have considerable strips of land on the opposite shore, within the British Dominions, bordering upon the river; these they have reserved to themselves, for hunting. The Iroquois Indians have a village upon the Isle of St. Regis, and another also upon the main laud, on the south-east shore; as we passed, several of the inhabitants put off in canoes, and exchanged unripe heads of Indian corn with the men for bread; they also brought with them some very fine wild duck and fish, which they disposed of to us on very moderate terms.
>
> On the fourth night of our voyage, we encamped as usual on the main land, opposite the Island of St. Regis, and the excellent viands which we had procured from the Indians having been cooked, we sat down to supper before a large fire, materials for which are never wanting in this woody country. The night was uncommonly serene, and we were induced to remain to a late hour in front of our tent talking of the various occurrences in the course of the day; but we had scarcely retired to rest when the sky became overcast, a dreadful storm arose, and by day break the next morning we found ourselves, and every thing belonging to us, drenched with rain.[2]

Wells and his companions took shelter in the home of an "old provincial officer," who lived with his daughters nearby. This would most likely have been Lieutenant-Colonel John McDonell. He had been a captain in Butler's Rangers during the War of the Revolution, and commanded Akwesasne warriors in battle. He was among the Loyalists who settled on the north shore of the St. Lawrence. The towering remains of his stone house watch over the community today.[3]

Akwesasne is mentioned in the first chapter in relation to the fate of Oswegatchie, the mission community at what is now Ogdensburgh:

> The Oswegatchies, at the time when the present class of settlers came on, were occupying a village of twenty-three houses, on Indian Point, in Lisbon, about three miles below Ogdensburgh. Spafford, in his Gazetteer, published in 1813, thus mentions them. "This village was built by the British government, after the Revolution, and when, of course, that government had no title to the land. The Indians remained here several years after the settlement of the country by the present proprietors, and were removed by order of the government of New York, on the complaint of the inhabitants. These Indians driven from New Johnstown, in Upper Canada, received this spot with improvements, in exchange from which

driven by our government, they became destitute of a local habitation and a name, and the Oswegatchie tribe no longer exists, although a few individuals remain, scattered among the surround ing tribes."

This dispersion took place about 1806, or 7, and the remnants of the tribe, or their descendants, are found at St. Regis, Onondaga, and elsewhere.

While in Lisbon, they were under the direction of one Joseph Reoam, a Frenchman, who spoke their dialect of the Iroquois language, and is said to have been a chief, and to have married an Indian woman. They planted corn on Galloo island, and elsewhere in the vicinity.

Their village is described by one who saw it in 1802, as consisting of a street, running parallel with the river, with the houses ranged in a regular manner on each side of it, all uniformly built, with their ends to the street, sharp roofed, shingled with pointed shingles, and with glass windows. Every house was built for two families, had two doors in front, and a double fire place, and single chimney in the centre, with a partition equally dividing the interior. In 1802 there were about 24 families.

These Indians were accustomed to spend most of their summers on Black lake, in hunting and fishing, returning to their cabins for the winter. They used bark canoes, which they carried around rapids, and across portages, with perfect ease. As many as forty Indians at a time were often seen in the settlement when new.[4]

Akwesasne is mentioned in the fourth chapter about the history of land titles, where Hough reviews the history of the "Macomb Purchase."

New York, May 2d, 1791.

I do hereby consent and agree, that the islands called Caleton's or Buck's islands, in the entrance of lake Ontario, and the isle Au Long Saut, in the river St. Lawrence, and a tract equal to six miles square, in the vicinity of the village of St. Regis, be excepted out of the above contract, and to remain the property of the state: Provided always, That if the said tract shall not be hereafter applied for the use of the Indians of the said village, that then the same shall be considered as included in this contract, and that I shall he entitled to a grant for the same, on my performance of the stipulations aforesaid.

ALEXANDER MACOMB.[5]

Akwesasne is mentioned again in the same chapter's discussion of Barnhart Island:

Barnhart's island, 1692.95 acres; two-thirds to David A. Ogden and one-third to Gouverneur Ogden, Dec. 15, 1815.

> This island, near St. Regis, lies very near the Canadian shore, and a considerable part of it north of the line of 45° N. latitude. It was accordingly regarded as British territory, and in 1795 it was leased of the St. Regis Indians, by George Barnhart, for a term of 999 years, at an annual rent of $30. The British government had made a practice of granting patents upon the issue of similar leases, and would doubtless have done so in this instance, had application been duly made.
>
> In 1806, a saw mill was built, and arrangements made for the erection of a grist mill, when the Indians became dissatisfied and insisted upon a renewal of the lease, at an increased rent. Accordingly a lease was given for 999 years, at $60 annual rent. Deeds had been granted by Barnhart, who with all the other inhabitants of the island, were treated as British subjects, until upon running the line between the two nations, after the treaty of Ghent, the commissioners assigned the island to the United States, as an offset for the half of Grand island, at the outlet of Lake Ontario, which in justice would have been divided. In 1823, D. A. Ogden and G. Ogden purchased the islands in St. Lawrence county, and with them Barnhart's island.[6]

The fifth chapter of the book focused on the new towns in the two counties. This brings us to a brief mention of Akwesasne in relation to the town of Waddington:

> Fish abound in the waters, and the wild fowl and deer appeared to have chosen this spot as a resort. As a natural consequence, the rude Indian here found his favorite employment of hunting and fishing; there are those of the St. Regis tribe still living, who remember with regret, the peculiar advantages for their pursuits, which the locality afforded, and a few of the race annually visit the island, and camp in the woods near its head. The island was once covered by a pine forest, and large quantities of valuable timber having been cut in early times, under the direction of the St Regis Indians. Mr. Joseph Edsall, agent for the town, forbid them to take it away. The Indians appeared to be anxious to settle the matter amicably, and accordingly in May, 1803, an instrument was drawn up between the agent and William Gray, Louis Cooke and Loren Tarbell, trustees of the Indians, by which Edsall was to be allowed to remove the timber then down, and to pay 60 cents for every tree, if the title to the island then in process of investigation, should be decided as belonging to the proprietors of Madrid.[7]

Akwesasne's neighbor to the west is Massena. Hough's account of its history mentions the "St. Regis Indians" briefly:

> The first settlement in Massena began as early as 1792, by the erection of a

saw mill on Grass river, a mile below the present village, on premises leased and owned by the St. Regis Indians. Amable Foucher, from Old Chateaugay, near Montreal, afterwards occupied them, and was in possession till 1808. The first dam built by F. was swept off up stream, by the back water from the St. Lawrence, thrown up by the obstruction of ice.[8]

The account of the town of Oswegatchie mentions the natives of the village of the same name issuing a lease for lands in 1785. Akwesasne chiefs signed off on it:

Onatchateyent, Totagoines, Onarios, Tiotaasera. Aonarta, Gatemontie, Ganonsenthe and Onente, Oswegatchie chiefs, at Grenville, U. C., June 1, 1795, in the presence of Joseph Anderson, John Stigman and Ephraim Jones, confirmed to Catharine and Frances, the wife and son of Capt. Verneuil Lorimier, a verbal lease, executed in 1785, of a tract on the south shore, hnlf a mile on each side of the small river called Black river, and tip to Black lake, for the yearly rent of one hundred silver dollars, or money equivalent thereto. This was a full warranty deed with covenant. Lorimier had been a French officer in command of Fort Presentation, and a tradition relates that he also possessed a French title, which with other papers, were scattered and lost in a gale of wind that unroofed his house. It having been reported the St. Regis Indians dis countenanced these proceedings. Watson and his associates wrote to them on the subject, and received the following answer, dated at St. Regis, April 10, 1795.
    "Sir—We were favored with your letter of the 9 March, and we have to inform you that no Indian of St. Regis ever will molest or trouble you on your present possession. You pay our brothers of the Oswegatchie, a tolerable rent, and as long as you will make good payment of the same rent to our brothers, who are the same in all respects as ourselves, we shall and ever will be happy to keep you in full possession; do not ever believe any thing to the contrary from any person whatever. We are with esteem, your brothers and friends,
        Tharonhiageton   Ononsagenra
        Asserontonkota   Tionatagekha.
    For ourselves and others of our village of St. Regis."[9]

The next reference, from the same chapter, is found in a letter written by Joseph Edsall to Samuel Ogden in September, 1796:

I have had all the chiefs of the St. Regis village to see and welcome me to this country, excepting Gray and two others, who are gone to the river Chazy, to receive the money from the state.
    They gave me a hearty welcome, and pressed me very much to pay

them a visit I treated them with the utmost civility, and sent them all away drunk. As to the Oswegatchie Indians, I have never heard a word from them upon the possession of their lands,—many of them have been here to trade, &c.[10]

The notice of Bombay, Akwesasne's closest neighbor, mentions the village of Hogansburg:

The first improvements in the town, except at St. Regis village, were, it is said, begun by Gordon, the founder of St. Regis, who about 1763 caused mills to be erected at what is now Hoganshurgh, but which then bore the name of St, Regis mills. From this place he is said to have sent rafts to Montreal. The tradition of this affair is obscure and uncertain. A mill was burned about 1804, said to have been old. In December, 1808, there were no mills there. William Gray, the Indian interpreter, was living on the west bank during the early part of the war and for many years previous, and the place then bore the name of Gray's mills. From information derived from Joseph Lefonduze, a Frenchman, who has resided for many years at Hogansburgh, it is learned that Frenchmen, named Beron and Bouget, owned the first mills erected since 1808, who were succeeded by one Soufacon and Jean Baptiste Parissien, who left in 1816.[11]

The last substantial reference to Akwesasne is found in the eighth chapter, which is devoted to biographical notes. In the notice of Nathan Ford, we find the following account of a rowdy night with some spirited men from Oswegatchie:

We have given some of the details of his settlement at Oswegatchie, from which it will be learned that he was a man of indomitable energy and force of character, which proved adequate to the trying emergencies which surrounded him, and which would have discouraged common men from proceeding. The Oswegatchie Indians often proved annoying, especially when stimulated by ardent spirits, and on one occasion a number of them in the night time, entered the old stone garrison which he inhabited, seized Dick his negro slave, and was about to put him into the fire which was burning in the room, but the cries of the frightened negro aroused Mr. Ford, who seized his sword, and without waiting to dress, he rushed into the room, and succeeded with the help he assembled, in driving out the intruders. This affair probably occurred in a drunken row, for after the Indians had been driven from the house they began to quarrel among themselves, and one Battise, said to be a chief of the tribe, got stripped and beaten till he was nearly dead. During the night he knocked at the door of Mr. Lyon for admission, and was allowed to enter and spend the night on the floor. In the morning as he arose to depart, he stooped down to the hearth, blackened both hands with coal, and rubbing them over his face, he with a whoop and a bound, sallied forth to avenge the injuries he had received on the previous night. These Indians were peculiarly addicted to intemperance, having for many years resided near a post where liquors were easily procured, and in consequence frequent quarrels arose among them, and the night was often made hideous by their bacchanalian riots and yelling. Two or three of their number got killed at these revels in 1796 and 7.[12]

Hough goes on tell us of another incident in the life of Ford. It concerns Akwesasne's William Gray, who threatened the "taking of scalps" over an issue with an island in the St. Lawrence river. Colonel Louis Cook came along and attempted to smooth things over. The people of Oswegatchie are mentioned in relation to this incident:

Early in 1803, a dispute concerning timber on Ogden's island, alluded to on p. 343, had reached such a pitch that life was threatened, and the affair necessarily came under the notice of Judge Ford, who wrote to Governor Clinton as follows: "Upon my arrival here, I availed myself of the first safe opportunity to forward the letter (your excellency did me the honor to commit to my care), to the chiefs of the St. Regis village. Upon inquiry, I found they had carried a very high hand respecting the island business, and absolutely went so far as to threaten the taking of scalps. This threat was made by Gray, and was previous to Judge Edsall's sending the express forward. Upon my being informed of this outrageous conduct, I wrote Gray a letter upon the subject, and wished to know how he durst throw out such threats against the citizens of this state; and told him it was absolutely necessary for him to come forward and make such concessions as conduct like this required; that harmony and good understanding the citizens of this country were willing to cultivate, but threats like this they would be far from submitting to, and the sooner he gave satisfactory explanations upon the subject, the sooner harmony would be restored. Had he resided in the county or state, as a magistrate) I should have pursued a different method with him. Col. Lewis, who was on his way home from Oneida, (and who had not seen your excellency's letter to the chief's, or mine to Gray), called upon me. I explained to him the subject of your excellency's letter, and also mine to Gray. I told him it was a matter of astonishment, that he and Gray should have to act in such open defiance of the laws of the state as they had done respecting the sale of the timber upon the island; had it been by common Indians, some little apology might have been made for them, but for him and Grey, there certainly could be none, because they knew better, and they as certainly could have no doubt resting upon their minds as to the islands being comprehended in the sale of those lands to the state; and as an evidence that at the time of the treaty, he and Gray applied to your excellency, to know if the islands would not be taken possession of before the corn which was then upon them would be fit to gather. This was too strong a circumstance to admit of a quibble, and too well grounded in their recollection to be denied. He attempted a weak apology, and concluded by saying, he hoped good understanding would not be broken up, and that similar conduct would not take place. I then stated to him Gray's threats, and the necessity there was of his coming forward and making satisfactory acknowledgements which should be made as public as his threats had been. This he assured me he should do, and accordingly Gray came up, and after making the fullest recantation, declared he never meant or intended harm to any of the citizens of this state, and that he must have been in liquor when so unguarded an expression escaped him, and hoped the thing might be overlooked. I then talked with him upon the subject of the island. He did not pretend but that the islands were contained in the sales to the state, but attempted to apologize by impressing the idea of a grant made to the St. Regis people of that particular island, by the Oswegatchie Indians. I found no difficulty to confound him in this specious pretext, for it has been his and Lewis's uniform declaration to me, that the Oswegatchie Indians never had any claim whatever, to lands in this part of the state, consequently they could not grant an island in the river. In consequence of his excellency's letter, the business of the island I hope is happily concluded, and I hope a similar occasion will not present itself. I consider it proper to give your excellency the earliest information upon this subject, and it was but yesterday that Gray came forward."[13]

Finally, there this final note in the appendix, which concerns itself entirely with the Mohawk language:

NOTE C.
[Referred from page 111]

Instead of continuing our account of St. Louis, a short space will be devoted to the Mohawk dialect of the Iroquois. As it exists in Canada, it is said to have but 11 letters, viz: A, E, H, I, K, N, O, R, S, T, W, for the last of which a character like the figure 8, open at the top, is used. It is remarkable for the combinations of which it is susceptible, and which arises from the fewness of the roots or primitive words. The natives having but few ideas, and these of the most common and familiar objects, when it became necessary to speak of abstract ideas, as those of a religious character, the missionaries were obliged to use figurative terms, and comparisons couched in language suited to their capacity. From this cause, the speeches delivered at treaties abound in rhetorical figures, especially in metaphors. Hence arises a flexibility and range of modification in mood, tense and declension said to be much analagous, especially in the verb, to the Greek. The following is an instance of combination:

Ka-o-nwei-a, signifies a boat of any kind, (hence our word *canoe*).
Wa-ten-ti-a-ta, any thing "that goes by fire."
He-ti-io-kea, "on the ground."
Ot-si-re, "fire."
Watentiata-hetiiokea-otsire, "a machine that runs on the ground by fire," i. e., a *rail road*.
Watentiata-kaonweia-otsire, "a boat that goes by fire," i. e., *steam boat*.

The Algonquin language has a relation with all those of the north and northwest. The dialect of this spoken at St. Francois, is the softest and most musical of all. For this reason the Iroquois call the latter sken-towa-ne, signifying a bird that soars and warbles. This arises from the prevalence of letter L, instead of R. The Iroquois called the Algonquin) in derision, Adirondacs, or "wood eaters," which term has been applied to the lofty chain of mountains in Essex county. Mt. Marcy, the highest peak, is, called Ta-ha-was, "that cleaves the sky."

The following are the numerals used in the Mohawk dialect, as given by Dwight, in the *Transactions of the American Antiquarian Society. vol. ii, p. 358*.

1, Oohskott ; 2, tekkehnih ; 3, ohson ; 4, kuhyayrelih ; 5, wissk ; C, yahyook; 7, chahtak; 8, sohtayhhko; 9, tihooton; 10, weeayhrlih; 11, oohskohyahwarrhleh; 12, tekkehninhyahwurrhlih; 20, toowahsun; 30, ohsonnihwahsun ; 100, oohskohtowenyaoweh ; 1000, towenyaowwehtserealahsuhn.

We are indebted to Dr. E. B. O'Callaghan, editor of the Documentary History of New York, for the following:

The Lord's Prayer in Mohawk.

(*From Davis's Translation of Book of Common Prayer, New York.* 1837. *p.* 80.)

Tagwaienha ne garon hiake tesiteron; Aiesaseennaien; A-onwe ne

Our Father who heaven in dwellest; Glorified be thy name; May come

Sawenniiosern; Tsinisarikonroten ethonaiawenne nonwentsiake, tsiniio
thy kingdom; Thy will be done earth on the, at

ne garon hiake; Niatewenniserake tagwanataranontensek; nok sasani
heaven in; To day our bread give us; and for-

konrhen tsinikon gwanikonraksaton; tsiniiot ni-i tsiongwanikonrhens
give us our trespasses; as we the trespasses forgive

nothenon ionk-hinikonraksaton; Nok tosa asgwatgawe nothenon aiong
those against us who trespass; And lead us not into

gwanikonrotago; Noktennon heren tagwariwagwiten ne gariwaksen;
occasion of sin; But us lead away from deeds evil;

Ise sawenniiosera, iah othenon tesanoronse, nok agwa saiataneragwit,
For tis thy kingdom, power, and the glory,

iah tegagonte etho neniotonhake. Amen.
for ever and ever.[14]

1 *A History of St. Lawrence and Franklin Counties, New York, from the Earliest Period to the Present Time.* Franklin B. Hough. Albany: Little & Co. (1853) 25. In a footnote, Hough cites "Aboriginal Monuments of New York, by E. G. Squier. Smithsonian Contributions to Knowledge. Vol. 2, Art. 6, page 16."
2 Ibid., 102.
3 http://www.biographi.ca/en/bio/mcdonell_john_5E.html
4 Hough. Ibid., 108.
5 Ibid., 254.
6 Ibid., 259.
7 Ibid., 343.
8 Ibid., 348.
9 Ibid., 370.
10 Ibid., 380.
11 Ibid., 482-483.
12 Ibid., 589-590.
13 Ibid., 590.
14 Ibid., 707-708.

"St. Regis" in Retrospect

Publishing again the history of Akwesasne written Franklin B. Hough allows us the opportunity and perhaps even the mandate to revisit the text in light of more than a century and a half of time since ink met paper.

There are many things worth noting about his work that explain why it has had such enduring value. Yet, there are also a few points of concern for the historian.

"St. Regis" begins with a vivid description of the village, a passage that reads like a novel. It is rich in detail about what the author saw as he made his way to the stone church. He painted a pretty picture of the landscape and scenery, but when a resident caught his eye, he saw only their poverty, which he attributed to their "indolence." He likened his visit to being in a "foreign land."

Hough next introduces the early history of Akwesasne, drawing from oral traditions that were generously shared. The community's origin is found in an "emigration from the mission of Caughnawaga, or Sault Saint Louis, about nine miles above Montreal."[1] We know this place today as Kahnawake.

Along with its mother community, Akwesasne was part of an alliance known as the *Seven Nations of Canada*. Hough presents a list of the Seven Nations shared with him by the local priest. Very little was known about the Seven Nations at the time. Today the topic is an important genre in the literature about native peoples.[2]

Hough covers in great detail the negotiations leading up to what is known as the *Seven Nations of Canada Treaty* of 1796. He includes numerous speeches made by native delegates and their counterparts from New York, as well as the words of the treaty itself. The transcripts reveal that New York played hardball with the native leaders, challenging their claims on the grounds that other natives had already sold this land without ever mentioning them!

Sales of reservation land continued in the early nineteenth century, diminishing Akwesasne's land base. Hough documents these sales by consulting the official record in Albany. His work has been of great benefit to the community's land claims, as many of these sales did not have the necessary federal sanctions.

The War of 1812 had a significant impact on Akwesasne. There was a skirmish that took place in the village of St. Regis early in the war. The border community was beset by factionalism and hard feelings long after Great Britain and the United States made peace. Hough's narrative give us the broad picture and details in equal measure.

Epidemics swept Akwesasne in the years and decades before his first visit. Dr.

Hough gave the grim statistics about these harrowing events. The people he first encountered in 1852 were recovering from outbreaks of cholera and smallpox in 1849 and typhus in 1850. Twenty-nine died from cholera. Five hundred were infected with smallpox, and thirty died from it. That may have been why they appeared less than energetic to his eyes as he ambled about the village.

Hough's account of Akwesasne's tumultuous first century is compelling, and perhaps at times astonishing, yet the historian in him holds back on any expression of emotion about the facts he is calmly stringing together. The little village on the big river turned out to have played an important role in the history of North America, but at quite a price. It may have only been a pawn in the great chess tournament of European colonization, but somehow it survived the playing.

Hough felt a strong a connection to the land in all its aspects, scientific or otherwise, and later in life made forestry his personal cause after realizing how many trees were being devoured by the growing nation. The people of Akwesasne may have sensed that about him early on. They shared with him the Mohawk names for rivers, streams, lakes, islands, and places, which he dutifully recorded. This allows us in the modern era to recover information that may have been lost over time.

He set a high standard for future scholars in his respectful approach and the positive relationship he established with his native informants. This carried over to documents he found in their possession. He made copies of materials that today may not exist.

That being said, historians today have access to documents that were beyond his reach during his lifetime. Measured against these materials, parts of his narrative turn out to be in error or incomplete. They are discussed below, in the same order as they appear in his text, not to discredit his otherwise fine work, but to correct the historical record.

The Tarbell Captives

The story of the Tarbell captives has long been associated with Akwesasne. In fact, Tarbell is the most prominent surname in the community, and always has been. The two accounts from oral tradition that Hough published about the Tarbell captives do not match up with what we know today. Hough wrote that the two boys were taken captive by Kahnawake warriors, but an older sister either managed to escape or evade capture. In reality, she was taken with her two brothers. Sarah Tarbell was sold to a French family shortly after her arrival in Canada and later entered a convent.

Hough did not learn the names of the Tarbell boys, John and Zecharia, or the year they were captured, 1707. He thought it happened a hundred and thirty years in the past, which would put it somewhere in the 1720s. He got the name of the town right but not much else.

Hough wrote that the Tarbell brothers were part of the first wave of Kahnawake people to move to Akwesasne at its founding, owing to some "petty quarrels" they were involved in with other "young Indians of their age." John would have been about fifty-nine years old when the move to Akwesasne began in 1754; his brother Zecharia would have been about fifty-four. Hough said they married the daughters of chiefs and brought their parents with them to Akwesasne. It may have been their children who were the actual "founders." One of the Tarbell captives was still in Kahnawake in 1771 when the community was visited by people from New England, who took one of his grandchildren and placed him in a school there. All of this was fleshed out in 1883 by Samuel Abbot Green, the author of *Groton in the Indian Wars*.[3]

To date, Akwesasne genealogists have not been able to verify when or where either of the captives died, or what their Mohawk names were.[4]

The Founding of the St. Regis Mission

Hough puts the founding of the St. Regis Mission in Akwesasne at 1760. Documents from New France pinpoint the mission as starting in 1754 and 1755, but they were not published until 1858, five years after Hough published his book.[5]

The Bell of St. Regis

Hough devoted several pages of the book to the legend of the "Bell of St. Regis," and even reprinted a poem about it. The legend says that when the town of Deerfield was raided in 1704, native warriors captured its bell as part of the spoils, bringing it fearlessly to Akwesasne, where it was installed in the church there. There was no bell captured in Deerfield, so it could not have been brought to Akwesasne. The Mission of St. Regis did not exist until almost a half a century after the Deerfield raid. Kahnawake has the same story about one of their bells, and that one is not true either.[6]

The Treaty with the Mohawks

Hough included the text of a federal treaty with the "Mohawk nation of Indians." This was a quit-claim of Mohawk territory in New York State by Captain Joseph Brant and Captain John Deserontyon. Hough gave the date of the treaty as "the twenty-ninth day of March, in the year one thousand seven hundred and ninety-five." He got the month and day right, but not the year. It was signed in 1797, not 1795. It is out of sequence in his narrative.[7]

The Seven Nations of Canada Treaty

There are discrepancies in the amount of money New York would pay the Seven Nations. According to Hough's transcript, "the people of the state of New York shall pay to them at the mouth of the river Chazy, on Lake Champlain, on the third Monday of August next, the sum of one thousand two hundred and thirty pounds, six shillings and eight pence, lawful money of the said state; and on the third Monday in August, yearly, forever thereafter, the like sum of two hundred and thirteen pounds, six shillings and eight pence."

The actual treaty says New York would pay "the sum of one thousand two hundred and thirty-*three* pounds, six shillings and eight-pence, *and the further sum of two hundred and thirteen pounds six shillings and eight-pence, lawful money of said state,* and on the third Monday in August, yearly, forever thereafter, the like sum of two hundred and thirteen pounds six shillings and eight-pence:"[8] (Italics are mine.)

The 1838 "Removal" Treaty

There is a curious absence in Hough's narrative about what is known as the Second Treaty of Buffalo Creek, or Treaty with the New York Indians. This was an attempt by outside interests, both public and private, to force the Haudenosaunee that were not already relocated to Canada to relocate to lands in the west. This "removal treaty" was signed on January 15, 1838 by various native leaders. Reverend Eleazer Williams signed on Akwesasne's behalf, but there is no evidence that he was authorized to do so.[9] This may explain why his attempt to start a school at Akwesasne in later years met with failure.

Readers may find other examples to add to the list. To his credit, Hough kept additional notes about the subject long after his book was published. He understood that history would always be unfinished business.

In this treatment of Hough's history of Akwesasne, the goal has been to be as comprehensive as possible. There is little more to be said about the work he published in 1853. Had he stopped there, it would have been enough. But this was not the end of it for him. He continued to explore and share its fascinating story for more than thirty years.

1 *A History of St. Lawrence and Franklin Counties, New York, from the Earliest Period to the Present Time.* Franklin B. Hough. Albany: Little & Co. (1853) 111.

2 "History, Historiography, and the Courts: The St. Lawrence Mission Villages and the Fall of New France" Jean-François Lozier. *Remembering 1759: The Conquest of Canada in Historical Memory.* Phillip Bucker and John G. Reid, Editors. University of Toronto Press: Toronto, Buffalo, and London. (2012) 110-135. Lozier summarizes the historical background of the Seven Nations, and provides an overview of the extensive scholarship about this alliance.

3 *Groton in the Indian Wars.* Samuel Abbot Green. Groton, Mass. (1883) 109-124.

4 René Garcia and Janeth Lazore Murphy. Personal communication. April, 2020.

5 M. Duquesne to M. Machault. October 31, 1754. *Documents Relative to the Colonial History of the State of New York.* Volume X. E. B. O'Callaghan, Editor. Albany. (1858) 266-267. See also M. Duquesne to M. de Vaudreuil. July 6, 1755. 301. (Same volume.)

6 http://1704.deerfield.history.museum/popups/artifacts.do?shortName=bell Accessed April 18, 2020.

7 *The Everett Report in Historical Perspective: The Indians of New York.* Helen M. Upton. New York State American Revolution Bicentennial Commission. Albany. (1980) 205.

8 *Indian Affairs. Laws and Treaties.* Vol. II. (Treaties) Compiled and Edited by Charles J. Kappler. Washington: Government Printing Office. (1903) 35.

9 Ibid., 373-380.

This Associated Press photograph depicts three Akwesasne men with the "Seven Nations of Canada" Treaty of 1796. Franklin B. Hough documented the negotiations leading up to the treaty in his book, *A History of St. Lawrence and Franklin Counties, New York* in 1853. The following is the caption included with the photograph. The identity of the men is reversed. (© The Associated Press.)

> Indians of the St. Regis Mohawk Tribe display a 1796 treaty at the state capitol, Albany, N. Y., in 1971. They are, from left, Standing Arrow, Harold Thomas and Larry Lazore. The treaty gives the tribe rights to certain lands in New York state, and the tribe is bringing a claim for 12,500 acres—one of many such Indian claims, which form America's longest continuous legal saga.

II

His Later Work

Franklin B. Hough Returns to Akwesasne

Just one year after Franklin B. Hough published *A History of St. Lawrence and Franklin Counties,* he produced another about Jefferson, the county southwest of St. Lawrence on Lake Ontario's eastern shore. As he did in his previous work, he addressed the topic of "pre-history" with an examination of the county's archaeology. The information he gathered in the field is useful to those working in the discipline today.[1]

With two major history books to his credit, Dr. Hough was hired by New York State as Superintendent of the Census. This work brought him back to Akwesasne to gather data. He wrote the report about the community that appeared in *Census of the State of New-York, for 1855,* published in 1857. He also wrote an article about Akwesasne in the *New York Times* that came out the year before, in January of 1856.

Dr. Hough returned to Akwesasne on March 3, 1856. He transcribed documents he found in the possession of Reverend Eleazer Williams on blank pages of the galley of his book about the two counties. (A galley is an advance copy of a book given to authors before it goes to press.) This was where he kept notes about the text for future reference. The annotated galley is preserved among the Hough Papers in the New York State Library.

The materials he copied from Williams were written in 1811, 1812, 1813, 1815, and 1821. They purport to be letters written by New York governors Daniel D. Tompkins and Dewitt Clinton, as well as Thomas Williams, William Gray, and others. Some of the recipients were the chiefs of Kahnawake and Akwesasne. Most of the letters were concerned with the War of 1812. Future researchers will be left to determine if copies of them exist elsewhere, or if they were generated by Williams himself.

Several interesting loose documents have been found in Hough's papers as well.

The "American Trustees" at Akwesasne allowed Hough to make a copy of an indenture for sixteen islands in the St. Lawrence river. It is dated November 28, 1796. Colonel Louis Cook's Mohawk name is among the Akwesasne chiefs listed in this document.

There is a copy of an appeal by an Oswegatchie chief, Gautinonty, to New York Governor Morgan Lewis, which he presented to the Senate on January 28, 1805. Gautinonty complained of his community's land being sold out from under it by the "Canawagas." This was no doubt a reference to the Seven Nations of Canada Treaty of

1796, which was signed in part by chiefs from Kahnawake.

As previously noted, Dr. Hough had been asked by the chiefs of Akwesasne to investigate their claim to Oswegatchie land when he first visited them in 1852, but he did not know much about it at the time. He went on to write about Oswegatchie in the first chapter of *A History of St. Lawrence and Franklin Counties,* in which he noted, "This dispersion took place about 1806, or 7, and the remnants of the tribe, or their descendants, are found at St. Regis, Onondaga, and elsewhere."[2]

The Gautinonty material is evidence that Hough kept an eye out for further information on this topic, but we do not yet know if he shared this information with the chiefs at Akwesasne. However, chiefs from Akwesasne talked about pursuing a claim, in conjunction with their Onondaga counterparts, to Oswegatchie lands in 1876:

Dundee, Dec. 6th 1876

Sir,

I have been requested by the chiefs of the British Indians of St. Regis, to communicate with you in regard to a certain portion of land lying about three miles to the east of the Town of Ogdensburgh, in St Lawrence County, in the State of New York, being in extent, three miles front and running back 12 miles, making thirty six square miles.

They state that the Government of New York State told the Indians (the Oswgatchies) there residing on that land, if they would give it up, they, the Gov. would purchase as much land for them from the British Government, the Upper Canada lands.

In the year 1796, the Indians moved to Georgetown in Ontario, the place selected for them, and they lived there for three years, but the Gov. of New York State did not purchase the land for them, and they were obliged to leave, some of them going to Onondaga, and the balance to St. Regis.

The Indians say that as the said Indians mixed with the St Regis and Onondaga bands and that they never received any payment for said tract of land, that it belongs to the two bands.

The British chiefs of St Regis wants the Department to let them have the sum of fifty dollars, to go to Albany, to prosecute their claim, in conjunction with the American Indians of St Regis, and the Onondagos.

The Indians profess to have some books or some things that establish their claim.

Probably the Department may know whether there is anything in the above or not.

I am sir,
Your obedient Servant,
John Davidson,

Indian Agent

E. A. Meredith, Esq.
Deputy of the Minister of the Interior,
Ottawa[3]

Another interesting document was one he wrote about Akwesasne's traditional government. It bears no date, but it mentions that in the previous year, 1855, Kahnawake's council had been "overhauled" by the Canadian government. It describes the different type of leaders at Akwesasne, and names the "bands" of the community as plover, bear, great and little turtle, and great and little wolf. He notes that there was support for elections at the time. An informal election had even been held by some of the young men, but the results were disallowed. This was more than a decade before Canada passed the Indian Act in 1867.

Hough's 1856 visit to Akwesasne, and the renewal of his acquaintance with Eleazer Williams, no doubt made him aware that his "Lost Dauphin" claims had begun to attract a lot of attention. A two-part series about Williams appeared in *Putnam's Magazine* in 1853 under the title, "Have we a Bourbon Among Us?" The author, John Hanson, went on to publish a book about the claim in 1854, titled *The Lost Prince: Facts Tending to Prove the Identity of Louis the Seventeenth of France, and the Rev. Eleazer Williams, Missionary Among the Indians of North America.*[4] Hanson was convinced the claim was true, whereas Dr. Hough saw through it immediately, and consciously ignored mention of it when he wrote of Williams's contributions to his own work.

Reverend Williams died on August 28, 1858, and was buried in Hogansburg. Historians are fond of noting that none of the mourners at his funeral were from Akwesasne.[5]

Shortly after his death, Hough published a limited edition book of 200 copies based on the biography Williams wrote about his father, Thomas. *Life of Te-ho-ra-gwa-ne-gen, alias Thomas Williams,* was released in 1859. He credited the book on its title page to "Rev. Eleazer Williams, reputed son of Thomas Williams, and by many believed to be Louis XVII, son of the last reigning monarch of France previous to the revolution of 1789."[6]

Hough was no longer keeping Williams's wild claims under his hat, but highlighting them with the publication of the biography. As he wrote in the introduction, "The strange romance that has been woven into the history of Eleazer Williams, and the numerous corroborating circumstances which have been adduced to sustain the theory that he is the son of Louis XVI, render everything connected with the parentage, education and life of this person worthy of the attention of the unprejudiced seeker after truth."[7]

He stated that the book was largely written by Williams, minus a few editorial corrections of spelling and grammar, and that nothing had been omitted. But a comparison of the original manuscript to the book reveals that not everything Williams wrote made it to print. Indeed, he was quite critical of the local priest and his flock. Hough may have figured he would return one day and did not need these comments to upset the good relationship with the community he had worked so hard to establish.

Another curious thing about the book is that it contained Williams's bizarre claims about his own role in the War of 1812, written in the third person. For example, he said that he held a commission as a lieutenant-colonel in the American army, and was responsible for the victory at the Battle of Plattsburgh. Hough's only comment about it was reserved in a footnote: "Historians will probably be inclined to differ from the author in some of these statements."[8]

Williams slipped mention of "Col. E. Williams" in the biographies he wrote about Colonel Louis Cook and William Gray as well. He also wrote a new journal of his alleged activities in the war, which John Hanson included in his book to support the notion that leadership has always been in his blood!

All of this leads to the question of why Hough did not publish a similar book about Colonel Louis Cook, who was much more important, historically-speaking, than Thomas Williams. The answer to that may never be known. What is known is that Hough continued to uncover information about him, as described in his 1861 book, *Proceedings of the Commissioners of Indian Affairs, appointed by law, for the extinguishment of Indian titles in the State of New York*.[9]

Proceedings is the documentary record of what happened to the Haudenosaunee Confederacy after the American Revolution, beginning with events just before the Treaty of Fort Stanwix of 1784. Colonel Louis Cook was then firmly established among the Oneida, having led their pro-American warriors throughout the war as their ranking officer. He is listed as present and speaking at various councils. In a footnote, Hough included a brief biography of Colonel Louis as well as an account of the various commissions he and his Oneida and Tuscarora comrades held.

Proceedings documented controversial land transactions in which Cook was involved. Hough followed up a few years later with another book, *Notices of Peter Penet*, that focused on one of the private merchants that Colonel Louis promoted during his time among the Oneida.[10] Both books are discussed in a later chapter.

Franklin Hough wrote an entry for Colonel Louis Cook in his 1875 book, *American Biographical Notes*:

> COOK, Louis, alias Atiatonharonkwen, St. Regis chief, and officer of the revolution; b. at Saratoga, about 1740, settled at Caughnawaga near Montreal, and in 1775 went to Boston to learn facts about the war; he was examined by a committee of the gen. Court, appointed lieut. Col., by Washington, and served with his Indians through the war, mostly on scouting parties; he removed to St. Regis, was a party to several treaties with that tribe, and in the war of 1812, again took up arms for the U. S.; he d. on the Niagara frontier during the war. (*Hough's Hist. St. Law and Fr. Cos., N. Y.*, p. 182.)[11]

Hough returned to Akwesasne in 1875 to conduct the census for that year. In his report about the visit, submitted to the United State Department of Education and published in 1888, he noted the changes that had taken place over time. For instance, he found the people to be more reluctant to talk about their clans as they had been in the past.[12] For Hough, this report would be a posthumous credit in his long list of accomplishments, and his last gift to us. He died in 1885 at the age of 62.

To complete our tribute to the work of Dr. Franklin Benjamin Hough, the above-mentioned texts, minus the entry for Colonel Louis Cook in *American Biographical Notes,* have been reproduced either in whole or in part in the pages that follow, presented in the order in which they were published.

The unpublished materials found in the Hough Papers are also included to represent the period following his work on the New York State Census of 1855. It has been arranged this way so that the biography Eleazer Williams wrote about his father, Thomas, appears in the book immediately before the published version, which is presented here in its entirety.

We will conclude this collection of documents with the entry for Franklin Benjamin Hough from the *Dictionary of American Biography,* written by Henry S. Gates, and published in the ninth volume in 1936.

1   *A History of Jefferson County, in the State of New York, from the Earliest Period to the Present Time.* Franklin B. Hough. Albany: Joel Munsell. Watertown: Stirling & Riddell. (1854)
2   *A History of St. Lawrence and Franklin Counties, New York, from the Earliest Period to the Present Time.* Franklin B. Hough. Albany: Little & Co. (1853) 108.
3   Library and Archives Canada. RG 10, Volume 2001, File 7372 St. Regis Reserve – Request for grant to visit Albany to dispute their claim against New York State for land near Ogdensburg.
4   *The Lost Prince: Facts Tending to Prove the Identity of Louis the Seventeenth of France, and the Rev. Eleazer Williams, Missionary Among the Indians of North America.* John H. Hanson. New York: G. P. Putnam. (1853)
5   *Professional Indian: The American Odyssey of Eleazer Williams.* Oberg, Michael L. University of Pennsylvania Press. (2015) 204.
6   *The Life of Te-ho-ra-gwa-ne-gen, Alias Thomas Williams, A Chief of the Caughnawaga Indians in Canada.* Reverend Eleazer Williams. Albany: J. Munsell. (1859)
7   Ibid., 5.
8   Ibid., 79.
9   *Proceedings of the Commissioners of Indian Affairs, appointed by law for the extinguishment of Indian titles in the State of New York. Published from the original manuscript in the library of the Albany Institute, with an introduction and notes.* Franklin B. Hough. Albany: J. Munsell. (1861)
10 *Notices of Peter Penet: and of his operations among the Oneida Indians, including a plan prepared by him for the government of that tribe, read before the Albany institute, January 23d, 1866.* Franklin B. Hough. Lowville. (1866)
11 "Cook, Louis, alias Atiatonharongkwen." *American Biographical Notices, being Short Notices of Deceased Persons, Chiefly those not included in Allen's or Drake's Biographical Dictionaries, Gathered from Many Sources, and Arranged by Franklin B. Hough.* Franklin B. Hough. Albany: Joel Munsell. (1875) 85-86.
12 "St. Regis Reservation" Franklin B. Hough. *U. S. Bureau of Education Special Report, 1888, Indian Education and Civilization, A Report Prepared in Answer to Senate Resolution of February 23, 1885 by Alice C. Fletcher Under Direction of the Commissioner of Education.* Washington, Government Printing Office. (1888) 561-567.

The New York Times
January 11, 1856

THE ST. REGIS INDIANS.

Interesting Account of the St. Regis Indians in Northern New York.

ST. REGIS—ITS HISTORY, STATISTICS AND PRESENT CONDITION.

The Indian village of St. Regis on the River St. Lawrence, is divided by the 45th line of north latitude, the church and greater part of the village being in Canada, while a scattered population extends over their reservation in the town of Bombay, in Franklin County, New-York; comprising about one-third of the entire native and half-breed population of the settlement.

Few places are more delightfully situated than this. It lies at the head of Lake St. Francis, just below the foot of the Long Sault rapid, on a point between the mouths of the St. Regis and Racket Rivers, by the aid of which in former times the natives in their light canoes could penetrate far into the interior, and have access to the finest hunting grounds in the country, and which afforded in their immediate vicinity the choicest fish in abundance. If to these be added a salubrious climate, a fertile soil, and ready access by way of the great river to the most remote regions of the interior, it must be admitted that the location was judiciously chosen, and that its first settlement must have enjoyed peculiar advantages.

The village was settled by Father ANTOINE GORDON, a Jesuit priest from Caughnawaga, near Montreal, in 1760, with a colony of Mohawk Iroquois, who had, some seventy years before, been induced to join the French in Canada. A few families had located in the vicinity previously, but nothing was done towards permanent settlement, until GORDON arrived with a large number of savages, and took possession of the place—which, from the patron saint of the day of their arrival, was named St. Regis. The natives call it Akwissasne,—"where the partridge drums,"—perhaps from the abundance of these birds, or more probably from the circumstance that in Winter, when the river freezes, there is often heard a rumbling sound from the passage underneath the masses of ice from the open rapids above. The "anchor ice" thus accumulating, often causes a sudden breaking up and overflow, attended with a fearful crash, the waters flowing over the banks in alarming violence, at times destroying lives, and often doing great damage to buildings near the river.

From its origin to the present day, St. Regis has been the seat of a Catholic mission—Gordon being, in 1775, succeeded by DENAUT, and afterwards by L'ARCHAMBAULT, R. MCDONNELL, RINFRET, ROUPE, J. MARCOUX, N. DUFRE NE(DUFRESNE), J.BALLE and F.X. MARCOUX—the last name of whom has resided in the village since 1830. The distinction of bands, as the Wolf, Great Turtle,

Little Turtle, Bear, and Plover, into which they are divided, is the only trace of their national customs that they may now be said to retain.

Until the War of 1812, they were governed by twelve chiefs chosen for life, sharing equally among them the annuities and presents of two Governments. The war created a distinction, which still continues, having descended on the male line from the parties as they were formed at that period.

The American Indians have for many years been governed by three Trustees elected annually, while the British party continued the former government until it was broken up in June of the present year, by the Superintendent of Indian Affairs in Canada, it having been found that the tenure for life led to many abuses of trust on the part of the Chiefs. These people have made but little progress in civilization, beyond the adoption of the dress of the whites, and the attainment of a few elementary modes of cultivating the soil. The mechanic arts are unknown among them. It is instructive to trace the origin of names and the recognition of personal and social rights in the transition state of society here observed; for, although they are recognized by both Governments as tenants in common, having no individual right of soil, yet there has arisen among them a code, which without they sanction of a statute, has not less an obligation by common consent upon those who come within its influence. The title or claim of British or American party, follows the father, and is lost by the woman upon marriage, when she acquires that of her husband.

A white man, upon marrying an Indian woman, acquires no right to share in the annuities; nor does the woman lose these rights to herself and children. But a white woman marrying an Indian acquires for herself and children the rights of her husband. If the husband be White, the oldest male child is considered the head of the family for receiving annuities. If there are no children, the wife is thus considered.

Any Indian, or white intermarried and living with them, may take up as much of woodland as he can clear and cultivate, which may be sold or devised to any one of the tribe whether British or American. He cannot, however, appropriate woodland to the exclusion of any Indian from the cutting of timber, which they have the common right to cut and take off, as well for their own use as for sale.

Pasturage is in common—there being on the reservation from one to two thousand acres of cleared lands; besides woodland and tracts that from neglect have been overgrown with bushes. Every person may keep in these commons as much stock as he pleases, and the chiefs sometimes admit the cattle of farmers in the vicinity, on being paid a stipulated price.

American Indians may reside on the island or other islands of the tribe in Canada, and the British Indians may, in like manner, hold lands in the State of New York, without losing their rights of distinction of party.

Other Indians may be admitted to their rights with the consent of the chiefs; and a person may change his party with the general approbation of those among he is received, but not otherwise.

The distinction of bands descends on the female side from mother to son. Since the discontinuance of the election of chiefs, this distinction has no practical application, but formerly each bond was entitled to elect three chiefs, (the Plover and Little Turtle voting together,) and a vacancy only be filled by the band in which it occurred.

The property of a father, upon death, is equally divided among his children, but formerly it was held that the household good belonged to the daughters, while the land belonged to the sons.

The British Indians receive rents for lands sold to Governments, or leased for long periods, and presents of blankets, cloth, powder, shot and firearms, but of late some of the latter have been withheld, and the tribe have been notified that these presents will soon be discontinued altogether.

The American party draw an annuity of some $2,100, and rents from lands leased for a few years, which, unless renewed, will soon revert, under cultivation and with improvements. The total amount of land belonging to these Indians in the State of New York is about 12,000 acres.

There are at the present time 643 British Indians, sharing in the rents and presents of that Government, and 585 American Indians, participating in the annuities paid by the State of New York, making the total number 1,178. Of these, 420 reside within this State, of whom 88 are of the British Party.

The census of this tribe recently taken by Dr. FRANKLIN B. HOUGH, first Clerk of the Census Department of the Secretary's Office, shows the following statistics of those living south of the provincial line:

Number of dwellings	67
Number of families	87
Number of males	209
Number of females	217
Born in Can. St. Regis	170
Born in Lake of Two Mountains	13
Born in Caughnawaga	9
Born in Northwest	2
Born in St. Francois	1
Born elsewhere in Canada	9
Born in State of N.Y.	207
Married	153
Widowed	13
Farmers	59
Hunters	2
Children bet. 4 and 21 who attend school	53
Children bet. 4 and 21 who do not	89

attend	
Persons over 21 who cannot read	117
Person who can read Iroquois	65
Catholics	339
Methodists	48
Belong to Wolf band	195
Belong to Clover (Plover) band	89
Belong to Little Turtle band	41
Belong to Big Turtle band	83
Belong to Beaver band	21
Acres cultivated, exclusive of pasture	1,804
No. of cows owned	72
No. of horses owned	102
Bush. Of wheat raised in 1855	1,010
Bush. Of Corn raised in 1854	708

For several years these people have been on the increase, and had not their numbers been repeatedly reduced by ravages of cholera, small-pox and other epidemics, they would have nearly doubled in numbers since the war of 1812.

A striking illustration of the rate of increase may be inferred from the fact, that of the 430 living within this State, 250 are under twenty year-of-age. Marriages are usually contracted at that age, and sterility is almost unknown.

In view of those facts, it becomes a matter of grave importance whether it be not the duty of our Government to bestow attention upon the improvement and elevation of these people to that grade of intelligence which will fit them for becoming freeholders an citizens, by the introduction of learning, and especially of a knowledge of the English language; a practical education of the youth, in the duties of the farmer and the house-keeper, an appreciation of the comforts of home, with the habits of industry necessary for attainment of those conveniences which distinguish civilized life, and the emulation in labor so essential to prosperity and happiness.

There are at present two schools supported by the State, at which but few of the children attend, and those few with very little benefit. The system needs reforming, and until a different and more efficient method is adopted, there can be little hope of improvement.
                       H.

St. Regis

Census of the State of New-York, for 1855;
Taken in Pursuance of Article Third of the Constitution of the State.
And of Chapter Sixty-four of the Laws of 1855.
Prepared from the Original Returns, under the Direction of Hon. Joel T. Headley,
Secretary of State,
by Franklin B. Hough, Superintendent of the Census.
Albany: Printed by Charles Van Benthuysen.
1857

St. Regis—The Indian village of St. Regis,[1] on the south bank of the river St. Lawrence, where it is intersected by the 45th degree of north latitude, was founded about the year 1760, or a little before, by a colony from Caughnawaga, near Montreal, under Father Anthony Gordon, a Jesuit priest of that mission.

A tradition is preserved at St. Regis, that in the early part of the last century, two little boys of the name of Tarbell were stolen by the Indians, while at play, in the town of Groton, Massachusetts, and [508] adopted and reared among the natives at Caughnawaga, acquiring their habits, language and manners. Upon reaching manhood, they married daughters of the chiefs; but from a difference of race, or other causes, a series of petty quarrels ensued between the young men and Indians of their age, which was finally quieted by their removal with their families to the site of the present village of St. Regis, where they were residing at the time of Gordon's arrival. The descendants of these Tarbells have ever since resided at St. Regis, and several have been distinguished as chiefs and head men of the tribe. One of them, named Leser Tarbell, was a prominent chief about fifty years since, and was very much esteemed by the whites for his prudence, candor, and great worth of character. The name occurs repeatedly in treaties and other negotiations which these people have held with the State of New-York.

The settlement at St. Regis was increased on the breaking up of the mission at Fort Presentation, (now Ogdensburgh) in 1760, and the removal of a part of the Oswegatchies, although the latter did not finally abandon their settlement until 1806. Both of these sources of emigration were originally formed by the removal of Indians from New-York to Canada, through the influence of the French, and the language at St. Regis at the present time, is the Mohawk dialect of the Iroquois. This emigration from New-York, was encouraged by the French, with the double view of securing the Indian trade, and of attaching the natives to the Catholic religion, which has since been sustained among them.[2] These people retain none of the festivals and ceremonies of their ancestors, but the ancient distinction of bands has been transmitted in the female line to the present time, the number in June 1855, on the American side of the line being as follows: Wolf, (Okawaho), 195; Plover, (Rotinesiio), 89; Little Turtle, (Rotisennakehte),

41; Big Turtle, (Ratiniaten), 33; Bear, (Okwari), 21; not known, 41.

The St. Regis Indians formerly claimed the title of the islands in the St. Lawrence above their village, as far as French Creek, and in the early settlement of St. Lawrence county, serious difficulties were apprehended between the grantees under the Indians, and the patentees under the State. Within a few years, considerable sums have been paid by the State, for the right which these Indians had lost in the transfer of their lands by the location of the national boundary. They also claimed an undefined territory in the northern part of the State, besides a large tract in Canada. By a treaty held in May, 1796, the "Seven Nations of Canada"[3] surrendered to New-York all their title to land, with the exception of six miles square at St. Regis, one mile square on Salmon river, at the present village of Fort Covington, one mile square at the mills on Grass river below the present village of Massena, and the natural meadows on Grass river. These reservations have since been reduced by successive sales, to a tract of about 14,030 acres, a part of which is leased to whites for a term of years, by virtue of an act passed in 1841. The American party received from the State of New-York for the lands ceded an annuity of $2,131.66, which is equally divided among them per capita, by an agent appointed by the Comptroller.

The lands of these people in Canada have been mostly sold, or leased, the rents of which amount to about $2 per head to the British party. In addition to this, the English government gives presents of blankets and pilot cloth to each person, of a value proportioned to their age. Powder, shot and guns are also given, but it is understood that these presents are to be hereafter discontinued.

To increase these slender revenues, which are often anticipated by the sale of certificates to whites at a great discount before payment is due, most families cultivate small patches of land, while a considerable number of the young men are employed, during the early months of summer, in conducting rafts down the rapids of the St. Lawrence. Some go out to labor among the farmers in harvest, and a few resort to the primitive mode of hunting and fishing for subsistence.[4] There are a few good farmers among these people, who manage their affairs with ability and success, but the greater number exhibit an indolence and apathy that promises little in the way of improvement, without a radical change in their circumstances, a practical education of the young in the language and arts of civilized life, and at a proper period, the division of the common lands into individual rights. An examination of the accompanying tables, will show an unusual proportion of children, and the enumerations annually made for the distribution of annuities indicate a gradual increase in numbers among them. This growth has been repeatedly checked [509] by the ravages of epidemics[5] to which their habits of life particularly expose them. Were it not for these unusual causes, their numbers would have ere this exceeded the capacity of their reservation for comfortable agricultural support.

Previous to the War of 1812, the whole tribe was governed by twelve chiefs, chosen for life, after their ancient custom, and the annuities and presents of both governments were shared equally among them. Upon the declaration of War, it was agreed with these people, that they should remain neutral, but in violation of this engagement, a company of about eighty warriors was raised for the British army, who served during the War. Several of the tribe afterwards joined the American army, among the most efficient of Whom was Col. Louis Cook, or Atiatonharonkwen, who had held a commission from the Commander in Chief, as lieutenant colonel in the army of thel Revolution, and whose wonderful native sagacity and energy of character, had given him a commanding influence with the Indian tribes.

The war created parties among the St. Regis people, which have continued till the present time. It also led to a change in the form of government, the British party retaining the old system of chiefs, with the number reduced to seven. This mode was continued until June, 1855, when it was abolished on account of the misconduct of those who had held the office many years, and it was ordered that in future there should be an annual appointment of chiefs by the English government. The American party are required by a law of the State, to elect three trustees annually, who have the general charge of public affairs. The election of these officers is often conducted with much spirit, the American Indians being divided into parties, chiefly on the policy of leasing their lands.

The distinction of party, which originated in the war, has been continued by hereditary descent on the fathers' side to the present time. By the consent of the chiefs, or trustees, a man can be transferred from one to the other, or Indians from other places may be admitted to the rights of either, but this is seldom done.[6] A woman loses her rights in one party, by marrying a member of the other, but acquires for herself and children the rights of her husband. A white woman, upon marrying an Indian, gains for herself and children a right to the same annuities or presents that her husband receives, but a white man on marrying an Indian woman acquires no right, nor does the woman, or her children, lose their right as Indians if they remain on the reservation. The presents of the British government are divided among British Indians only, and the amount varies with the age of the person. The annuities paid by the State of New-York, are shared equally among the American Indians Without reference to age. The lands of both parties are held in common, and families of either party may reside in the territory of their own or the other government without losing their rights.[7] Although the law recognizes no individual rights to the soil, custom has sanctioned the holding of land for the exclusive benefit of families, and these rights are bought and sold among themselves. A white person marrying and living with the Indians, is sometimes allowed to acquire this conventional title to land. Formerly it was held, that upon the death of a father, the house and furniture belonged to the daughters and the right of land to the sons, but the children now share equally in the division of property.

Any Indian may appropriate for cultivation so much as he pleases of the Woodlands on the reservation, provided he clears and occupies it, and the improvements on the land so assumed may be sold to others of the tribe. Indians may pasture upon the commons as many cattle as they please, there being no regulation as to the number to which any person shall be limited. Whites frequently hire the privileges of the common, by paying the chiefs, or trustees, a price agreed upon, which is usually an eighth of a dollar a week or two dollars for the season per head. Woodlands are held as common property, and every Indian has the right of cutting wood wherever he pleases, either for his own use or for sale.[8] It is evident that these regulations could only exist among an indolent and semi-barbarous people, and that with the least enterprise or emulation in the acquirement of property, their reservation would soon be appropriated altogether, by individuals and conflicting claims would quickly lead to discord and confusion. This community of landed interest is undoubtedly a bar to further improvement, and until it is changed, there can be little prospect of advancement in civilization. The State of New-York has maintained for several [510] years two schools upon the reservation, but these are very poorly attended, and little or no benefit is now derived from them.

1   The natives call their village Ak-wis-sas-ne, "where the partridge drums" alluding, not as would appear, to the abundance of this game, but to a peculiar rumbling noise heard in winter, occasioned by the passage of masses of ice from the rapids above under the solid ice opposite the village. In extremely cold weather ice dams form occasionally very suddenly, causing a destructive overflow of the river and much injury to property along the banks. St. Regis is named from Jean François Regis, a native of Languedoc, who joined the Jesuit order and spent several years in zealous missionary labors among the poor in France. He died in 1640, and was canonized in 1737. His festival occurs on the 16th of June.

2   At St. Regis, the succession of Catholic missionaries has been as follows: Anthony Gordon, 1760 to 1775, after which the mission was without a priest for four or five years. Fathers Denaut, (afterwards Bishop of Quebec,) Lebrun and L'Archaumbault, occasionally visited the place in this interval. In December, 1785, Roderick McDonnell succeeded and remained until his death. He has been followed by Fathers Rinfret in 1806, Jean B. Roupe in 1807, Joseph Marcoux in 1812, Nicholas Dufresne in 1819, Joseph Vallé in 1825, and Francis X. Marcoux, the present incumbent, in 1832. The number reporting themselves as belonging to the several religions in 1855, was: Catholics, 339; Methodist, 48; Episcopalians, 8. The Canada census of 1852, gave 978 Catholics, 21 Episcopalians, 56 Presbyterians and 8 Baptists, as residing in the Canadian portion of the village, including both whites and Indians. A Methodist mission was established at Hogansburgh, on the border of the Reservation, in 1847, '48.

3   Of these settlements composing these seven nations, only that at Caughnawaga ever participated in the treaties with New-York or shared in the annuities paid under them. A further account of these treaties will be given under the head of "Cessions of land by the Iroquois."

4   These people seldom or never become chargeable to the town or county in which they live.

5   In the spring of 1829, the small pox swept off great numbers. On the 29th of June, 1832, the cholera broke out among them, accompanied by typhus fever, and about 340 cases occurred, of which 134 were fatal. In 1849 the cholera again appeared, destroying 29, and the same year 500 cases of small pox occurred, proving fatal to 30. In 1850 typhus fever prevailed the whole summer.

6   The nativities of those living on the American side in 1855 were as follows: St. Regis, Canada side, 179; ditto, American side, 201; Lake of the Two Mountains 13; Caughnawaga 9; Northwestern country 2; St. Francis 1; Oneida 1.

7   In June 1855, there were 374 American and 38 British Indians living in the State of New-York. The number of American Indians living in Canada was 160. The whole number of Indians drawing annuities from New-York was 535, and of those receiving rents and presents from the British government 643. The number of the American party during several years has been as follows: 1846, 452;—1847, 465;—1848, 495;—1849, 487;—1851, 498;—1852, 497;—1853, 470.

8   Within a few years large quantities of wood have been taken from the reservation. An intelligent citizen of Hogansburgh estimates that between four and five thousand cords were taken off within the last year. It is mostly sold at Montreal. The destruction of timber has since been rapid, and promises soon to lead to serious altercations and difficulties.

Documents from the Franklin Benjamin Hough Papers

In 1911, fire swept the New York State Capitol, destroying many early government records. Five years later, the New York State Library received a generous donation to help them rebuild their collections. The Franklin Benjamin Hough Papers were meticulously organized by the librarians, and housed in the Manuscripts and Special Collections department in 116 boxes.

With the assistance of the finding aid and the staff, the collection was searched for materials relating to Akwesasne. Several important items emerged, which have been transcribed and assembled here.

One item requires a bit more care in its presentation. It has been mentioned briefly already. It is the "galley" of *A History of St. Lawrence and Franklin Counties, New York.* This was where Hough wrote notes for future reference in the margins and blank pages. Some seem superfluous while others are noteworthy. Several are presented below.

The first two notes relate to the founding of the community and Father Mark Anthony Gordon, S. J.:

Page 110. From a passage in the "Memoire Sur le Canada" p. 140, giving an account of the expeditions of the English against Canada in 1759, it would appear that Gordon had settled St. Regis earlier than I have stated in the text.

"x x x P. Gordon a Jesuit who dwelt at St. Regis was ordered to engage those of his village to go into the woods, watch on the route to German Flats and cooperate with those of la Presentation."[1]

p. 124 Col Claus, writing from Montreal April 30, 1764, says – after noticing a visit to Gov. Burton:–

"He was pleased with their (the Indians) going by way of Lake George, as they might be corrupted by some disaffected French or Indians going up the river. He looks upon the Jesuit of Aughquissasne as a dangerous bad man, and intends to remove him from thence." Reference is here evidently made to Father Gordon, whose French instincts and sympathies were doubtless restrained with difficulty under English rule.

153

[MSS Sir William Johnson Vol IX][2]

Several galley notes relate to Colonel Louis Cook, the first to his military commission in the War of the Revolution:

Page 189   On the 5th of June 1779. Congress resolved:–
"That one more blank commission be sent to the commissioners of Indian Affairs in the northern department to be filled up with the name of such faithful Chief as they shall deem worthy of that honor," In pursuance of this order a commission of Lieut. Col. in the Army of the United States was granted to Louis Atayataronghta, to rank from June 15, 1779.
   Gen Knox March 8, 1791 stated to Congress that Louis had been settled with for his commutation and for his pay, to the same period that the State of New York settled with those under a previous act. {American State Papers. Ind. Affairs. Vol. 1. Page 123}[3]

On the land bounty he was paid an officer for his service to the United States:

Page 193. Colonel Louis drew Jan 29, 1791 the following lots on the military tract by virtue of his commission as Lieutenant Colonel. (Balloting Book P. 75.)
   The titles were delivered to Michael Connoly. And the lost drawn were in the town of Junius.
Seneca Co. 926.).
   Lot 72 ------- 600 acres
   "   55 ------- 500 "
   "   11 ------- 500 "
   "   34 ------- 600 "
   "   98 ------- 600 "   Total 2,800 acres[4]

On the negotiations he entered into with New York State. This note relates to page 129 of the book:

"Resolved. That his Excellency the Governor be requested to inform Col Lewis and others a deputation from the St. Regis Indians, that the object of their mission will be determined upon with all convenient speed – and that their further attendance upon the legislature is unnecessary: And that his excellency the Governor take proper measures to ascertain and defray the expenses which the said Indians may have incurred, whilst attending in this city, and furnish them with the necessary means of returning home, not exceeding the sum of one hundred dollars: and that this legislature will make provision for the payment thereof."

"Resolved, as the sense of this committee, that a committee be appointed to prepare and bring in a bill, appointing, commissioners to examine into the claims of the St. Regis Indians, to any of the lands in this state, and to report to the legislature of the state, extent and situation of the said claim."

Col Lewis and the others were to be informed of these resolutions.
(Assem Journal. 1794. P. 132—[5]

The next note concerns the same negotatiatons:

Page 129.
March 13, 1794 a committee consisting of David Brooks of Dutchess Co John Bay of Columbia and Wm North of Albany appointed to prepare a bill appointing commissioners to examine the claims of St Regis Indians and to report.

March 9, 1795. in Assembly.

Resolved as the sense of both houses of the legislature that it is advisable a future meeting at such time and place as shall be deemed most convenient should be appointed by his Excellency the Governor to be held with the Indians generally known and distinguished as the Indians of St Regis in order to treat and finally to agree with the said Indians touching any right or claim they may have or make to any lands within the limits of this State; and further that the Governor in addition to the request contained in the concurrent resolution of both houses of the 3d inst be also requested to cause the twelve Indians mentioned in the said concurrent resolution to be furnished with such sum of money as may be requisite to defray the expenses of their journey to this city and on their return home, and also that his Excellency the Governor be requested to cause such presents or gratuities as he shall deem proper to be given to the said twelve Indians in behalf of the State, and that the Legislature will make the requisite provision for carrying these resolutions into effect."[6]

On the governor's acknowledgment of the completed treaty, as related on page 146 of the book:

The governor in his next annual message remarked of this treaty:

"It gives me pleasure to inform you, that at a treaty held in this city, under the authority of the United States, a final agreement has been concluded between this State and the Indian tribes, who call themselves the Seven Nations of Canada. Although their title to the territory they claimed was not unquestionable, yet it was judged more consistent with Sound policy, to extinguish their claims, and consequently their animosity, by a satisfactory settlement, than leave the state exposed to the inconveniences which always result from disputes with Indian Tribes. Besides considering our strength, and their comparative weakness, every appearance of taking advantage of that weakness was to be avoided."[7]

On treaties that followed the Seven Nations of Canada Treaty of 1796. This note refers to page 170 of the book:

The Caughnawagas never pretended to Claim any share of the annuities under treaties subsequent to 1796.[8]

On Colonel Louis's last words:

His last words were addressed to his son in which he besought him "not to disgrace the memory of his father."[9]

On the likeness made of him:

An excellent likeness was taken by an artist for Mr. Parish at Ogdensburgh It was given away to one of the servants three or four years since and it is doubtful whether it be still preserved.[10]

On census data taken at Akwesasne:

Census of St. Regis Indians 1845
Taken by James B. Spencer

Heads of families	48
Male persons, including head of fam.	126
Females including heads of families	134
Married females under 45	44
Unmarried females 16-45	5
--------do------------ under 16	67
Births the year previous male	[0?]
do ----------do-----females	7
Deaths ------do-----males	5
" -------------females------	3
Born in the State of New York	125
" " British possession	135
Children from 5 to 16	81
Acres of improved lands	591 ¼
do --------------barley ---------	¾

do -------------peas -----------	27
bushels of peas -------------	105
acres of beans --------------	11
Bushels of beans ----------	18
acres buckwheat ----------	8
acres turnips---------------	[?]
acres of potatoes----------	20 5/8
bushels of potatoes------	410.
Acres of wheat ---	42 ½
bushels of wheat --	195
acres of corn --------	658 ½
acres of oats -----------	51
bushels of oats---------	290
number of meat cattle --	90
Under 1 year old	17
Over 1 year old	16
milked cows ------	43
Horses	50
Hogs	112[11]

In addition to the above, the galley was where Dr. Hough copied various letters that were in the possession of Reverend Eleazer Williams in 1856. These will be found under a separate heading in later pages of the present volume.

1 Hough Papers, NYSL. Box 74. Item 1. History of St. Lawrence and Franklin Counties, vol. 1, annotated galley, 1853. 367.
2 Ibid., 385.
3 Ibid., 366.
4 Ibid., 339.
5 Ibid., Attached to 129.
6 Ibid., 339-340.
7 Ibid., Attached to 146-147.
8 Ibid., 170.
9 Ibid., 197.
10 Ibid., 198.
11 Ibid., Attached to 201.

Indenture for Islands in the St. Lawrence River
1796

(From the original in the possession of the American Trustees, St. Regis)

This indenture made the twenty eighth day of November in the year of our Lord one thousand seven hundred and ninety six by and between Tharoningethon, Teganiatarogen, Sategaienton, Arenhisas, Atiatoharongewen, Onwaniente, Satorawane, Oriwagate, Ganotenti, Thoiennogen and Ganenewatase being chiefs of the Indian Village called and known by the name of St. Regis lying & being situate at the confluence of the River St. Regis with great River St Lawrence on the southerly side thereof about Eighty English miles above the city of Montreal do for ourselves our children our heirs and assigns our successors in office and in behalf of the Tribe of the St. Regis Nation of Indians whom we represent being part of one of the Seven nations so called being assembled in full council of the first part – and Thomas Tonsey Abraham Baldwin & Acariah Tonsey of Vergennes in the county of Addison & state of Vermont merchants in company under the firm of Tonsey Baldwin & Company & Timothy Johnson of Cornwall in the County of Stormont & Province of Upper Canada Physician & William Gray of said St Regis Indian Interpreter of the second part <u>Witnesseth,</u>

    That the aforesaid Indian Chiefs in their capacity aforesaid for the considerations and and agreements and agreements hereafter mentioned and entered into hath demised granted and to farm letten and doth hereby demise grant and to farm let unto the said party of the second part their heirs executors administrators and assigns [2] the following Islands lying and being situate in the said River St. Lawrence between this place and pointe Iroquois and are described as follows (viz.)

Name of Island	No.	No Acres	
Rocky Island	1	1/2	An Island which we name Rocky Island because it is mostly a barren rock rising out of the St. Lawrence opposite to lot number twenty in the first concession in the Township of Cornwall aforesaid reckoned to contain half an acre of land be the same more or less
Mill Pond Island	2	2 1/2	An Island which we call mill pond Island because it lies in Messr's Shiek's & Dixon's mill pond [ ] the most northerly branch that issues out of the Long Saut, and is about half a mile wide as near as we can judge below the head of said branch being an oblong piece

			of land of a fertile soil and contains two & half acres of land be the same more or less
Scrub Island	3	0 1/2	A small Island which we call Scrub Island lying opposite the foregoing described Island and nearer to the large Island which forms the aforesaid branch of the river issuing from the long sault and contains half an acre of land be the same more or less.
Ford Island	4	2	A small Island which we call Ford Island because the water between it and the British shore is very shoal and narrow and is situate directly at the head of the aforesaid branch of the river where it issues from the Long Sault. Contains two acres of land more or less [3]
Long Sault Island	5	640	A large Island which we call Long Seault Island because it lies near the middle of the Long Sault extending up the St. Lawrence beyond the head of sd. Long Sault having a great number of pine trees thereon & contains six hundred and forty acres of land be the same more or less.
Swan's Island	6	16	An Island which we call Swans Island because many of these fowls have been observed to visit it lying about two thirds of the way up the Long Sault Island on the northerly side thereof and is a rising stony ground at the upper end rich and fertile in the middle and low ground at the lower end containing sixteen acres of land be the same more or less.
Meadow Island	7	2	A small Island which we call Meadow Island because there is a long narrow meadow extending into the river from the lower end thereof situate a little lower down the river than Swan's Island and nearer to the Long Sault Island and contains two acres of land be the same more or less.

Barge Island	8	10	An Island which we call Barge Island because it lies directly at the head of Long Seault Island seeming to to attend the same as a barge does a ship. The French call this Island L'isle du petite Chenail Ecartie. It contains ten acres of land be the same more or less.
Eddy Island	9	940	A large Island which we call Eddy Island because a large eddy is formed in the river adjoining it. The French call this Island L'isle du Grand Renoux. The Indians call it Tsiteganegatases the soil is good and contains nine hundred and forty acres of land be the same more or less. [4]
Burnt Island	10	1	A small Island which we call Burnt Island, that being the interpretation of the Indian name Siiotewenogwatshon lying near to what the French call Pointe a la Barbue; it is very stoney & contains one acre of land be the same more or less.
Ash Island	11	2	A small island which we call Ash Island lying opposite to lot number fourteen in the first concession in the township of Williamsburgh, contains two acres of land be the same more or less.
Goose Neck Island	12	275	An Island which we call Goose Neck Island because the upper end terminates in a sharp peake something resembling the neck and head of that fowl and lies nearly opposite or quite opposite of the centre of Sd. Williamsburgh is of fertile soil, and contains two hundred and seventy five acres of land be the same more or less.
Round Island	13	32	A small Island which we call Round Island as it lies nearly in a round form and opposite to lot number twenty three in the first concession in said Williamsburgh of a fertile soil and contains thirty two acres of land be the same more or less.
Snipe	14	10	A small Island which we call Snipe Island because

Island			we saw a bird of that kind there. It lies opposite to lot number thirty three in said Williamsburgh and contains ten acres of land be the same more or less.
Duck Island	15	32	A small Island which we call Duck Island lying upwards of the last mentioned Island and not far from opposite to lot number thirty four in said Williamsburgh contains thirty two acres of land be the same more or less.
Rapid Plat Island [5]	16	740	A large Island which we call Rapid Plat Island because it lies in a rapid clearing that name and nearest to the United States shore containing seven hundred and forty acres of land be the same more or less.
		2705 ½	

The whole of the above mentioned Islands being sixteen in number, are by agreement of the aforesaid parties computed to contain two thousand seven hundred and five and an half acres of land be the same more or less.

The have and to hold the said demised premises with all the mill, water & other privilidges and appertenances thereunto belonging, or in any wise appertaining (we hereby engaging that we have good right to lease the aforedescribed land according to tenor of this lease) to them the said Tonsey Baldwin & Company & Johnson & Gray, their heirs and from and after the day of the date hereof during the term of nine hundred and ninety & nine years fully to be completed and ended, we the chiefs aforesaid reserving to ourselves & posterity all the mill priviledges of water on the aforesaid Long Seault Island & Barge Island but not on any other of the above said Islands. Also the point of land on the sd. Long Seault Island which the Indians call Tsiitsiagutha containing three acres of land to be taken off directly from said point & is reserved for a fishing. The lessees may also have free liberty to fish when the lessors are not actually occupying the same.

And the Lessees for themselves their heirs and assigns for & in consideration of the use and improvement of the lands and priviledges contained in this lease on the first day of January in each year, twenty seven dollars & five cents in specie and forty bushels &The whole of the above mentioned Islands being sixteen in number, are by agreement of the aforesaid parties computed to contain two thousand seven hundred and five and an half acres of land be the same more or less. The have and to hold the said demised premises with all the mill, water & other privilidges and appertenances thereunto belonging, or in any wise appertaining (we hereby engaging that we have good right to lease the aforedescribed land according to tenor of this lease) to them the said Tonsey Baldwin & Company & Johnson & Gray, their heirs and from and after the day of the date hereof during the term of nine hundred and ninety & nine years fully to be completed and ended, we the chiefs aforesaid reserving to ourselves & posterity all the mill priviledges of water on the aforesaid Long Seault Island & Barge Island but not on any other of the above said Islands. Also the point of land on the sd. Long Seault Island which the Indians call Tsiitsiagutha containing three acres of land to be taken off directly from said point & is reserved for a fishing. The lessees may also have free liberty to fish when the lessors are not actually occupying the same. twenty two quarts & one pint of wheat Winchester measure which payment is to be made at the [6] Council House in St. Regis on the following conditions and reservations (viz.) If any inconvenience should arise to the lessees their heirs or assigns so that they should not pay on the said first day of January in each year the month of January is allowed as a day of grace, and payment may be made on the first day of the February following without any penalty on the part of the lessees their heirs or assigns. Further in case payment is not made on the first day of February there shall be a further time allowed to the lessees their heirs and assigns of six calendar solar months which brings it to the first day of August at which time if they appear and pay up the back rent to the first day of the preceding January together with one tenth more than is really in arrear as a penalty for the delay the payment shall be deemed good and the lessees continue in possession of the aforesaid land and priviledges but in case payment is not made on or before the said first day of August no further time of grace shall be granted but the lessors shall have a right to reenter and enjoy the premises contained in this lease in the same manner as though this instrument had not been given.

Always provided that in case of hostility or war among any of the nations whatsoever so that in consequence thereof it is reasonably believed to be unsafe for the lessees to appear at time and place and make payment of all back rents due without any penalty they shall continue in possession or if out of possession reenter and enjoy the premises & priviledges conveyed by this instrument in as ample a manner as though no such failure of payment had happened. [7]

Also provided that in case any Government shall sieze all or any part of the aforesaid premises or priviledges so that the lessees are deprived of them or if the lessees are disturbed in the peaceable possession thereof they shall pay no rent for such part as is taken away but continue in possession and pay in proportion as the remainder of the aforesaid lands is to the whole nor shall they be liable to rent while they may be disturbed by other claimants as aforesaid.

The lessors their heirs and assigns do hereby give the refusal of all mill and other priviledges reserved in this writing to the lessees their heirs & assigns and engage not to improve or dispose of the same until they have been first fairly offered to the lessees their heirs and assigns (the said Priviledges) and the parties cannot agree.

And further the Lessors for themselves their heirs and assigns agree with the lessees their heirs and assigns never to erect any mills or water works on that point on Long Seault Island which is reserved in this lease as a fishery.

And further the lessors agree not to take rent on those Islands now leased to Mr John Hoople until his lease or right to cut timber expires which will be in July next and the lessees to have from this date all right to the same not granted to Mr Hoople, or that he will consent to part with to the lessees.

And further the lessors on their part agree not to dispose of this bargain without first notifying the lessees of their intention and obtaining their consent if they will reasonably give it, and the lessees also on their part, agree not to sell their lease, meaning the whole, [8] to one purchaser without notifying the chiefs and obtaining their consent if they will reasonably give it.

And be it remembered that the said William Gray is entered in this lease, as one of the chiefs above named in full council assembled at the council house in our village of St Regis have hereunto set our hands and fixed our seals on the 28th day of November in the year of our Lord 1796.

Signed Sealed & Delivered in presence of	Tharon X iagethon (L.S)
Mo. French	Teganiatargen (L.S.)
Samuel Mitchell	SateX ganenthon (L.S.)
David Sheik	Aren X hises (L.S.)
Gabriel Descoteaux.	Atiato X harongwen (L.S.)
	Tehotgengerenton (L.S.)
	Tehaton X wentsiaongoththa (L.S.)
	Nihasogwaho (L.S.)
	Niratenenraha (L.S.)
	Onwanren X te (L.S.)
	Sota X rowane. (L.S.)
	OriwaX gete (L.S.)
	Gaho X tenti (L.S.)
	Thoiennogen (L.S.)
	Ganon X watase (L.S.)

An Appeal by Gautinonty, a Chief of Oswegatchie
1805

[Among the Franklin Hough Papers in the New York State Library were two copies he made of a document "in which the claims of the Oswegatchies are thus mentioned." The community of Oswegatchie figured prominently in the first chapter of *A History of St. Lawrence and Franklin Counties, New York, from the Earliest Period to the Present Time.* Hough mentioned Gautinonty briefly in reference to Iroquois claims to land on page 38 of *A History of Jefferson County.* The following transcript was made from the official source rather than Hough's handwritten copy.]

Assembly of the State of New-York, at their twenty-eighth session, begun and held at the city of Albany, the sixth day of November, 1804. p. 48.

[Monday, January 28, 1805]

Gautinonty, a savage, styling himself chief of the Oswegatchie Nation, is now in this city, representing a grievance, which he prays the government to redress. He states that his tribe is the parent stock of the Onondagas and Cayugas; that they possessed, from time immemorial, a tract of country extending along the St. Lawrence from the mouth of Ganonoque river to Cat Island, a distance of about seventy miles. That the boundary between them and the St. Regis or Canawaga Indians was, by consent of the parties, fixed and established by Sir John Johnson, who, for that purpose, erected a monument on the said island. That the British Government built for them twenty framed house, near the Oswegatche river, where some of them still remain, deriving a subsistence from agricultural pursuits. That the state claims title to their lands by virtue of a purchase of the Canawagas, who had no right to sell to them, and that they have never received any compensation. That persons claiming title under the state have ordered them to quit their habitations. That it is their wish to remain where they are, and that the state would secure to each of them a farm, with a competent portion of hunting ground.

From documents on file in the executive department it would appear that this is not a novel claim. That its being disregarded, is the consequence of a declaration of the St Regis Indians that those of Oswegatche were their tenants at sufferance. Opposed, however, to the truth of this assertion is the attempt made by the Canawagas, in 1803, to justify trespasses committed on *Rapide Plat* islands, by pretext of a purchase made by them of the Oswegatches.

An examination of this claim in some mode which the wisdom of the legislature shall suggest I have ventured to assure the chief and his followers will not be denied them. They wait the result of this communication.

Notes on Governance at Akwesasne and Kahnawake circa 1856

[This document was in the hand of Franklin B. Hough and had no title.]

In former times there were elected twelve chiefs by the St Regis Indians. Each of the four bands chose three.

Of these, the women chose one head chief in each band The warriors chose one chief warrior in each band, and one messenger, or runner in each. The latter were young men; their place in council near the door, and their duty to act as messengers to assemble their tribe for council, convey intelligence and services of like kind

They were in due time promoted to war chiefs or head chiefs. The practice of election by women was discontinued in St Regis very many years ago. All the chiefs held for life. The Rev Mr Marcoux is not certain that chiefs were ever elected by women in St Regis.

Although there were five of six bands they were only entitled to elect in four parties.

The Plover and the Little Turtle elected one of each kind.

The Bear elected one of each kind.

The Great and little wolf elected one of each kind.

The Great Turtle elected one of each kind.

Vacancies could only be filled by the band in which they occurred. At Caughnawaga the head chiefs alone were recognized by government. At St Regis it was the custom of Mr Solomon Chessley Indian Agent to regard them all of equal power.

Till 1812 there was but one set of chiefs at St Regis and both British and American Indians shared equally in the annuities and presents of the two nations.

Since 1812 there has been until recently 12 chiefs among the British Indians. Of late years, vacancies have not been filled when they occurred, and the number had been reduced to seven. It had been decided by the British government that the number should then be allowed to reduce itself to five. The tenure for life, had for many years been complained of, especially by the young men, who declared that the old chiefs had [2] abused their power, and misapplied or embezzled the property of the tribe where and as often as opportunity occurred. To redress this, Col. Napier came up from Montreal in company with the Governor's aid and other gentlemen, and on the 26th of June 1855 called a council, arraigned the old chiefs who plead guilty of the charge, deposed them, and appointed five others. (Some of whom however had before been chiefs) and gave them to hold their office on trial for one year. Opportunity to be given for making accusation against them, and they are liable to removal at any time. They are numbered from 1 to 5, in the order of Seniority, and are to sign papers &c. in this order. One chief is to belong to each band. They are equal in authority. The British agent, was saluted by the discharge of cannon (as is the custom) on his arrival. The British Indians have a piece kept for this and similar purposes.

The British Government in 185_ bought of the Indians a large tract of land north of the St Lawrence in Glengarry (which had for many years been leased by the Indians to whites) sold it to the settlers in order to make them citizens and invested the money due the Indians in 6 per cent stocks. There is another tract between St Regis & Salmon Rivers, from which the Indians draw rents regularly and of which the Government has nothing to do. It has been stated that the Government proposes to discontinue their Indian Department at Montreal and to stop paying presents. The agency (of Mr Cahoun) on the north shore opposite St Regis is not supported by the government, but the agent is paid by a percentage in the funds which pass through his hands.

It is now a year since the chiefs at Caughnawaga have been overhauled by Government. There are seven there equal to the number of the bands. The Indians were denied the privilege of electing their chiefs at St Regis, a cause they were very anxious to take. Anticipating this the young men a few weeks since held an informal election which the agent refused to sanction, telling them that he could allow no elections.

Documents in the Possession of Reverend Eleazer Williams

[The materials presented here were found in the annotated galley of *A History of St. Lawrence and Franklin Counties, New York*. No attempt to verify them with other sources has been made. A few minor adjustments have been made to the format. They are introduced by Dr. Hough.]

The following documents, (pages 356-365) were taken from originals in the possession of the Rev. Eleazer Williams March 3, 1856

"Brothers.
I have received your friendly talk, and am highly gratified go find that you are still friendly to the people of the State of New York. We in return continue to Consider you as friends and brothers.
Brothers,
The wicked representation which has been made to you that in case the Americans should come into Canada they would drive you off and take your lands, is without foundation & entirely false. The Americans wish you to remain peaceably upon your lands, and have always assured you so, and this will be their wish as well if they were in Canada as while they are in the United States. You need not fear any disturbance or molestation from your American brothers.
Brothers,
Through the medium of [357] this answer, I take you by the hand and greet you all as brothers and friends.

Albany January 5, 1815

            Daniel D Tompkins.

To the Chiefs of the
Chanawage Iroquois}
...

  Brothers
I have received your friendly address and am pleased with the sentiments in

contains. Your determination not to take an active part in the war which has taken place between the United States and Great Britain meets the approbation of your brothers of the State of New York

Brothers,

The people of this State always have been and yet are your sincere friends.

They advise you to persevere in refusing to raise the hatchet on either side, under present circumstances.

Brothers

Your brother, hearing your address, has been entertained according to his wishes and we have endeavoured to make his road comfort able & smooth to his brethren [358]

Brothers.

May the great spirit preserve you in health and friendship, amongst yourselves and with the people of the State of New York.

Daniel D Tomkins.

To the Chiefs of the Coghnawaga Nation.

…

1821
Albany 14 December

Sir,

You may draw on me thirty days after sight for Two hundred and fifty dollars on account of contingent expenses incurred by me relative to affairs of Oneida Indians. This is in pursuance of an assurance heretofore made and with a view of facilitating the arrangements of the Oneidas relative to a removal.

I congratulate you on the success of your Mission

Your letter would have been answered before but I have lately returned from New York.

On getting this letter send me a receipt immediately in the following words to wit.

"Received of Governor Clinton Two hundred and fifty dollars on account of [359] expenses attending Indian Affairs. Dated 14th December 1821"

Let me hear from you immediately

Rev. E. Williams   Dewitt Clinton

…

French Mills. Nov. 27, 1815

Sir, In answer to your request about furnishing seventeen rations per day I have on reflection concluded that I will undertake it at twenty two cents per ration (whiskey excepted) on condition that I can issue them once only per week [?] have four months to pay in advance, on giving good security to perform the contract on my part. From my long experience in the same business during the warr, taking into view the small number of rations to be issued, the scarsity and [high?] price of provisions the present season I do not think that any less than the above price will be an object more than sufficient to compensate for the trouble. I make this offer on condition of beginning the first of January next and continue for 16 to 17 months thereafter.

                                                      I am with respect
                                                          Yours

Mr. Eleazer Williams   [Varcham?] Hastings

...

[360]
       Indian Chiefs letter to Thomas Williams.
       Great Brother.
We have received a short letter from you, in which you stated that the sums [which] we have authorized you to borrow are not sufficient your and your son's expences on the road we have requested you to take. We therefore by the consent of the Chiefs and Councilors of the Seven Nations, authorize you to borrow of the Indian Agent, seventy five dollars and if it is necessary that you should have more, you are at liberty to borrow thirty dollars more. As we have authorized you to receive the annuity during the present war. You will account the same. You will endeavour to be faithful, and replace the money at the time you shall appoint for that purpose by doing this the credit of our nation will be respected.

       We have appointed your youngest son to be interpreter of the Seven Nations in the room of the late William Gray.

       We wish that you and Col Louis would confirm the appointment. Your son shall have the same pay that Mr. Gray had.

       You will be careful by whom you send your letters to us, for the last you sent came very near falling into the hands of a British Officer.

       Brother. We wish you much prosperity

[361]   In the name and behalf of the
                                                     Caghnawaga Chiefs
                                                     Peter Thegaronwe

October 18th. 18[11].

...

                    New Williamstown Block House April 10 1813
Dear Sir,
       I received yours bearing date the 7th Instant and there find your anxiety to heer from the Cahnawagos. I am surprised that this is the first of your writing to me for this my third letter to you since you [were] at this Place and twice I have wrote since your father arrived here. He is with us and all the family there making sugar, not far from this place but draw provisions here

       Your mother says that she has come so far to see you and if you wish to see her you must come the other part of the [way.] There is thirty or that the chiefs tels me that have applied to take protection with us. Their names that I know is Garoniatsigowa Sagoiewatlha Awannaratie and your father that have been here to see if they may be promoted and finding they could, have gone for their families. There was a number of the young men at the village of St. Regis I understand that was on the same business, but there [362] was some misunderstanding to place by meens of the young [Coln] it is said and they did not come to the mills so that I did not see any of them

    I have nothing strange to write to you but remain your friend and well wisher,

                    William Gray

To Eleazer Williams

...

              Plattsburgh. May 27. 1813.

    Sir,

    Since I saw you this morning in Company [with] General Mooers, I have seen Mr. Hastings the sub contractor under Mr. Anderson and have concluded an arrangement with him to supply the Indians with rations as heretofore at the French Mills.

    Altho' this has been done on very unfavorable terms to Mr. Anderson, yet I have taken the responsibility upon myself, rather than to adopt a course which might possibly create uneasiness or irritation among friendly Indians.

    My official station in relation to the government who employs me has induced me to take this measure upon myself, which I trust will be considered by the Indians, as an evidence of the friendly care which the government is willing to extend to all its neighbors who wish to maintain just and amicable relations with it.

    You will therefore be pleased to [363] recal the order, vervally communicated by General Mooers for the removal of the Indians to this place

            Accept Sirs the assurance of my regard

                    Elihu Genkins

Mr. Ezekial Williams

...

                1813

        Constable Blockhouse June 4

Dear Uncle. I received your letter by the hand of Captain Spencer wherein you request me to advise with our Brothers of Cahnawaga I am sorry to tell you that [by] information from there it is not safe for me to call there My wife and I was laying out to have gone down to Cahnawaga as soon as we finished hoeing corn by my friends here in this village advise me not to go as there is none at home that I can depend on as friends.

    The [Caughnawages] has all been obliged to take up arms and go to Kingston and said that the British wanted them to go farther to the west but they refused and some of them turned back.

    It is said however we expect to hear soon more about that business and will write as soon as we hear

I have nothing more to write at present only Concerning mogasons tharitha wrote to me to get made   I did not understand where the pay is coming from as I have nothing to get them done with   I wish you to write to me [364] how I am to pay for making. My family and yours are all well and desire to be remembered to you all. I am very thankful to you uncle for the good usage we receive from our brothers throu William Gray he has done every thing he possibly could to make our families comfortable so no more but remain your dutiful

                                        nephue   Thomas X Williams

Endorsed by Gen. Louis Cooke Plattsburgh.

…

                     Albany November 7th 1812

Brothers

Your deputation has communicated the views and wishes of your nation with respect to the war which exists between the United States of America, and the Great Britain. Your wishes are reasonable and convince me of your friendship for our people and of your prudence in preferring to remain neutral in the war and to cultivate your fields peaceably. So long as you act according to that disposition you will be protected by the government of the United States in your property lives and privileges.

I am informed that some of your young men have imprudently taken up the tomahawk, and have gone to Montreal [365] or some other place and joined the British

For this we do not blame you as a nation but are satisfied that it was contrary to to the opinions and advice of a great majority of the Sachems and Chiefs, and I hope that those young warriors will see the impropriety of their conduct and return to their homes

    Brothers.

I advise you to remain quiet and not interfere in the quarrels of wars of the white people, and I believe our father of the United States and our national Council entertain the same opinion with harty wishes for your peace and welfare. Should any others of your young warriors be determined to take part in war and prefer joining the Americans standard they must apply to the President of the United States for advice and direction as I have no authority to employ or organize or pay them.

    Brothers.

Your kind and friendly treatment of our people has always been gratifying to me and I invite you to a continuance of that line of conduct and wish the enjoyment of peace and prosperity

                                                Daniel D Tomkins

To the Chiefs Sachems and
Warriors of the St. Regis Nation}

Biographies Written by Reverend Eleazer Williams

The notoriety of Reverend Eleazer Williams will live on through the ages, thanks to author Mark Twain, who lampooned the "Lost Dauphin" in the classic American novel, *Adventures of Huckleberry Finn*. Had he lived to see it, he probably would have been amused by the attention.

That brings us to another mark the wily missionary made on history. These were the biographies he wrote of Colonel Louis Cook, William Gray, and his own father, Thomas Williams, at the request of visiting historian Franklin B. Hough.

For those who study indigenous involvement in that last major colonial wars, they are of great value, not only because of the native participants they memorialize, but by the close relationship the author had with them. There are very few such items written in a native hand.

Considering the author's reputation for exaggerated claims, the biographies should be used with caution. Hough thought them sturdy enough a foundation to construct his own account.

The New York State Library allowed photocopies to be made of the original manuscripts so that the following transcripts could be produced. The unique spelling and idioms the author employed have been retained. The only modification has been to capitalize the first word in various sentences, and a few word suggestions in brackets.

The texts are presented in the same order that Franklin B. Hough used in *A History of St. Lawrence and Franklin Counties*. The manuscript about Thomas Williams is immediately followed by the text of the book Hough published in 1859, *Life of Te-ho-ra-gwa-ne-gen, alias Thomas Williams, a Chief of the Caughnawaga Tribe of Indians in Canada*.

Lewis Cook

Leiut. Col Lewis Cook must have been born about 1737 at Saratago.[1] His father was coloured man & his mother an Indian woman of the Mohigan or Abaniquis tribe. The attack made on Saratogo by the french & Indians in November 1745, the parents of young Lewis were among the captives. A french officer Mr Le Corn[2] seized the Boy and would claim him as his captivated property. But his mother unceasingly cry out "iih Nihawa" i.e. "He is my child" "No, no," said the officer, "he is a Negro and he is mine." The afflicted mother made an appeal to the Iroquois chief warriors for the restoration of her child, who immediately demanded of the officer to deliver up the child to them as one of their own people, who reluctantly gave up his prize. The mother, out of gratitude to her Iroquois friends would accompany them with her child, on their return to their country. She lived & died at Cahnawaga, and after her death, the Jesuit father of that Mission, persuaded young Lewis to reside with him as his attendant, which was accepted. Here Lewis acquired the french language of which he spoke with ease. He grew up pretty much as other Indian Boys of the place. He was early discovered as having inquisitive mind. In his youth he was often seen in councils to hear the orators of the day and to learn the object of their deliberations. From these councils, he often said in his old age, that "he learned the Lessons of wisdom." Living as he did with the Jesuit father of the Mission, he was taugh the faith of the Romish church, and was somewhat partial to its mode of worship yet he did not believe all her dogmas &. was liberal towards other religious sects.

The war which commenced in 1755, between Great Britain & France, Lewis was among the Indian warriors on the side of the french who were detached to watch the movements of the English on the Lake George. Early in the spring of 1756, he being in the vicinity of Ticondaroga and was one of the scouting party and out to spy out the enemy, and was met by the English under Major Rogers who, were on a similar errand, a skirmish ensued. The contest was maintained with a great obstinency by both parties for nearly one hour but finally, they seperated. In this affair, Lewis was wounded which troubled him for a considerable time. From this period, he was considered to be a warrior of the first order as to courage & bravery.

He was with the french troops at the defeat of General Braddocks on Ohio, where a french officer was saved by the brave and skillful conduct of Lewis. He was also at the taking of Fort Oswego with General Montcalm in 1756. In 1758, but few of the Iroquois warriors had reached the fortress of Ticonderago, when General Abercrombie appeared before it, with 7000 British regulars & ten thousand colonial troops.

In this unequal engagement, Lewis was for the first time, made a commander of the Iroquois party and the choice was not misplaced. General Montcalm and Chevalier de Levy commended him as a good soldier for the french and a brave warrior for the Indians. In April of 1760, he accompanied with the french army under Chevalier de Levy when an attempted was made by the french to retake Quebec and was engaged in the battle on the Plains of Abraham, where the English were defeated under Gen.

Murray. After the conquest of Canada his war spirit entirely ceased. He once more, to gain his livelihood, resumed the chase. In the mean time, he was much respected by his Brethren, the Indians as well as the french, where ever he was known.

Lewis was so much attached to his old military friends, the french, he was never reconciled under the English Government. He would sigh, when speaking of the English conquest of Canada. He watched with intense interest at the movements of the American Colonies [ ]the expected rupture between England & her American subjects. Once or twice he took a journey to Albany for information. The Late Gen. Schuyler & John Bleccker, he would confer and from whom he derived all the information he desired. Many of the cahnowaga chiefs, on his return became friendly to the American cause from the information they [received] from him. [The] above mentioned gentlemen were known to them & highly respected.

The long expected hostilities between Great Britain and her colonies, finally reached Lewis, with which he seemed to be roused from his lethargy, and his martial spirit was once more on the wing. He was sure that the Americans would suceed. He knew they were brave people, (by experience) he had met them in a battlefield, when they fought with unequal numbers, like tigars. He was sure, they would swept the English every where and show them what is to be a soldier. "They will fight," said he, "for their liberties, their country, their wives & children and for their church." "The King of England" said he, "would make slaves of them, and their country as a nursery to keep up the strength of his army & navy and as a treasury to enrich his Kingdom." To these, they will never submit. Their cause is a good cause, and they will be victorious."

After the skirmish at Lexington and the battle of bunker hill, and General Washington had assumed the command of the American army at Cambridge, several of the Cahnowaga chiefs would visit the American General & his camp and this visit Gen. Washington mentioned it in one of his letters to Congress+ (+which see in the I Vol. of his Letters.)

Lewis was one of the party. He had exerted to persuade & encourage the chiefs to make this visit. He suceeded as to get the party in a motion and their arrival at Crown point where they remained for several days where most unfortunate event occurred which would to destroy his peace & comfort for a time. although done innocently, he and a young man of the party, in a play, was killed. In consequence of this sorrowful event, Lewis, was dejected & appeared to be in a gloomy state of mind. But after the interview with the American General he assumed his former vivicity [ ] which he appeared to be highly gratified what had passed between the Gen. and his party. His war spirit was rekindled in his breast & his whole soul appeared to be to defend the Americans cause. General W. was pleased with his speech which was delivered in a council with him, which unfortunately is not preserved. The Rev. Mr. Kirkland Missionary to the Oneida Indians (it so happened he) was present & acted as an interpreter on the occasion, from him we learn, something what it passed between the Gen. W. & the Indian council with the Iroquois from Canada and the Oneidas. "One of the Cahnowaga chiefs rose & said, He perceived that there was a war cloud rising in the

East which may make much trouble and bring a great distress upon the American people, on account of which his very soul troubled him. War was an great evil to any nation or people. He knew this by sad experience. In the war between the English & France, which ended in the conquest of Canada by the former, the french people, in Canada were brought to the very verge of destruction, and it was happy for them, that they were conquered at the time and that this saved them from further distress, and lost of lives. He rejoiced to see that the Americans had such a independent spirits as to take up arms & defend their rights and liberties, and that they would seceed because, he believed that God was on their side. and that this must be gained at expense of much blood and a great distress upon the people. That the King of England was strong & powerful King, yea, so powerful was he as to conquer the french King in Canada, but that the King of heaven is a stronger than any Earthly King and will defend the oppressed." And then with a strong voice, added, "Brother Bostoinans, Be strong & courageous. Your cause is good. you will assuredly be supported by the Great Spirit above, whose omnipotent arm will defend you, and in the end will give you a victory. A victory that will resound through all the Earth, and this shall be a noteable day with you & your children and it shall be ceribrated with joyful hearts as long as the true Americans spirits shall beat in their hearts. Your true Indians friends from the north will do what they can in your favour. Indians are free born people. They love liberty, yes, they would wish to live as free as the deer in the forest and fowles in the air. Brother Bostonians, you are a great people, you are sensible of this as to dare to meet the King of England in a battlefield. We the Indians, are now in feeble state in comparison of what we were once, you will I hope, always remember the feeble people, once the Lords of this soil, but who are now much reduced as to numbers & strength. The war spirit, which is naturally in us, is still so, and we will therefore exert ourselves to our uttermost to aid you when an opportunity shall offer, even to the destruction of our village, by the British your enemies. Remember, Brother, Bostonians, the words of your Brothers at Cahnowaga. Never forget that a portion of them are your true friends at heart, & pray to the Great Spirit that you may become free people as your Brothers, the Indians.

  It is said, by those who heard the foregoing speech, that it was delivered with great modesty, but it was with much animation. General W. pronounced it to be sensible, judicious & friendly speech. It was [received] with much satisfaction by all present, especially by the officers of the army. Other friendly speeches which were somewhat more eloquent were delivered on this occasion by the cahnowaga chiefs, but the above was the only one preserved. The chiefs were regaled during their stay at the expense of the Continental Congress. They returned by way of Albany, where a Council was held by Gen. Schuyler with them and John Bleecker acted as an interpreter. There Lewis made known to the party of his intentions to remain and join the American forces in the contest. four others volunteered with him. The remainder ten returned to Canada with strong appearance to be friendly and to render secret service to the American Colonies. So they did, on various occasions. Governor Carlton & his Indian angents were jealous of them. But Indian sagacity & activity were not to be thwarted by "slow & long thought

Englishmen." They carry out their plans & projects in defiance of the vigilance of the British agents. The information they communicated to Lewis, he to Gen Schuyler & General W. were seasonable & important.

In 1775, he accompanied with the American army when Gen. Schuyler invaded Canada, but who was prevented by sickness. He left the army at Aux Isle Noix and was suceeded by Gen. Thomas. After the reduction of Montreal, Lewis was active among the Indians & Canadians in sustaining the American cause. He assisted Col. Livingston and Haven in raising volunteers from the french. one or two Regiments of them were received into the service.

In the spring of 1776 the commanding General of the American forces would erect a fort at the Cedars, with which Lewis attempted in strong language to dissuade him as impolitic, & unsafe with so small detachment he had sent to erect the works & to defended it.

Knowing as he did, that the British were still in possession of Oswegatchie under Capt. Foster, a viligant & brave officer, although he had but few regulars with him yet, he had one thousand Indians warriors were at his command. As predicted by Lewis, the unfinished works were attacked by Foster & his Indians & some Tories. Col. Biddle being absent from his command & had gone down to Montreal to bring up reinforcement—and Major Butterfield made but a feeble ressistance and surrendered. There was a massacre a goodly number of the prisoners by the western Indians. Col. Biddle corps was advancing at the time & a portion of them had reached at St. Anna's Church where the enemy's Indians had already emassed. A skirmish ensued. Lewis with Cahnowagas fell with them on the right flank and as soon as the British Indians heard the war whoop, they fled and at the same instant, the Americans pressed forward, the English also gave away and retreated to their Boats and were fired upon so long as the Indian rifles could reach them.

In June Governour Carlton having received large reinforcements, and the Americans were compelled to retreat. Lewis was deeply affected with event. He left Canada once more and directed his course for Albany, accompanied with 16 Cahnowagas. From this period, he watched with intense interest, the preparations & movements of the enemy under the command of Gen. Burgoyne.

In the winter 1777 he was in a feeble state of health, and this may be attributed to his having passed through so many hardships in his several expeditions. But in the spring his health was restored. As the Oneidas had taken headquarters at Schenectady, so he resided with them when not in actual service. He gave an early intimations (in June) to General Schuyler of the movements of the enemy on Lake Champlain. With his Indian friends, they were in two battles which was fought at saratoga and shared with the Americans the joyful event in beating and taking the English army.

In the winter of 1778 or 9, when it was contemplated by Congress to invade Canada one more time with an army under the command of General La Fayette, and to prepare the minds of friendly Indians & french in that quarter of such an event and to obtain information the strength of the enemy in that quarter, Lewis and Capt. John

Vincent were dispatched on this dangerous expedition. They were Indians and the country they were traverse was known to them. They reached Chateaugay River and there Vincent was left with a friendly french Canadian and Lewis alone proceeded accompanied by the frenchman and in dark ness met the American chiefs as they were called and delivered to them Letters and the message from General Schuyler and La Fayette which were received with peculiar satisfaction. Before the dawning of the day and in the midst of a snow storm, he left the village and was once more on his way toward Albany accom panied by Vincent. They struck into deep forest and bent their course for Lake Champlain which they gained at the nor end of Isle Motte. as they entered upon the [Lie] of the Lake they were discovered by the British piquet guard at Rouse's Point and heavy guns were fired. This hastened their steps and in a few hours they reached Onion river which they followed up and so on to Connecticut river.

It would appear that Lewis went on a similar errand in the winter of 1777 and extended his journey as far as river Boquet in Essex County and there met him according to previous agreement a Messenger from the north, and there they interchanged the communications entrusted to them. Lewis reached the camp of his friend in a state of starvation, as he had lost his provision bag in crossing one of the branches of the hudson river.

He could not hunt on the way, as the British had Indian scouts from Lake Champlain to Fort Edward. But he was relieved by his forest friend, who had plenty of venison, Bears Greese & with all, his friend had preserved two bottles of Brandy for him. After spending three days in merriment, they separated on the fourth at noon, each one bearing an important & confidential communications to their respective friends. Lewis crossed the Lake & took his course for Coose Country, as some Letters were directed to President Wheelock of Dartmouth College & his friend Col. Biddle of Haverhill, by whom the dispatches were immediately for warded to Albany.

In June following he visited Gen. Washington's camp where he was much respected for his patriotism and was often with Gen. Washington in a private walk. Lewis, "worth to our cause," said Gen. Washington to some of his officers, "cannot be too highly appreciated."

In 1780 he recieved a commission from Congress as Leiut. Col. of the Calvary with which he had merited for the important services he had rendered to the American people.

After peace in 1783, he & his Cahnowaga friends accompanied with the Oneidas on their return to their country, where he resided until 1784 and the removed with his family to St. Regis. He gave preference to this place (which being near the great territorial line) instead to that of Cahnawaga, where in all probility he would not live in peace, in consequence of the great prejudice existed among the British officers in the Indian Department and the Tories.

The Cahnowaga, who had so nobly volunteered in the American cause, where left to find home where they could, as no special provision was made for them by Congress as they had done for the french Canadians. These patriotic Indians for years wandered here & there homeless. Some of them finally went to St. Regis. This act of ingratitude on the part of Congress is indilable stain in the view of the Indians upon the character of that Honorable body. Congress may yet retrieve its character by granting something to their descendants.

A spirit of unfriendly feelings was created between Col. Lewis & Col. Brandt during the Revolution. They were in opposite parties. This feeling was cherished by Brandt to unmanly degree. After Lewis' return to St. Regis he was often disturbed by the British Indian agents. Although living peacably with his Indian friends, yet, his former course in the american struggl was not easily forgotten by the tories who had taken a refuge in the Province.

Col. Brandt at Montreal in 1797 made a visit, with a large party of the Mohawks & held a council with Sir John at La Chine. The Mohawks were heard with threats against the life of Col. Lewis. Some of the friendly Cahnowagas, gave timely notice to Lewis of those threats. As it was expected, on the return of Brandts party, they crossed the St. Lawrence from Cornwall with a view to execute those threats uttered at La Chine. But he was secured by his friends. An account of which there was a fray with the Mohawks by some of the St. Regis Indians.

Lewis received a military grants in land from the State, like other officers, and a hand tract from the Oneidas and several sums at different times from General Government.

The claims to some lands in the state of New York was [adjudicated] by the Iroquois Indians in 1789. To favour the claims of the Cahnowaga Volunteers, for services rendered to the U. States, in the revolution, Lewis, who had been their late commander would sustain their claim. With this view, he, Thomas Williams & W. Gray, the interpreter, formade themselves into an association to effect this charitable and friendly act in behalf of the long neglected Indian Volunteers, if effected, not only for their benefit but for all those who may hereafter be in a similar situated. To give home to the Indian Volunteers as well as to manifest some gratitude by the americans towards them was one of the most powerful arguments which moved the Legislature of the state to give hearing to the pretend claims and finally, to go into a treaty, with seven nations of Canada, as they termed themselves, who were to realize five hundred dollars per ann. and this was all it was provided for them. But the land was given up for the benefit their american friends, which tract all lay within the state of New York. Although the treaty reads as if it was surrendered to the "St. Regis Indians" who were all living within the British Province, and the name of the place ie. village was over the territorial line, and this only shows that the commissioners intended for their own volunteers friends as a place of refuge then & hereafter. This tract was within the town of Bombay and Missina. The arguments used by Lewis, Williams & Gray with the Legislature for a grant certainly favours this idea & construction of the treaty. It was intended for those who may live within the state of New York and by those who had rendered service. When Lewis & Williams objected to the term of St. Regis Indians, being used but the commissioner replied, that the name was nothing, which being in Canada and the state of New York had nothing to do with it. And the same was used in [consequence?] of Lewis and some of the volunteers being at the place, who intended to reside in the tract specified and for whose benefit the state had repurchased from Macomb, Constable &c.

The treaty was finally consummated at the head of Lake George in 1796 between the commissioners of the state, with the consent of the Gen. government with the Deputies & chiefs from the North. On this occasion Lewis appeared to a great advantage and much notice was taken of him by the several officers & soldiers of the revolution who were at the place.

From this period of his life, nothing worthy to our notice, excepting from 1801 to 1811 he was greatly troubled & perplexed the course had been taken by the St. Regis chiefs in relation to the lands within the state. Its those, for whose especial benefit, it was granted, had not occupied excepting three or four, nor were disposed to centraul it as they (& with Lewis) might have done. The power of centrouling the same was assumed in a gradually manner by the chiefs of the St. Regis village. Many of these were [ ] and ever deposed to sell it, which they knew it was not granted them. They commenced to sell those lands on Solmon River to some french men, and which give the name french mills after words. To these sells, Lewis was opposed and from necessity was often compelled to put his signatures to those sels. The St. Regis Indians became so tinacious "of their sole right" to the tract of land within the state as to attempt to exclude those for whose benefit it was granted, even the heirs of Col. Lewis, Williams & Gray are suffering under it to this day. This spirit of ingratitude & usurpation over the rights of others, manifested by the St. Regis Indians, may be attributed to two causes, vis: Religious & political principles of those men whose rights they would disclaim. Those patriotic men, who were liberal in thier religious sentiments and above all, they loved the Americans. The Romish Priesthood & the British functionaries, have ever cherished this spirit of discord & usurpation in the tribe.

In the war of 1812, Lewis was once more called upon to manifest his love for the americans & his Indian Brethren. The Indians at St. Regis were called upon by the British Governour to take up arms for his Britanic Majesty. To this Lewis strongly opposed it. In accordance to the policy and wishes of the american government, he would have them to be neutrals in the present contest. He and Thomas Williams at Cahnowaga were in unison in the sentiments. But on this account, Lewis was compelled to withdraw himself from the tribe & repaired to Plattsburgh, where he drew his rations from the government stores. Being now aged, he could render no active service to his american friends yet his influence was some use.

"On the 17th August 1813, a body of volunteers, under commande of Major Chapin had a skirmish with the enemy, near Fort George, in which the Latter was defeated & completely routed. The American Indians captured 12 of the British Indians, & four whites. In the former there were four Cahnawaga Indians, and the latter, a Capt. De Lorimie of the Indian Department (whose father was the principal agent at Cahnowaga). The captivity of the four Cahnowagas excited much interest among them, as two of those were chiefs & men of consideration in their village. A belt & a branch of peace, or in other words charity and mercy for the prisoners was sent to the neutral party of the St. Regis Indians, for their [interference] (if possible) in favour of the prisoners. Col Lewis was applied to for an advice, and who, out of humanity, consented to repair to Niagara and make an attempt to do something in their favour. His young friend Col. E. Williams was not consulted upon the subject, who was somewhat surprised at the hearing of Lewis mission. Seven or eight warriors from St. Regis accompanied him to Oneida where in a council he made known to the chiefs the object of his mission. After several hours in consultation, he was dissuaded by them to dropt the subject and not make further known the object of his mission. As the six nations had in a formal manner declared war against the English so that they could do nothing for the prisoner, they must be left with the American Government. To this Lewis assented, but would proceed to Niagara.

In the meantime, Col De Lorimie of Cahnowaga writes to the an officer in the American army, in which he stated a chief, by name Lewis, a resident in the Province, was on a secret mission in that quarter. The letter was calculated to rouse the spirit of jealousy among the American officers against patriotic Lewis. The Letter had reached Niagara before his arrival. When he presented himself at the fort he was detained as a prisoner, his old friend in revolution Gen. Dearborn had been recalled. The old patriotic was held as a prisoner eight days when some officers arrived from Plattsburgh who knew him and were surprised to find, he was suspected. They would have a further investigation into his case. According a court of enquiry was instituted. Only three were known to him, and the rest entirely strangers. When it was represented of his patriotism & fidelity in the revolution, and with all that he bore a commission. All these were doubted. He stood before them with great modesty. Several questions were put to him by the young officers. One of them more officious than the rest. His questions roused the war spirit in Lewis. With a strong voice and with a commending aspect, said, Gentlemen officers, you see I am old and your are young. Yes, your are in the service of your country, your know but little of that service, but I am worn out & know it much by experience. You seemed to doubt of what I have been & what I am now. It is right for your to guard the rights of your country and with whom you have to do in the time of war. My history you shall have. There are living witness to the East in this state, who I am confident will declare to you that I am the same man now that I was during the revolution, in which you gained your independence. General Mooers Gen. Dearbor who were acquainted with me in those days, Gov. Thompkins, and Col. E. Williams, the Superintendant General of the Indian Affairs at the north, will be able to give you the information of my attachment to the American people and thier cause in the present contest. Gentlemen, I do not blame you for examining me so close in regard to the object of my coming here. I have no secret. I understand that Col. De Lorimie's Letter is the cause of this examination. This infamous agent of our enemies, has effected in some measure to [injure] me and his sole object was to destroy me. I will state the real cause in the beginning of my taking this journey, but my brothers, the Oneidas make me see the impropriety of interfering in the Governmental concerns. But I would extend my journey into these frontiers in order to visit the six nations who have declared war against the common enemy. I have learned since I left St. Regis that it was by the advice of De Lorimie that an application was made to me to take such a mission as I did when I left St. Regis in behalf of the prisoners and one of them is his own son. But mark Gentle men. Immediately on my departure he writes that infamous Letter, and to whom was it directed, to a American officer. How comes he being an enemy, to write to his enemy. This is a new thing with me. For an enemy to write his enemy and appraise him that there is a man from his own country going to do him a mischief. If my words and statements are not sufficient, here are my credentials and these will show you what I have done for your country and how I am viewed by those who are now in authority in civil & military. He then with a heavy hand laid large black pocket Book on the table. "please Gentlemen" said he, "examine them". There were found his commission as a Leut Col. of the calvarey, Gen. Washington's commending Letters, Gen. Schuyler's, Gen Gates, Gov. G. Clinton, Gen Knox, Gov. Tompkins, Gen. B. Mooers. A certificate (in parchment) as a regular member of Gen. Washington's Military Masonic Lodge. To satisfy the commanding officer of the American army in the Naigara Frontier Lewis insisted that Letters should be addressed to different persons at the north by way of inquiry as to his character & standing. Although the Gentlemen were more than satisfied of his patriotism, yet to gratify him Letters were written and one to Col. E Williams at Plattsburgh, who replied. "I am astonished that Col. Lewis Cook should be suspected of his fidelity to the American people. He is now suffering on account of it. He has been driven from home, and I believe, as old as he is, he is ready to sacrifice his life to sustain the honor of the American flag. I fear there is an intrigue in operation against him by his personal as well as common enemy in Canada. I have regretted much, that the object of his Indian mission to the west, was kept from me. Of this, I am satisfied it was not for want of confidence in me, but from various circumstances, which were urgent in their nature, that his departure was somewhat in haste."

  In autum, on the arrival of Gen. Wilkinson with his army at the french Mills (now Fort Covington), in 1813 he repaired thither, and when the army vacated the place January 1814, he followed Gen. Brown's devision for Sacket Harbour. In June following he & his sons & several others of the St. Regis Indians went to Buffaloe. When the American army under Gen. Brown crossed into Canada side, he and a detachment of the warriors of the six nations, accompanied the army. He was present at the battles of Chippewa & Lundy's Lane. After the retreat of the American army to Fort Erie, he soon after recrossed to Buffaloes being now in a feeble state of health, where he was attended to with much kindness and care by the Government Physicians. Age & other infirmities were making a slow progress upon his strong constitution. He desired to be carried to the Indian settlements, as he wished, as he said, to give his last advice to them, and to breath his last breath among them. Col. Moody Biddle of the 11th Regiment, the son of his former old friend in Coos Country, often sent to know his welfare. Lewis at length sent for the Col. who hastened to his wigwam & found him in a dying condition but able to speak. Lewis said to him, "My Col. you see I am about to leave the world, leave all my dear friends, to die in the midst of the American camp as I have always wished. Pray remember me to Gen. Brown & other officers here. I think much of my family at St. Regis and the American part of the tribe, but they are under the superintendance of Col. E. Williams, they are safe if they will adhere to his councils. He is a true friend to them & to the Americans. Col. Williams is following my steps, and I trust, he will live & protect the Indians at St. Regis. As you are about to return to Plattsburgh remember me to my Indians there, Gen. Mooers, Sailly, Col. Isaac Clark."

After a few minutes, said, Col. as your Honoured father was a soldier, & brave one too, I hope you will prove to be a worthy of his descendant." Several other officers now made their appearance, but was able to say but a few words. In three hours after the party left him, he breathed his last, in the month of October 1814. His death was announced by heavy guns in the American camp.

William Gray

Capt. William Gray was a native in Washing. county in this state. Where he was born, it is uncertain. He was taken by the St. Regis Indians at Whitehall in 1781. He was then but a youth and adopted into one of the Indian families of that tribe. What little education he had he improved much by reading & studying closely all the books that fell in his way. He learned the Iroquois language perfectly, so that eventually he became an interpreter to the tribe. His manners were pleasing and by his friendly disposition he gained many friends among them & the whites in vicinity of his residence. He was often consulted by the chiefs, who benefited from his councils. His mind was clear and penetrating which made him able & judicious counsellor for the Indians. By these he raised himself in gradual manner in their view. Much confidence was placed in his decisions. He had a heart. He was kind & liberal to all his friends. As he advanced in life, so his popularity increased. He connected himself for a time with a commercial house in Montreal, but finally, he became the sole propriety of the little establishment under his charge.

He married with one of the tribe, and several of his children are now living at St. Regis.

He appeared conspicuous as an interpreter, in the negotiations of Col. Lewis Cook & Thomas Williams with State of New York in the claims which they set up in behalf of the northern Indians, and which was finally affected.

It was unfortunate for him that he took an oath of allegiance to the British Government and this no doubt proved fatal to him.

He continued in his mercantile business and keep a public house, which was keep in good order and a great convenience to the travellers who had occasion to pass through St. Regis. He built a sawmill at Hogansburgh rapids to which after a while he made his residence. This prosperity at times led him astray by attaching himself to strong liquors. Still, he was William Gray, ever ready to attend to his business and at the call of his Indian friends. In his political principles he was republican. He was true American. In the War of 1812, he would place himself under the American flag, and resided as he did within the state of New York, supposed there was no danger yet he was disturbed and compelled to retire to Fort Covington. He was employed by Gen. Mooers, under Col. E. Williams, as an interpreter in behalf of the Government. In the winter 1813, as he was approaching the village of St. Regis, he was ambuscaded and taken by the hostile Indians under the command of Capt. Le Clear, of the Indian Department.

He was taken to Montreal, hence to Quebec, where he was put in close confinement. Such a sudden change from a life of activity to a sedentary life, and to a different mode of living, his health & constitution were soon affected & and in a gradual manner, he sunk under them. He expired in April or May following. In his death, the tribe lost a true friend, able counsellor, & useful interpreter and the Americans a faithful & sincere patriot. No notice has been taken of his services by the American Government.

Thomas Williams

Thomas Williams, alias, Tehoragwanegen, an Iroquois chief warrior, was born about 1758 or 9, a third descent of the Rev. John Williams of Deerfield, Mass., who with his family and Parishioners were captivated by a party of three hundred french & Indians when they made an attack upon Deerfield in the night of February 28, 1704. A party of them then broke into the house of the Rev. Mr. Williams, who, as soon as he was awakened from sleep, snatched his pistol from the tester and put it to the breast of the first Indian, that approached, but it missed fire. The savages seized and bound him. Two of his children, and a negro woman of his family, were taken to the door and murdered. His wife, the only daughter of the Rev. Eleazer Mather of Northampton, and all his children, excepting his eldest son, with himself were compelled immediately to begin their march towards Canada.

In wading a small river, on the second day, Mrs. W., who had scarcely recovered from a late confinement, fell down; and soon afterwards one of the Abinaquis or St. Francis tribe killed her with his hatchet. At length after witnessing the most agonizing scenes, during a journey of 300 miles, he arrived in Canada. One of his daughters (Eunice) he was unable to bring with him. She became assimilated to the Indians, and afterwards by the instigation of some of the Jesuits, married one of them, a young chief, by name De Roguers, by whom, she had three children, viz., Cathrine, Mary, & John. Mary was the mother of Thomas, who dying when he was fifteen months old and his aunt Cathrine took the charg of the orphan child and of whom he ever considered as his mother. He being born and grew up among the Indians as he did, he of course imbibed all the Indian habits, customs & manners. He was springly & active boy. He was early instructed in the faiths & dogmas of the Romish church. It was fortunate for him, to have such an affectionate aunt, by whom he was cherished with the greatest care & tenderness; who, although married to a noted chief, (X. Rice) but had no heir, therefore, he had no competer in the family. He was cared for as their only child.

In 1772, the Rev. Levi Frisbie, was sent into Canada as a Missionary by the Rev. Dr. Wheelock of Dartmouth College, who visited Cahnowaga, & took particular notice of Thomas, whose descent & family in New England was well known to him. After much negociation, he, finally, obtained a consent of his adopted parents to take him to Hanover, and place him in the Moore's Charity School, connected with the above college. To fulfill his instructions, Mr. Frisbie visited the Indians at the Lake of Two Mountains and during his absence, Thomas was attacked with the small-pox and this prevented of his accompanying with the Rev. Mr. Fr. on his return which was greatly regretted by the youth.

As his adopted father was a great hunter, so by being with him often in the chace, he, himself, became very fond of life in the forest, and sporting with its wild inhabitants. His hunting grounds were those near Crown Point, Lake George, & in the vicinity of Fort Edward. After his marriage he was frequently absent from his village from one to two or three years. All this time his living was at the very best and what he took in the chace, enabled him to clothe his family & to exchange the same for flour, pork, [etc].

In the commencement of the revolutionary war, although he was then only at the age of eighteen years of age, he accompanied the warriors of his tribe in the various expeditions by them to disturbe the peace and to annoy the inhabitants of the Northern frontiers of the American Colonies. It has been said that he was secretly instructed by his grand mother Eunice to follow the Indian detachments, with a view of preventing if possible, the massacre of feeble and defensiless women and children. So he did. On various occasions he exerted himself to create in the feelings of the warriors, humanity & kindness towards all the Americans who fell into their hands.

In 1777 he was promoted to a rank of a war chief of his band. This gave him a greater power & influence. As he was brave & energetic in his all his movements, so he was beloved by his Brother warriors and highly respected by the British officers, particularly by Major Carltonand Capts. Horton & Ross. They were his friends during the war.

In October, 1776, he headed his band, when the armed vessels of the British and Americans came to action opposite of the Valcour Island, (near Plattsburgh) Thomas & his warriors had a full view of the battle, and was much animated at the bravery of the Americans. He exclaimed one time, "These brave Americans will have what they want, liberty."

In the spring 1777, when he was called upon to prepare himself and his warriors to cooperate with Gen. Burgonyne's army, which was now assembling at St. John or Isle None, he appeared to be in a great despondency. The cause of this, various reasons were assigned by his friends. It was solved at length. Knowing as he did, that Gen. Burgonyne's had a formadable force under his command and if resistance was made by the Americans in his invasion of their country, of which he was well aware, they would, that much blood would be shed and thousands of valuable lives be lost. The best feelings of humanity were now [ ] in his breast, which was accompanied with sadness in his countinance. But said he, "I will indeavour to serve God in this affair & to do good, equally to all my fellow creatures." At Cumberland head he & his corps joined the royal army where he met his friends, Capts Horton & Ross.

In the retreat of the Americans from Ticonderoga, he & his Indian corps among others were ordered in pursuit of them. On the rout, he discovered the course the Americans had taken, he instead pursuing their course, he took his rout more to the left under the pretence of falling upon them on their flanks when overtaken. But the circuit made by the detachment was too great to have a share in the action, which took place between Colonel Warner & Gen. Fraser. The object of this manouvre by the Indian capt. Was undoubtedly gained.

In August Gen. Burgoyne detached from Saratoga Colonel Brown, with five hundred men, and one hundred Indians, under the command of Thomas. On the 16th, at Bennington Col. Brown was attacked by General Stark, Thomas arrived with his Indian warriors soon after the action had commenced, & his sagacious eye discovered immediately that the Hessian Colonel would be defeated, and he accordingly manouvered his warriors that they many not be encircled by the Americans. He kept them in the woods and kept up for a time a scarrering fire, & that too great distance to be effectual. One hundred of the Americans took a secret path & had gained almost in their rear, when they opened a heavy fire upon the Indians which caused them to retreat in great confusion, and made no further resistance, as Col Brown by this time had ceased to fire. Four or five of the Indians were killed & several slightly wounded. Among the latter Capt. De Loromie, who was an Indian Agent & a Capt. In Indian Department in the British service. Thomas met Col. Breyman, who had already learned the fate of Col. Brown, but would proceed if the Indian warriors consent to sustain him.

But Thomas refused. "We are defeated," said he, "and it is no use to met with a superior numbers." "If you proceed, you will [ ] with the same fate."

Capt. De Loromie, who acted as an interpreter, rather joined with him in the view he would taken. Col. Breyman received these expressions in the most ungracious manner. A stormy arose between the young chief-warrior & the Col. But it was finally amicably settled by the interference of the officers, and the Col. retraced his steps.

It may not be amiss to state here, that in the Death of Miss McCrea near Fort Edward it was viewed & reviewed with greatest approbation by Thomas. Capt. Jones once applied to him for assistance, to have the young Lady taken & brought within the British lines by his Indian warriors, but Thomas Williams refused to undertake so delicate & dangerous enterprise. Jones was put off with this. "Capt. Jones, you have come to conquer the country, if so, when the country is conquered, you will have your white squaw. She is now safe and to attempt to take her by force by our Indians, her life may be in danger, as there may be a skirmish in doing this. Therefore she had better remain where she is now." In a few days after this Capt. Jones applied to Capt. Langlad, who had the charge of the western tribes viz: Ottawas, Chippeways, Menominies, and Winnibagoes. The latter were employed by Capt. Langlad to captivate & bring Miss McCrea into the camp. Two chiefs of the different bands of the tribe were employed on the occasion, but they were ignorant of each other, the object of their enterprise. One of the parties succeeded and had the young lady safe in their hands, and the other party coming up and found the object of their pursuit was already obtained. The head warrior demanded of the other party to give her up to him & his friends, as they were sent by Capt. Jones to bring her to him. The other replied, "we on a similar errand & the Bird is in our hands." upon this a contest ensued between the head men, and in the fray the lady was murdered. It is entirely mistake, by some late writers, who have attributed this murder to the St. Regis Indians.[3]

Williams urged upon the Iroquois chiefs present to call upon Gen. Burgoyne & request him to put an end of such inhuman & unchristian like conduct. He was heard, and the British Gen. rebuked the western tribes on the account of the murder, who were highly incensed with the language held out to them; so that it was not long before he was deserted by them.

He was present on the 19th of September and on the 7th of October at Saratago when the two armies met in battle. On the 8th at midnight he called his corps together stated to them that he had consulted with the old chiefs on the expediency of retreating immediately as he foresaw that the King's army would be compelled, either to retreat or be taken, and that he believed, the latter would be its fate. At two o'clock the Indian corps left its encampment and took its course by way of Lake George.

His humanity would not permit him to have one sick warrior but all were brought away in litters and were carried safe to their village. In autumn 1778, he went with a party to Oswego at the call of Col. Johnson with a view of invading the country bordering on Mohawk river; but which was give up.

In 1779, he accompanied with the detachment under the command of his friend Capt. Horton. On this occasion, he refused to have any command, it was given to another, and no reason was assigned for this this strange conduct of his. He would go as a private warrior. The party went into Vermont as far as White river. They ravaged several small settlements, particularly Royalton and took a number of prisoners, of for when he made every exertion to have them treated with humanity, by his party, the Indians. Many houses & barns were saved by his influence. This was noticed by Capt. Horton, who pleasantly observed, "My friend, I am not surprised at this, you have Bostonian blood running in your veins."

He replied, "Yes, and I glory in it, as it is tinctured with humanity, which you know is the principles of Christianity." He defended two females from being abused by three of St. Francis Indians. And an aged man would have been killed had he not defended him.

In February 1780, he headed a party of Iroquois and St. Francis Indians, and were all by Captain Raynier of Quebec, on a secret mission to Penobscot river, with dispatches. Raynier had despatches from Gov. Carlton for the commandant of the Fort at the mouth of that river. It was a great journey, being in the midst of hard winter. Rackets were used to enable them to perform their jouney. They passed the American guards under the pretence of belonging to the Penobscot Tribe and Raynier entered the fort on the island in the night & delivered his despatches; and the party returned safe. The good conduct of thomas as head of the party was applauded by the British Governour. The party were regaled by his Excellency during their stay in the city, beside, with large presents in gold, with blankets, linnin of the first quality, rifles, kettles, knives, and silver broaches and with all silver medals.

Thomas remained but seven days in his village and was again called upon to head his band, to accompany Sir John Johnson in his expedition to the Mohawk river, and this was the last in revolutionary war in which Thomas Williams was engaged in favour of the British.

He was present when the attack was made upon the dwelling of Colonel Vitcher, at the mouth of Schoolhare creek, who was scalped and left for a dead man, but he revived and lived many years afterwards. His two Brothers were killed & the house was burnt. Thomas and Col. Lewis had an interview with Col. Vitcher in 1795, which was moste friendly. "We met once," said the brave Col, "as enemies, but Colonel Vitcher still lives, and we will now meet over his good wine and brandy as friends, for we are commanded from above to forgive our enemies." His friends responded with *Amen*.

Although in this last campaign he would be as [humane] as formerly, yet he was unable to go to the extend the desires of heart, as there was a positive orders from Sir John to burn all the buildings on their rout. In consequence of this order and the depradations & ravages committed upon the defenceless inhabitants & these were under the eyes of Sir John, and encouraged by him, it produced no good feelings between him & Williams. As the latter disapproved of such inhuman and disgraceful conduct of the tories & some of the Indians, who were not under the control of Williams. Sir John from this period had ever a jealous eye upon him, but Williams stood so high in the view of Governor Carlton & the officers of the army for many & important services he had rendered to the British government, he did not dare "to come to open rapture with him. Knowing as he did being merely a refugee in Canada and had no service of any consideration but only to plunder and abuse his former fellow citizens of New York. He was proud, haughty, selfish and covetious to a disgraceful degree. For these, he was despised by the Canada Indians and more so, on the account of his partiality for the Mohawks, who had emigrated from the river which bears their name. Who were formerly his neighbours, over whom his father, Sir William had acted as an agent for near half a century. The fire of hatred kindled in this campaign between them never ceased to burn in their hearts during their lives. The result of this may be seen, what happened with Williams in the next war between Great Britain and America.

From this period it would appear he attended to his usual vocation, and after peace in 1782, he soon commenced with several of his friends to hunt in the vicinity of Crown Point and Lake George. Often visited Albany with his peltries and always had a friendly intercourse with Gen. Schuyler. This gentleman was once a pupil of the Rev. Dr. Stephen Williams of Longmeadow, Mass. who was the brother of Eunice, the grand mother of Thomas.

In 1783, after having hunted a great part of the winter in the vicinity of Lake George, he descendant to down to Albany with his friend and co-hunter <u>John Baptist Taietakhenontie</u>, with whom, he proceeded, after receiving recommending letters from General Schuyler and other Gentlemen in Albany, to New England to visit his relatives for the first time. He arrived at Stockbridge in Mass., at the house of the Rev. Dr. West, where he happily met the noted Rev. Samuel Kirkland, the missionary to the Oneida Indians, who understood his language perfectly, and acted on the occasion as interpreter, where he passed two days in a most agreeable manner with several respectable families who claimed to be his kindred. With a strong recommending Letters from the rev. gentlemen & others of the place, <u>to all whom it may concern</u>, on his route to Longmeadow, to the place of his destination.

His object was to visit & have an interview with the Rev. Dr. Stephen Williams, the venerated Brother, of his grandmother Eunice. But on his arrival he found, to his sorrow & regret, he was dead. He died on the third of June, 1782. He had & presented Letters addressed to him, written in December of preceeding year from his beloved & unfortunate sister Eunice, who addressing him in a most affectionate terms, said "My beloved brother, once in captivity with me, and I am still so, as you may consider it, but I am free in the Lord. We are now both very old and are still permitted by the goodness of God to live in the land of the living. This may be the last time you may hear from me. Oh, pray for me that I may be prepared for death, and I trust we may meet in Heaven with all our godly relatives." Her brother as it was believed, was already there, waiting for her to enjoy with him the full fruition of God.

From this period Thomas visited, occasionally, his kind relative in New England, till 1806. After the removal of the Rev. Dr. Samuel Williams from his professorship of the Harvard University, to Rutland, Vermont, he made his house one of his stopping places on his rout. This Rev. Gentleman was in equidistance with Thomas in their descend from the Rev. John Williams of Deerfield, who was taken captive in 1704, as before stated. With this Gentleman he had a peculiar regard. He often said that Professor Williams was the glory of the Williams family, on the account of his learning. Dr. Williams, in his history of Vermont, it has been said, that under the article of Indians, he had made use of the information which he had derived from Thomas, in relation to their customs, manners, habits, laws, government and religion. If so, it may be relied upon as a just representation, coming, as it did, from one who is well acquainted with them.

The claims of land by the Indians in the state of New York which they considered were taken from them by force & contrary according to an eternal principles of justice & equity was a subject of much discussion among them at St. Regis and Cahnowaga. But no one knew how to proceed to put up this claim. Col. Lewis, Williams, & W. Gray, were called upon for their opinions upon the subject in 1789. It was left with them entirely as to the course to be taken to lay this claim before the Legislature of N. York. A long correspondence ensued between the Governor of the state and the three deputies. Many long & tidious journies were taken by them for seven years, City N. York, Philadelphia & Albany were visited by them. At length this difficult & perplexing affair was settled by the state in a treaty with the seven nations of Canada, as they stile themselves, at Lake George in 1796. The land bordering on the Great Territorial line in 45 deg. From Salmon river to Messina was awarded to the St. Regis Indians. The state repurchased the tract from Macomb, Constable, &c as she had previously sold the same to them. To induce the state to relinquish the tract, the Indian negotiators asserted strongly it was in part for the benefit for the Cahnowaga volunteers who were in its service in the revolutionary war, and for those who may hereafter be brought in a similar situation. This was plausible argument yet the St. Regis Indians afterwards, would claim the tract as belonging entirely to them, and have manifested an ungenerous disposition towards those who were instrumental cause in procuring the tract, which they now occupy and from several sales they have made to the state, they now receive annuity for more than $2000.

The existence of this ungenerous & selfish feelings among them, two causes may be attributed. 1. The British influence is still felt by a portion of the tribe, and the royal Indians maintain their position strictly in political view, as they did during the war. They have no good feelings toward the American part of the tribe. The lands they occupy, which was formerly a common property, is now entirely under their control. This seizure of common property is approved by the British government and that contrary to one of the articles at the treaty of Ghent in 1814.

2. The Romish religion, or church, have had tendency to keep the tribe in the turmoil state. The influence of its Priesthood, who are generally tenacious to the dogmas & ceremonies of their church, and no charity for other sects and who would control the consciences of the poor & ignorant Indians, and lest departure from its rules he is denounced as a <u>Heritic</u> and unworthy to be a member of the holy church. A person of different sentiments, even their own tribe must suffer more or less by the influence of its Priesthood from the Confessional Box.

As these Indians are now generally emerging from the trammels in which they had hitherto been held, they would be free in their religious sentiments, so, this produces a scene at hand & unpleasant feelings among all parties. The Protestant part of the tribe are increasing and have a desire to have their children educated, but they are feeble as to means & it was hoped they would be assisted by the Christian Philanthropists.

The tract of land before mentioned given up by the state to the St. Regis Indians was effected with great difficulty but by perseverance and a great exertions of Thomas Williams & his friends it was finally consummated. His white relatives by [consanguinity?] and his extensive acquaintance with the gentlemen in both houses of the Legislature, undoubtedly were the means of securing & obtaining the objects for which he had exerted himself for a series of years: yet the Catholic & British influence he & his heirs are denied to have the same rights to the land and annuity which is now enjoyed by the American part of the tribe. It is hoped that the Legislature will correct this ungenerous act of those for whom he had laboured so faithfully for their benefit. In the first payment of $500 made by the state at Chazy in 1797, $100 was only appropriated as remuneration for the monies he had expended & for services rendered during the seven years. No other compensation was received by him.

In August 1798 he was called upon by the British authorities to head a party on a secret mission on Lake Champlain. The government of Canada had been disturbed of its peace in consequence it was contemplated to take Quebec by surprise by the emissaries of the french [revolutionists], headed by one M'Cler but the plot was detected and M'Cler was beheaded & quartered. It was reported that large party were in preparation on Lake Champlain, to descend to Quebec with rafts, under the cover of their being raftsmen, but the real object was, when all assembled at the place, to surprise the military guards in the night & take the city. The object of Thomas Williams's mission was to watch the motions of the attacking party and if possible of certain their numbers. He was to appear among them as a hunting party and to mingle with them as friends. He performed this mission to the satisfaction of the Governor and other functionaries of the Canadian Government.

In January 1800 he once more visited his relatives in New England states, which he took two of his boys and left them there to be educated by them, as they had always been [desirous] to have some of their family to be brought to them for that purpose. It might not be amiss to state here that "one of the youths (Eleazer) aged about 14 or 15 has been doubted, whether, he really is the son of Thomas Williams. It is supposed he is an adopted child of a high descent, who in the destruction of the Royal family in the french Revolution, he & a sister were saved from the guilotine of the Revolutionists. It is a mystery yet to be solved, whether, he is the son of Louis XVI King of France, and at this distant period, perhaps it will never be. There are, however, many circumstances in the history of this unfortunate youth; which goes to prove, that, there is a possibility of its being true. The Rev. Eleazer Williams rendered some important services to the government of the U. States in the late war and in time of peace, the Episcopal church, in whose service he acted as a Missionary for more than thirty eight years to the Oneida & St. Regis Indians in the states of New York and Wisconsin. He is now labouring in the same capacity among the latter at St. Regis.

To save the live of the youth, as well as his rescuers & other friends from the bloody hands of the anti Royalists, a profound secrecy was necessary to be observed both in Europe & America by those who were interested in his preservation. This one of the hidden things are yet to be revealed.

"Unfortunate youth,
born in a palace
and nourished by the
Royal Queen
Yet transported to a foreign
clime—and
there to be cherished and
sustained by an Indian warrior!"

In the year 1801 Thomas headed a band of hunting party of the Cahnowaga Indians in the service of the North west company. He went at first as far as the Red river & thence towards the rocky mountain and traversed partly of the Grand Prairie. In the spring he had a grand view of the immense prairie of the majestic peaks of the mountains to the west and the numerous herds of Buffaloes in the natural meadow which stretched far beyond the eye could reach. He often said, "in these he saw the mighty works of the Great Spirit above and was led by them to adore & worship him as the one supreme creator & upholder of all things. That him only he would serve, and devote his whole heart to obey his blessed will." He was a man of a few words. He thought and meditated of what he said, and what he uttered he was sincere.

In 1804 he visited with his wife, his sons in Longmeadow Mass. where they were at school. He was highly pleased the improvements they had made in the American manners and the progress they had made in learning. N. Ely, Esq, a gentleman of wealth and who had married the grand daughter of the Rev. Dr. S. Williams formerly minister of the Parish who were eminent for piety, and who not only had endeavoured to improve & advance in the Education of the youths committed to their charge, but to instill into their minds of the great truths of religion. But unfortunately the youngest, John, for whom the mother appeared to have a peculiar partiality, was taken away and carried back to

Canada with them. This was made against the will of the father, and to the great regret & sorrow of Eleazer, who protested in the strong terms with his mother of his being separated from John. But that the Priest of her parish would excommunicate her from the church, if he did not bring the boys back and she hoped, that if one was enough away from her native country, she might escape from the censurer of the holy Catholic church.

The Rev. Dr. Nathan Williams of Tolland, Rev. Dr. Nathan Strong of Harford, the Rev. Dr. McClerer of East Windsor, Rev. Dr. S. Stors of Longmeadow, and the Rev. Dr. Joseph Lattrop of West Springfield, N. Ely of Longmeadow and Justin Ely Esq of West Spring, Gov. Trumbull of Connecticut and G. Strong of Massachusetts, were the gentlemen made strong efforts that Eleazer should remain & pursue his Education and they were successful.

From this period there is a chasm in the historical part in life of Thomas to 1812. We find nothing worthy of notice of him until after the decleration of war between Great Britain & America of the above year.

It was the wish of the Americans, as they also endeavoured in a former war, to induce the Indians to be neutral. Humanity and civilisation plead in favour of a principle which would not add savage barbarity to the other evils of war; but, unfortunately, the policy of a "magnanimous" enemy, was different. The Americans soon learned that the enemy had leagued himself with the ruthless savage of the wilderness and the domiciliated in the Provinces, as they were termed, the warfare of the tomahawk & scalping knife was to act in concert with the modern invention of rockets; in short all means within the power of the enemy, were to be combined against the people if the United States.

The first act in which the allied Indians and British signalisised themselves was in the taking of the fort of Michilimackinac on the 19th of July 1812, where some of the Cahnawagas were present, from L. Canada.

Governor Provost of Lower Canada, in July issued proclaimation to the Indians in the lower province to take up arms in behaf of his Britanic Majesty and through Sir John Johnson, this proclamation passed to Thomas Williams, which was indignantly rejected. Soon after Col. De Loromie sub-superintendent of the Indian Department, reported that Thomas Williams & others at Cahnawaga, as well as Lewis Cook & others at St. Regis, were refractory. The Indians at St. Francis and the Lake of Two Mountains manifested in some measure with the same disposition. The French Canadians on the Island of Montreal, were disposed to resist to take up arms against the Americans & the affair at La Chine in August, when fifteen hundred of them had skirmish with the royal troops, manifested strongly that they had no good will to adhere to the proclamation of the Governor General. How far Thomas Williams was concerned & connected in this affair, is uncertain; he was, however, within two miles when the action commenced with few of the Indians. But such was the timidity or treachery of the french commander, who would not seize the King's stores, containing arms &c. which were then completely in his power and with a formadable force, who were first at hand in comparison with the royal troops to oppose him, yet after ten minutes of canonading & the fire of muskets on both sides the french commander ordered the whole corps to withdraw. It was obeyed with great reluctance for those in the front line and in the amidst of aloud murmuring of the volunteers in the rear, who were eager to come in contact with the english troops and who were determined to [march on] with the same spirit of soldiery with those of their mother country under Bonapart. They were for charging with bayonets hand to hand, that the work of warfare maybe finish as soon as possible! But they had sommilly engaged to obey they commander, and when the orders were given to retreat, they obeyed, supposing to take a more suitable position for an action where they were to display their courage and soldiery like conduct. But after the retreat, & had taken a position, they found the commander had deserted them. They were thrown into a confusion and a disperson of the whole corps followed. It has been asserted, from high respectable sources, that if the American Government had sent two thousand regular troops into the Province at this particular time, the whole of lower Canada would fallen into their hands excepting Quebec, as the whole french population would have take up arms in their favour.

In August 1812, a provisional agreement was entered into by General Dearborn with Colonel Baynes, the British Adjutant General, that neither party should act offensively before the decisions of the American Government should be taken on the subject. This suspension of hostilities was grounded on a Letter from Sir George Provost Governor of Lower Canada, to General Dearborn, suggesting the probability of of a general suspension of hostilities in consequence of a proposed suspension or repeal of the British orders in council, of which Mr Foster, late minister to the United States had received advices on his arrival at Halifax. The American Government, viewing the British proposition as coming in an indirect manner, offering no satisfactory security for its observance, and adhering with little variation to their former pretences, did not hesitate to disagree to the proposal. The armistice terminated on the 8th of September.

While adjutant General Baynes being at the head quarters of General Dearborn Lieut. Col. Eleazer Williams, was sent off in haste to the lines, near Rouse's point, where he met, according to previous agreement, with Sir John Johnson, the Superintendant General of the Indian affairs in the Canadas, and Williams appeared in the same capacity on the American side for the northern frontiers. The object was for neutrality of the Indian tribe in the present contest. This proposition of Gen. Dearborn's was respectfully refused by Sir John. It was, however, left, finally, to the decision of Sir George Provost.

In relation to this affair, it was remarked by Sir John, that young Williams argued like a young Lyon upon the subject. That he not only plead upon the principles of humanity, civilisation, but religion, which would not add savage barbarity to the other evils of the war.

"Your king," said he, "styles himself, the defender of the Christian faith, and will he league himself with the ruthless savages of the wilderness, whose tender mercies are to be manifested by the tomahawk & scalping knife and that not only upon the wounded & captivated of the American soldiery but upon the defenceless women and children? Sir, I have too exalted an opinion of the British humanity and the principles of religion with which the English nation is governed to admit this unholy alliance. England is the bulwork of the Protestant religion. Yes, Sir, she may well glory, that she is the imporium of Bible and missionary societies. In the midst of this corrupt age and the bloody strife among the nations of the Earth, she is sending forth the word-giving life to the dark corners of the Earth, and her Messengers of the cross are proclaiming, "Peace on earth and good will to men."[4]

The sole object, it would appear, at this period of the war on the part of young Williams was, to save the St. Regis Indians, who were peculiarly situated, being on the lines, & were within striking distance of the two contending parties. He succeeded. Sir George Provost was compelled from circumstances, to permit the neutral party to remain in peace in their village. A portion of them however, took up arms afterwards and joined Gen. Hampton's army in 1813, and were with him in the skirmish on Chateaugay river.

It is said "that General Dearborn and Dr. Eustis, the Secretary of War, were highly pleased & gratified with the management of their young & native negotiator. The policy and humanity of the American government towards the unfortunate Indians, were so well represented. Gen. Mooers in his report in relation to this affair, to Gen. Dearborn & Gove. Tompkins, was enthusiastic in favour of young Williams."

At this period of the war, by the agency of Gen. Dearborn, as a commander-in-chief of the Northern army, Gen. Mooers of the New York division & and Gov. Tompkins and Judge Pliny Moore of Champlain, Thomas Williams, an Iroquois chief, was invited by the American Government to retire from the British Province and place himself and family under the protection of the American flag, with an assurance of honorable support; and whatever losses he might sustain in personal property, and the interest he might enjoy in common with his tribe, the American government solemnly engaged to make up to him and his family. With these honorable offers and assurances made, he left the British Province in 1813, and warmly engaged in the American cause and by his influence, many of the British Indians became [ ] in her interest. His influence was strongly felt in the invasion of New York at Plattsburgh in 1814 by George Provost, with 14000 regulars and 700 Indians, who refused at Champlain to advance any farther with the royal troops. They knew Thomas Williams their beloved war-chief with his sons, were with the Americans at Plattsburgh. This refusal on the part of the Indians to advance is a established fact and the cause was then secret. While at Champlain, although within the American lines, they committed no depredations, but conduct themselves in respectful manner towards the inhabitants, particularly to Judge Moore and Col. Mix.

Although Gen. Brisbane the commander of the advance division of the army, pretended to Silas Hubbell of Champlain (a Magistrate) that the Indians were kept in the rear out of humanity; yet in a council of war at La Cole river, held by Sir George Provost with the war-chiefs, he was told in strong language of the propriety of their remain in the rear of the army and so determined were they, his excellency was compelled from necessity to submit to their decision. At the same place on the retreat of the royal army after their defeat before Plattsburgh, the officers of the Indian department made a strong effort to obtain volunteers from the Indians with a great reward, to retake the ships of war captivated by the Americans, with the assistance of the few remaining gun boats, but this application was rejected by their alliances.

Thomas Williams after this affair, in his address to them, says, "Brothers, I have not deceived you in the result of the [late] campaign on the part of the red coats. I told you they would not succeed, but a defeat would follow with such an attempt. Saranac (or Plattsburgh) is safe, and its fortresses arc spangled with their flags, and the eagle & its stripes are floating in the air with all their glory. If the British army had remained four days longer at the place, it would have been Burgoyned, and had I been with them, I should have fled in the night, as I did in 1777 at Saratoga, after the last battle with the brave Yankees. They beat the English then & gained their independence, and be assured they will beat them again."

His son John who was in a honorable office in the British service, but soon followed his father into the U. States and several others of the Caughnawagas. This son was a brave and fearless volunteer. On the morning of the 5th September, at Beekmantown, he was in advanced rifle corps, which opened the first fire upon the enemy, & in his advance retreated & disputed every inch of ground, until the corps reached the main force under General Mooers, when the general action commenced by cannonading from the American line, with two hundred and fifty regulars troops under Major Wool, who maintained their position with great obstinacy untill they were completely outflank by the superior force of the enemy and were compelled from necessity to retreat and that in a good order and disputed the ground for 5 miles with the advancing columns of the enemy. Col. Willington leading the British column, of Brisbane's brigade, was shot down within two miles from Plattsburgh, and this shot is supposed to be from Capt. John Williams, whose aim, was sure of its object. Who was said to say on the occasion, that "the American rifles knew their way when their contents are properly sent forth, as well as the heavy English muskets." There other feats of valor performed by this young man in the service of U. States which are worthy of notice but no room have to insert them.

The other son, Col. E. Williams (the Superintendant general) when a general attack was made at Plattsburgh by the enemy by land & water, he had a charge one of the moveable batteries, which played furiously and answering to one of the enemy batteries on ferris point and was at the close of the cannonading slightly wounded.

It must not be omitted to mentioned here, that in all probability he rendered an important service on that day, which saved from a complete discomfiture of the American force and the captivity of the forts and their defenders.

After the surrender of the enemy's fleet and the recall of the royal troops from the battle field, a concil of war was called by Sir George Provost, at three o'clock, by which, to sustain the honor of the army & the British flag, it was concluded & determined upon, to carry the forts by stormy at the point of the Boyonetts on the next day at the dawning of the day. To effect this, scaling ladders were prepared and 8000 of the best troops were divided into three columns, commanded by Generals, Brisbane, Powers and de

Rottenburgh, and 3000 of the regulars were selected, and 1000 of the light corps to contend with the American militia.

But in the mean time, a <u>coup de main</u> was played upon Sir George, which completely disconcerted his former plan. This was planned by Col. E. Williams, the confidential & secret agent of the government, and approved by the Generals Macomb and Mooers, who urged, most earnestly to have the plan immediately carried into effect. No means where with held in the hands of the two commanders to have the plan consummated. It was a delicate and dangerous experiment, but it was in the hands of a judicious and sagacious hand, with an eagle's eye, he foresaw the good it might be derived from it if properly executed. With a faithful and patriotic co-operators, it was accomplished. By then, Sir George was alarmed at 5 o'clock, that the Governor of Vermont was on his march with ten thousand men and ready to enter the village of Missisquo Bay with the intend to get into his rear, and 700 batteauxs from Burlington (which were known to him that number existed at that place) were on their way to Plattsburgh to take the troops to descend with the fleet to <u>Aux Isle Noix,</u> and that the Americans in his front, were hourly expecting to be reinforced with 8000 men of the best troops and those that were on the ground were eager, in consequence of the defeat of his fleet & the retreat of his troops from the battle field, were encouraged and animated, and ready to meet him or follow him into the province, and under the command of Gen. Mann, from Franklin and St. Lawrence counties in the west, were their march 3000 and would fall in his rear that very night or the next day at Champlain, and that the whole American force of the northern frontier, were in motion to oppose him. That every hour was the greatest importance to his Excellency. This unexpected intelligence alarmed Sir George, whose fleet had been taken before him and in consequence of this unlooked for disaster, had recalled the attacking troops, he most reluctantly gave orders for the whole army to retreat that very night, which, saved by the <u>coup de main,</u> played upon him by Col. E. Williams, the forts at Plattsburgh, the honor of the American troops and the flag of the United States. It is very evident, had not this taken place the forts would have been carried & their defenders taken captives and the militia defeated and dispersed.

This is only verifying the truth of one of the military maxims, that "with judicious management, whole armies have been taken or defeated. How far this important service is appreciated by the American government it does not appear.

At the time and in the historic pages, it has been boasted that the discomfiture of the enemy and his retreat is attributed to the bravery of the Vermont and New York volunteers, but every living man, who had the knowledge of the affair must acknowledge <u>that there is a mystery connected</u> with the sudden retreat of the enemy, who with 14000 of the best troops, and accustomed to conquer and with a formadable train of artillery, and who had suffered so little on the 11th, as to be taken on no amount with his remaining strength for a battle with raw raw and undisciplined militia; therefore there must be other reasonable causes of his sudden retreat than a heavy skirmish which occurred that day. The light corps of the Third of the Buffs as they were termed were only engaged and brought to action, and the remaining force of ten thousand were in a motion when they were recalled. In estimating the number of militia then in the field, with the best disciplined troops of England, they must have yielded on that day, to such overwhelming force; and the victory would been on the side of the enemy. Gen. Brisbane wanted only 20 minutes with his three columns to carry the American works. But to the great mortification of this brave & active gen. he was recalled. He remarked in the council of war, that it was his wish to retain the honor of the army, and if possible, in some measure, to retrieve the tarnished fame of the fleet, by attacking & carrying the American works, which he justly remarked were in an unfinished works and that in 20 minutes all would be in the hands of his majesty's troops!

The author or the planner was too modest to make it known or as a pretext to raise himself in the estimation of the government. It has been stated, that this important affair had been <u>kept down</u> by Generals Macomb & Mooers, lest their own fame in the victory of Plattsburgh may be lessened in the public view. But the American government is too magnanimous to forget those who have rendered her valuable and important services like this! By this judicious maneuvre, her honor was sustained, her troops, with immense quantity of property, were saved, and the whole northern frontier was relieved from a troublesome enemy.

But to return to the Biography of Thomas Williams.

In December 1815 he repaired to Albany accompanied by his son Col. E. Williams to consult with Gov. Tompkins & Lieut. Gov. Tayler of the propriety of his reminding the government of their engagements with him. He was advised to proceed to City Washington and present his claims. With recommending letters from the two Governours and military officers at that place, and with assistance of the state funds, he proceeded to the capital of the Union, where he was received with great cordiality by the President and other officers of the Executive Departments, particularly by Mr. Dallas of the State Department and Mr. Crawford, Secretary of war. But for want of suitable papers conformable to the Laws in relation to his claims, it was recommended to him to procure them, and the secretary of war was engaged to present them to congress; but they were mislaid, and the old & patriotic chief suffered much from the infidelity of the government towards him, and died without being compensated as he was promised, and his aged widow is now applicant for relief on his account.

Thomas Williams after having served his own people, the British & American governments, died in his native village, August 16, 1749.[5] In person he was above the common size, with a countenance manly & bespeaking with intelligence. In his politics he was a strenuous republican. For his attaching himself to the American cause in the war of 1812, he lost the good graces he had of the British government in the Canadas, and its functionaries in the Indian department ceased not to trouble him on that account. It was clearly an act of bigotry and persecution. His memory will be cherished by his American friends.

1 NEW NOTE: The year of his birth was written as 1740. The author crossed out 40 and wrote 37 above it.
2 Brother of the noted St. Luke Le Corn. Note by the author.
3 During the residence of the Rev. E. Williams at Green Bay, a Winnebego chief related to him more than once of his having a hand in this murder. Note by the author.
4 Judge Moore and Col. Mix of Champlain, were permitted to be present on the occasion, reported to General B. Mooers, as one of the most interesting scene which called their attention at the commencement of the war. There was a great contrast between the negotiators in appearance and dress. Sir John aged about 65, and Williams 23 or 4. The former in scarlet with abundance of gold lace with high military hat, decked with lace & feathers and with all his broad sword. Whereas the young American with a plain frock coat and round hat, with his elegant hunger aand pocket pistols. But with his good sense & powerful arguments Sir John had enough of it. After a good cheer the parties separated. Note by author.
5 NEW NOTE: Eleazer Williams wrote 1749 as the year Thomas Williams died. It was corrected as 1849 in the book, *Life of Te-ho-ra-gwa-ne-gen, alias Thomas Williams, a Chief of the Caughnawaga Tribe of Indians in Canada.*

LIFE OF TE-HO-RA-GWA-NE-GEN, ALIAS THOMAS WILLIAMS,

CHIEF OF THE CAUGHNAWAGA TRIBE OF
INDIANS IN CANADA.

BY THE
REV. ELEAZER WILLIAMS,

Reputed son of Thomas Williams
and by many believed to be Louis XVII,
son of the last reigning monarch of France previous
to the Revolution of 1789

ALBANY, N. Y.:
J. MUNSELL, 78 STATE STREET.
1859.

INTRODUCTION.

In the summer of 1852, the undersigned, while preparing for publication a History of St. Lawrence and Franklin counties, N. Y., applied to the Rev. Eleazer Williams, who was residing upon the Indian Reservation of St. Regis, for such facts as he might be able to furnish concerning the history of these people and of his own family, who were known to be descendants of a captive daughter of the Rev. John Williams of Deerfield. [4]

A few weeks after, this gentleman sent, with other papers, a manuscript narrative of the life of Thomas Williams, with full permission to make such use of them as might be deemed proper; but expressing a wish that, if published, the language should be slightly amended, and grammatical errors corrected, as the papers had been hastily prepared and time had not been found to give them the necessary revision for the public eye.

Believing that this permission justified the present use of these papers, the undersigned has copied them with the sole view of correcting the slight irregularities in the style, or the "Indian [5] idioms" as the author termed them, which they contained; but in so doing has preserved the original meaning in all cases, and has neither added, omitted or corrected, except in the way of notes.

The strange romance that has been woven into the history of Eleazer Williams, and the numerous corroborating circumstances which have been adduced to sustain the theory that he is the son of Louis XVI, render everything connected with the parentage, education and life of this person worthy of the attention of the unprejudiced seeker after truth. It is not certain that these pages will add any [6] thing to what has been previously written concerning him, further than as they indicate the character of the man under whose protection he was reared to manhood, and the circumstances in which his early habits and associations were formed.

To the inhabitants of the section in which Mr. Williams resided, the story of his noble birth was received with very general distrust; and with but few exceptions, it was regarded as an artful invention of some ingenious dealer in romance. This fact can not be received as evidence in the case, since but few, if any, who knew him personally, could claim acquaintance in [7] his early youth. At the time of his alleged introduction into the family of Thomas Williams, the whole of Northern New York was an unbroken wilderness, and there is not probably a single person living in the county where Mr. Williams resided, who has had any personal knowledge of it earlier than the beginning of this century. Any opinion they may have formed concerning the personal history of Eleazer Williams must therefore have been derived from secondary and uncertain authority, and should be received with suitable allowance for the errors it might possibly involve.

Aside from the principle of human [8] nature which inclines us to undervalue the fame that may attach to those with whom we are personally acquainted, and which is so forcibly implied in the statement of scripture, that "a prophet is not without honor, save in his own country," another cause existed, which may have had its influence in determining the local opinion with regard to the reality of the reputed identity.

While we would touch lightly upon the faults of the dead, and would fain allow the grave to close over whatever of error in education or habit there may have been in the living, it can not be denied that many persons who have [9] formed and expressed opinions upon personal acquaintance with the subject of these remarks, in the locality where he resided, had at some period of their lives sustained the relation of *creditors*. How far this circumstance might bias opinion, is left to the decision of the mental philosopher; to what extent this trait, if admitted in the full degree, and conceded as hereditary, would disfavor the theory of descent from the Bourbon family, is referred to the historian for *settlement*.

The acquaintance of the editor of these pages with Mr. Williams, continued from the time above mentioned to a few months previous to his death, [10] which occurred at Hogansburgh, N. Y., on the 28th August, 1858. The impression made during this intercourse was, that he possessed a kind and generous heart, an unusually large fund of general information concerning American history and the character of prominent individuals who have figured in public life, a retentive memory of events during and subsequent to the last war with Great Britain, an acute perception of motive and character in those with whom he was brought in contact, and a desire for public notoriety. It was evident that he dwelt upon the romantic story with pleasure, and that allusions to the subject, [11] with complimentary appellations of royalty, were received with satisfaction.

However the story of his titled ancestry, suffering, and sequestration, may have originated, it is believed no person intimately acquainted with Mr. Williams will deny, that he possessed an ingenious faculty for collating the plausible coincidences which make up the warp and woof of the narrative, and that few who heard from his own lips the various incidents which tended to confirm the theory, could withstand the conviction that the whole chain of evidence *was extremely like truth.*

It is a fact of public notoriety, [12] in the locality where he lived, that Mr. Williams was regarded with distrust and apprehension by those who professed the religion of his father, and that efforts have been uniformly made, in speaking of him, to disparage the pretensions which have been set up in his behalf.

His influence with the St. Regis Indians was chiefly limited to the Protestant portion, who form a very small minority; and, for this cause, few opportunities occurred in that place for the exercise of the functions of a clergyman among the people with whom he had been associated the greater part of his life. [13]

For a few years before his death he resided at Hogansburgh, mostly alone, near the edge of a grove, in a neat cottage erected by friends subsequent to the publications which excited so general an interest in 1853. His habits of domestic economy were such as might, under the circumstances, be alike expected in one reared as a prince or a savage; and his household presented an aspect of cheerless desolation, without a mitigating ray of comfort, or a genial spark of homelight. His neatly finished rooms had neither carpets, curtains nor furniture, save a scanty supply of broken chairs and invalid tables; boxes filled with [14] books, the gift of friends, lay stowed away in corners; his dining table, unmoved from week to week, and covered with the broken remains of former repasts, and his pantry and sleeping room disordered and filthy, left upon the visitor an oppressive feeling of homeless solitude that it was impossible to efface from the memory.

Franklin B. Hough.

Albany, May 10, 1859.

[15]

TEHORAGWANEGEN.

Thomas Williams, alias Tehoragwanegen, an Iroquois chief warrior, was born about 1758 or 9, and was the third in descent from the Rev. John Williams of Deerfield, Mass., who, with his family and several parishioners, was captured by a party of three hundred French and Indians, on the night of February 28, 1704.[1] [16]

A part of the assailants broke into the house of Mr. Williams, who, as he was awakened from sleep, snatched his pistol and presented it to the breast of the first Indian that approached ; but it missed fire. The savages seized and bound him. Two of his children, and a negro woman of his family, were taken to the door and murdered, and his wife (the only daughter of the Rev. Eleazer Mather of Northampton), and all his children, except his eldest son, were, with himself, compelled immediately to begin their march towards Canada.

In wading a small river, on the second day, Mrs. W., who had scarcely [17] recovered from a late confinement, fell down, and was soon after dispatched with a hatchet by one of the Abenaquis or St. François tribe. At length, after witnessing the most agonizing scenes, during a journey of three hundred miles, they arrived in Canada. Upon his return, he was unable to bring one of his daughters (Eunice) with him. She became assimilated with the Indians, and afterwards, by instigation of some of the Jesuits, married a young chief by the name of De Roguers, by whom she had three children, Catharine, Mary and John.

Mary was the mother of Thomas; she dying when he was fifteen months [18] old, his aunt Catharine took charge of the orphan child, by whom she was ever regarded as his mother. Being born and reared among the Indians, he of course imbibed the Indian habits, customs and manners. He was a sprightly and active boy, and was early instructed in the faith and dogmas of the Romish church. His affectionate aunt reared him with the greatest tenderness. Although married to a noted chief (X. Rice), she had no heir, and he therefore had no competitor in the family circle, and was treated by his foster parents as their only child.

In 1772, the Rev. Levi Frisbie was [19] sent as a missionary into Canada, by the Rev. Dr. Wheelock of Dartmouth College, and visited Caughnawaga, where he took particular notice of Thomas, with whose descent and family connection in New England he was familiar. After much negotiation, he finally obtained the consent of his adopted parents to take him to Hanover, and place him in the Moore Charity School, connected with the college above named. In the fulfillment of his instructions Mr. Frisbie proceeded to visit the Indians at the Lake of Two Mountains, and during his absence Thomas was attacked with the small-pox, which prevented his accompanying [20] him on his return ; an occurrence greatly regretted by the youth.

This adopted father was skilled in the chase, and by following him on his journeys the youth became very fond of the forest, and of watching its wild inhabitants. Their hunting grounds were near Crown Point, Lake George, and in the vicinity of Fort Edward. After his marriage he was often absent from his village, from one to two or three years, living upon the best that the forest afforded, and earning sufficient to obtain by exchange clothing and food for his family.

At the beginning of the Revolutionary war, although then but about [21] eighteen years of age, he accompanied the warriors of his tribe upon various expeditions against the inhabitants of the northern frontiers of the American colonies. It has been said that he was secretly instructed by his grandmother Eunice, to follow the Indian detachments, with the view of preventing, if possible, the massacre of feeble and defenceless women and children ; and on various occasions he exerted himself to excite feelings of humanity and kindness towards the Americans who fell into their hands.

In October, 1776, he headed his band when the armed vessels of the British and Americans came to action [22] opposite Valcour's Island, near Plattsburgh. Thomas, with his warriors, had a full view of the battle, and he was much animated at the bravery of the Americans, and exclaimed, "These brave Americans will have the liberty they want!"

In 1777 he was promoted to the rank of a war chief of his band, which gave him greater power and influence. As he was brave and energetic in his movements, he soon came to be beloved by his brother warriors, and highly respected by the British officers, especially by Major Carleton, and Captains Horton and Ross, who were his friends during the war. In the [23] spring of this year, while called upon to prepare himself and his warriors to cooperate with General Burgoyne's army, then assembling at St. Johns and the Isle Aux Noix, he appeared to be in great despondency. His friends assigned various reasons for this, but knowing as he did that Gen. Burgoyne had a large army under his command, and that resistance would be made by the Americans against the invasion of their country, in which much blood would be shed, and many valuable lives lost, the better feelings of humanity were awakened in his breast, and sadness appeared in his countenance. He however resolved to [24] serve God in this affair, and to deal equally with his fellow-man.

At Cumberland Head he and his corps joined the royal army, where he met his friends Captains Horton and Ross. In the retreat of the Americans from Ticonderoga, he and his Indians were among others ordered to pursue them ; but discovering the course they had taken, he took his route more to the left, under the pretence of falling upon their flank, but the circuit was too great to allow them to take part in the action between Colonel Warner and General Frazer. The object in view by the Indian captain was undoubtedly gained. [25]

In August, General Burgoyne detached Col. Baum with five hundred men, and one hundred Indians, under the command of Thomas ; and on the sixteenth the former was attacked at Bennington, by General Stark. Thomas arrived with his Indian warriors soon after the action had commenced, and his sagacious eye immediately discovered that the Hessian colonel would be defeated, and he accordingly took precaution not to be surrounded by the Americans, and held them in the woods, where they kept up a scattering fire for a time, but at too great a distance to be effectual. A party of the Americans having taken a secret path [26] gained their rear, and opened upon the Indians a heavy fire, which caused them to retreat in great confusion without further resistance, as their white allies had by this time ceased to fire. Four or five of the Indians were killed and several of their party slightly wounded, among whom was Captain De Loromie, an Indian agent, and an officer in the Indian department in the British service, who acted as an interpreter. Thomas met Col. Breyman as he was advancing to sustain Colonel Baum, but would not consent to turn back with him. "We are defeated," said he, "and it is of no use to meet with superior numbers, and if [27] you proceed you will share the same fate." De Loromie rather joined in this advice, which was received by Colonel Breyman in a most ungracious manner, and an angry dispute arose between the young chief-warrior and the colonel, which was finally settled by the interference of the officers, and the advancing party retraced their steps.

It may be proper to here state, that the murder of Miss Jane McCrea, near Fort Edward, was regarded with strong disapprobation by Thomas. Captain Jones once applied to him for assistance in bringing the young lady within the British lines, but he declined to [28] undertake so delicate and dangerous an enterprise, and replied : "You have come to conquer the country; if you succeed you will have your white squaw: she is now safe, and to attempt to take her by force by our Indians may endanger her life, as there may be a skirmish in so doing; so she had better remain where she now is." A few days after this, Captain Jones applied to Captain Langlad, who had charge of the western tribes, consisting of Ottawas, Chippeways, Menominies, and Winnebagos, and the latter were employed to bring Miss McCrea into the camp. Two chiefs of different bands were employed in this service, each [29] ignorant of the object of the other in the enterprise. One of these had succeeded in getting the young lady safely into their hands, when the other party coming up found the object of their pursuit already obtained, and their head warrior demanded of the other party to give her up to him and his friends, as they had been sent by Captain Jones to bring her in. The former replied, "We are on a similar errand, and the bird is in our hands." Upon which a contest ensued between the leaders, and in the affray the lady was murdered. It has been entirely through mistake that some late writers have attributed this murder to the St. [30] Regis Indians.[2] Williams urged the Iroquois chiefs, then in camp, to wait upon General Burgoyne and beg him to put an end to this inhuman conduct, and the British general rebuked the western tribes in such a manner that they were offended, and soon after deserted from the army.

He was present at the battles of Saratoga, on the 19th of September and 7th of October, and on the night of the 8th, after consulting with the other chiefs, they left the encampment [31] at about two o'clock, and took up their march to Lake George. His humanity would not permit him to leave one sick warrior, and all were brought away on litters, and carried safely to their village.

In the autumn of 1778, he went, at the call of Colonel Johnson, with a party to Oswego, with the view of invading the Mohawk country; but the design was given up. In 1779 he accompanied a detachment under the command of his friend Captain Horton, as far as White River, in Vermont, where they ravaged a number of white settlements, among which was Royalton, and took a number of prisoners. [32] His influence was exerted to have these treated with humanity, and through his efforts many houses and barns were saved, two females were protected from abuse at the hands of three St. François Indians, and an aged man was spared, who would have been killed had he not defended him. Observing this, Captain Horton pleasantly observed: "My friend I am not surprised at this; you have Bostonian blood running in your veins." He replied, "Yes, and I glory in it, as it is tinctured with humanity, the true spirit of Christianity."

In February, 1780, he headed a party of Iroquois and St. François Indians, [33] under Captain Raynier of Quebec, on a secret mission to the Penobscot river, with dispatches from Gov. Carleton to the commandant of the fort at the mouth of that river. This was a fatiguing service, in the midst of a hard winter, and was performed upon raquettes.[3] They passed the American guards upon pretence of belonging to the

Penobscot tribe, and Raynier, entering the fort on an island in the night, delivered his dispatches. The party returned safely, and their good conduct was applauded by the governor. During their stay in the city, they received [34] large presents in gold, with blankets, linen of a fine quality, rifles, kettles, knives, silver broaches and silver medals.

After remaining seven days in his village, Thomas was again called upon to head his band in an expedition under Sir John Johnson to the Mohawk river, and this was the last of his services under the British during the revolution. He was present at the attack upon the dwelling of Colonel Vischer, where the latter was scalped and left for dead, but revived and lived many years afterwards. His two brothers were killed, and the house was burned. Thomas and Col. [35] Louis had a friendly interview with Colonel Vischer in 1795. "We met once," said the brave colonel, "as enemies; but Colonel Vischer still lives, and we will now meet over his good wine and brandy as friends, for we are commanded from above to forgive our enemies." His friends responded with *Amen*.

The Indians, on this occasion, received positive orders from Sir John to burn all the buildings on their route, and he was prevented from being as humane as formerly, and the ravages committed upon the defenceless inhabitants under the eye of Sir John and with his encouragement, produced no [36] good feeling on the part of Williams, who disapproved of such inhuman conduct on the part of the tories and some of the Indian warriors.

Sir John, from this period, regarded him with jealousy, but Williams stood so high in the esteem of Governor Carleton and the officers of the army, for the important services he had rendered to government, that he dared not come to an open rupture. He was proud, haughty, selfish, and contentious to a shameful degree, and was the more despised by the Canadian Indians from his partiality to the recently emigrated Mohawks, his former neighbors, over whom his father, Sir [37] William, had acted as agent for nearly half a century. The hatred engendered in this campaign never ceased to burn, and influenced the conduct of Williams in the subsequent war between Great Britain and America.

From this period he appears to have followed his usual vocation, and after the peace of 1783 he began, with several of his friends, to hunt in the vicinity of Crown Point and Lake George. He often visited Albany with his peltries, and always had a friendly intercourse with General Schuyler, who was once a pupil of the Rev. Dr. Stephen Williams, of Longmeadow, Mass., the brother of Eunice the grandmother of Thomas. [38]

In 1783, after having hunted a great part of the winter in the vicinity of Lake George, he went down to Albany with his friend and fellow hunter John Baptist Toietakherontie, with whom, after receiving letters of recommendation from General Schuyler and other gentlemen in Albany, he proceeded to New England to visit his relatives for the first time. He arrived at Stockbridge, Mass., at the house of the Rev. Dr. West,[4] where he happily met the [39] noted Rev. Samuel Kirkland, missionary to the Oneida Indians, who understood his language perfectly, and acted on the occasion as interpreter. Here he passed two days in a most agreeable manner with several respectable families who claimed to be his kindred, and with strong recommending letters from the reverend gentlemen and others of the place, "to all whom it might concern," they continued on their route to Longmeadow, the place of their destination. [40]

His object was to visit the Rev. Dr. Stephen Williams[5], the venerated brother of his grandmother Eunice but on his arrival he found, to his sorrow and regret, that he was dead. He died on the third of June, 1782. He had, and preserved, letters addressed to him, written in December of the preceding year, from his beloved and unfortunate sister Eunice, who addressing [41] him in most affectionate terms, said "My beloved brother, once in captivity with me, and I am still so as you may consider it, but I am free in the Lord. We are now both very old and are still permitted by the goodness of God to live in the land of the living. This may be the last time you may hear from me. Oh, pray for me that I may be prepared for death, and I trust we may meet in Heaven with all our godly relatives." Her brother, as it was believed, was already there, waiting for her to enjoy with him the full fruition of God.

From this period Thomas visited, [42] occasionally, his kind relatives in New England, till 1806. After the removal of the Rev. Dr. Samuel Williams from his professorship in Harvard University to Rutland, Vermont, he made his house one of his stopping places on his route.[6] This reverend gentleman was equidistant with Thomas in descent from the Reverend John Williams, of Deerfield, who was taken captive in 1704, as before stated. For this gentleman he had a peculiar regard, and he [43] often said that Professor Williams was the glory of the Williams family, on account of his learning. Dr. Williams, in his history of Vermont,[7] has, it is said, in his article on Indians, made use of the information which he derived from Thomas, in relation to their customs, manners, habits, laws, government and religion. If so, it may be relied upon as a just representation, coming, as it did, from one who was well acquainted with them.

These Indians claimed a considerable amount of land in the state of New [44] York, which they felt had been taken from them by force, and contrary to the eternal principles of justice and equity, and this became a subject of much discussion among them at St. Regis and Caughnawaga. None of them knew how to set up their claim, and Colonel Louis, Thomas Williams and William Gray, were in 1789 called upon for their opinions on the subject, which was left in their hands to bring before the proper authorities, in New York.

A long negotiation ensued, and the three deputies made many tedious journeys to New York, Philadelphia and Albany, during seven years, before [45] this perplexing affair was settled by the state, in a treaty with the Seven Nations of Canada, held at New York in June, 1796. The land bordering on the national boundary line of 45 degrees, from Salmon river to Massena, which the state repurchased from Macomb, Constable, and others, was awarded to the St. Regis Indians.[8] [46]

The personal acquaintance of Thomas Williams with various members of the state government, and their knowledge of his ancestry, are believed to have had an influence in obtaining a favorable result in the negotiation. Yet, notwithstanding this, from causes to be presently noticed, his heirs have been denied a share in the lands and annuities enjoyed by the American portion of the tribe. It is hoped [47] legislature will correct this wrong towards those who have labored so faithfully for their benefit. In the first payment at Chazy, in 1797, only $100 was applied as a remuneration to Thomas Williams for the money and time he had expended during several years in these negotiations. To induce the state to relinquish this tract, the Indian negotiators strongly asserted that it was in part for the benefit of the sixteen Caughnawaga volunteers who entered the Continental service in the Revolution, and for such as might hereafter sustain a similar relation. Notwithstanding this plausible argument, the St. Regis Indians afterwards [48] claimed the whole tract as belonging to themselves alone, and have manifested an ungenerous feeling towards those who were instrumental in procuring the tract they now occupy, and the annuities, amounting to over two thousand dollars, that they enjoy.[9] [49]

This ungenerous and selfish feeling may be attributed to two causes. First. The British influence is still felt by a portion of the tribe, and the Indians of that party maintain their relations as they did during the war, and have no good feeling towards the American part of the tribe.[10] Second. [50] The Romish Religion, to which most of the tribe are subject has a tendency to keep them in an unquiet state, and the influence of the priesthood, who are generally tenacious of their dogmas [51] and ceremonies, has the effect of keeping the Indians opposed to those of different sentiments.[11] The Protestant part of the tribe are increasing, and have a desire to educate their children, but are feeble as to means, and it is [52] hoped will be aided by Christian philanthropists.[12]

In August, 1798, Williams was called upon by the British authorities to head a party on a secret mission on Lake Champlain. The government of Canada had been disturbed by an attempt to surprise and take Quebec by some French revolutionists headed by one McCler. It was reported that a large party was preparing on Lake [53] Champlain, to descend the St. Lawrence to Quebec upon rafts, in the guise of raftsmen, and when a considerable number of men had thus assembled without attracting notice, they were, at a preconcerted signal, to attack the military guard by night and seize fortress. The instruction to Williams, to appear among the parties in the character of a hunter, and to mingle with them as friends, and to ascertain their numbers and intentions. This service be performed to the satisfaction of the Canadian government. The leader of the conspiracy was beheaded and quartered.

In January, 1800, Williams visited [52] his relatives in New England, and took with him his two boys, to be educated by them, as they had before urged him to do.

It may be amiss here to state, that of "one of these youths (Eleazer) aged about fourteen or fifteen, it has been doubted whether heis really the son of Thomas Williams. It is supposed he is an adopted child of high descent, who in the destruction of the royal family in the French revolution, was, with his sister, saved from the quillotine of the revolutionists. It is a mystery yet to be solved whether he is the son of Louis XVI, king of France, and at this distant period [55] perhaps it never will be. There are, however, many circumstances in the history of this unfortunate youth which go to prove that there is a possibility of its being true. To save the life of the youth, as well as his rescuers and other friends, from the bloody hands of the anti-royalists, a profound secrecy was necessarily observed, both in Europe and America, by those who were interested in his preservation."

Hidden things are yet to be brought to light. This is one of the "Unfortunate youth born in a palace and nourished by the royal queen, yet transported to a foreign clime and there to be cherished and sustained by an Indian warrior!" [56]

In the year 1801, Thomas headed a hunting party of Caughnawaga Indians in the service of the Northwest Bay Company, and went as far as the Red river, and from thence towards the Rocky mountains, and traversed part of the grand prairies. The view of these immense prairies in the spring season, covered with numerous herds of buffaloes, and stretching farther than the eye could reach, and of the majestic peaks of the western mountains, filled his mind with wonder, admiration and awe, and he often said, that in these he saw the mighty works of the Great Spirit above, and was led to worship him as the only supreme [57] creator and upholder of all things; that him only would he serve, and to him devote his whole heart and obey his blessed will. He was a man of few words. He thought and meditated on what he said, and what he uttered was sincere.

In 1804, with his wife, he visited his sons in Longmeadow, where they had been left at school, and was highly pleased with the improvement they had made in American manners, and their progress in learning. N. Ely, Esq., a gentleman of wealth, who had married a grand daughter of the Rev. Dr. S. Williams, formerly minister of the parish, took a deep interest in [58] the education of the youths, and particularly in endeavoring to instill into their minds the great truths of religion. But, unfortunately, John, the younger of the lads, who appeared to be the mother's favorite, was taken back with his parents to Canada, much against the wish of the father, and to the great regret and sorrow of Eleazer, who protested in the strongest terms against being separated from him. But her parish priest had threatened to excommunicate her from the church if she did not bring the boys back with her, and she hoped to escape his censure if she returned with one.

The Rev. Dr. Nathan Williams of [59] Tolland, the Rev. Nathan Strong of Hartford, the Rev. Dr. McCluer of East Windsor, the Rev. R. S. Storrs and N. Ely, Esq., of Longmeadow, the Rev. Dr. Joseph Lathrop and Justin Ely, Esq., of West Springfield, the Rev. Mr. Howard and Dr. William Sheldon of Springfield, Gov. Trumbull of Connecticut, and C. Strong of Massachusetts, took a deep interest in the welfare of Eleazer, and succeeded in retaining him for the purpose of continuing his education.

From this period there is a chasm in the historical incidents of the life of Thomas Williams, till the declaration of war in 1812, as nothing in this interval occurred worthy of note. It [60] was the wish of the Americans that the Indians should remain neutral in this as in the former war. Humanity and civilization pleaded in favor of a principle that would not add savage barbarity to the evils of war; but unfortunately, the policy of their enemy was different, and they soon learned that the British had leagued themselves with the ruthless savages of the wilderness and the domiciliated native tribes of the provinces;

in short, that they had exhausted every resource from the warfare of the tomahawk and the scalping-knife to the latest improvements of modern art, which they were preparing to use against the people of the United States. [61]

The first act in which the allied Indians and the British signalized themselves, was the taking of the fort at Michilimackinac, on the 19th of July, 1812, at which several Caughnawagas from Lower Canada were present.

In July, Governor Provost of Lower Canada issued a proclamation commanding the Indians in that province to take up arms in behalf of his Britannic Majesty, and this order was by Sir John Johnson[13] transmitted to Williams but indignantly rejected. [62] Col. De Loromie, Sub-Superintendent of the Indian Department, soon after reported him and others at Caughnawaga, as well as Col. Louis Cook and others at St. Regis, as refractory.

The St. François Indians, as well as those as well as those of the Lake of Two Mountains, evinced in some degree the same spirit ; and the French Canadians on the Island of Montreal were by no means inclined to take up arms against the Americans. The affair at La Chine in August, in which fifteen hundred of these people skirmished with the royal troops, strongly indicated the ill-will with which they received the proclamation of the Governor General. How [63] far Thomas Williams was concerned in this affair is unknown. He was within two miles of the place where the action occurred.

Such was the timidity or treachery of the French commander upon this occasion that, neglecting to seize the king's stores and arms as might have been done, as his force was much more formidable than that which opposed him, he ordered his forces to withdraw after ten minutes firing. His order was obeyed with reluctance by those in the front line, and with loud murmurs by the volunteers in the rear, who were eager to be brought into action with the English troops, and [64] determined to evince the same spirit that was evinced by those of their mother country under Bonaparte.

The retreat threw them into disorder, and the whole body quickly dispersed. It has been asserted, from highly respectable sources, that if the American government had sent two thousand regular troops into the province at this particular juncture, the whole of Lower Canada must have fallen into their hands, except Quebec, as the French population would have taken up arms in their favor.

In August, 1812, a provisional agreement was entered into between Gen. Dearborn and Adjutant Gen. Baynes, [65] that neither party should act offensively until the decision of the American government could be obtained on a question then pending. This armistice was grounded upon a letter from the governor, Sir George Provost, to General Dearborn, suggesting the probability of a general suspension of hostilities in consequence of a suspension or repeal of the British orders in council, of which Mr. Foster, late minister to the United States, had received advices on his arrival at Halifax.

The American government considered the proposition as indirect, and offered no security for its observance, [66] and the cessation of hostilities terminated on the 8th of September.

While Adjutant Gen. Baynes was at the head-quarters of Gen. Dearborn, Lieut.

Col Eleazer Williams was sent off to the lines near Rouse's Point, where he met, according to previous agreement, Sir John Johnson, Superintendent General of Indian Affairs in the Canadas, and Williams appeared in the same capacity on the American side, for the northern frontiers. Their object was to arrange for the neutrality of the Indian tribes; but the proposition of Gen. Dearborn was respectfully declined by Sir John, and finally left to the decision of Sir George Provost. [67]

In relation to this affair, it was remarked by Sir John, that youn g Williams argued like a young lion upon the subject; that he not only pleaded upon principles of humanity and civilization, but of religion, which would not add savage barbarity to the other evils of the war. "Your king," said he, "styles himself the *Defender of the Christian Faith,* and will he league himself with the ruthless savages of the wilderness, whose tender mercies are to be manifested by the tomahawk and the scalping-knife—and that not only upon the wounded and captive of the American soldiery, but upon defenceless women and children? Sir, [68] I have too exalted an opinion of British humanity, and of the principles of religion by which the English nation is governed, to admit this unholy alliance. England is the bulwark of the Protestant religion! Yes, sir, she may well glory that she is the emporium of Bible and Missionary societies. In the midst of this corrupt age and bloody strife among the nations of the earth, she is sending forth the word giving life to the dark corners of the earth, and her messengers of the Cross are proclaiming 'Peace on earth, and good will to men.'"[14] [69]

The sole object of young Williams, it would appear, at this period of the war, was to save the St. Regis Indians, who were peculiarly situated, being on the line, and, as it were, within striking [70] distance of the two contending parties.[15]

He succeeded, and Sir George Provost was induced, under the circumstances, to permit the neutral party to remain in peace in their village. [71] A portion of them, however, afterwards took up arms and joined Gen. Hampton's army in 1813, and were with him in the skirmish on Chateaugay river.

It is said that General Dearborn and Dr. Eustis, Secretary of War, were highly pleased with the management of their young native negotiator, as the policy and humanity of the American government towards the unfortunate Indians was so well represented. Gen. Mooers, in his report of this affair to Gen. Dearborn and Gov. Tompkins, was enthusiastic in his praise of young Williams.

At this period of the war, by the [72] agency of General Dearborn, as commander-in-chief of the Northern army, Gen. Mooers of the New York division, and Gov. Tompkins and Judge Pliny Moore of Champlain, Thomas Williams, the Iroquois chief, was invited by the American government to retire from the British province, and place himself and family under the protection of the American flag, with an assurance of honorable support; and the American government solemnly engaged to make up to him and his family whatever losses he might sustain in personal property, and the interest he might enjoy in common with his tribe. With these honorable offers and assurances [73] he left the British province in 1813, and warmly engaged in the American cause; and through his influence, many of the British Indians became attached to their interests. His influence was strongly felt in the invasion of New York at Plattsburgh in 1817, by Sir George Provost, with 14,000 regulars and 700 Indians, who refused at Champlain to advance any farther with the royal troops.[16] They knew that Thomas Williams, their beloved war-chief, with his sons, was with the Americans at Plattsburgh. This refusal on the part of the Indians to advance is an established fact, and the cause was then secret. While at Champlain, although [74] within the American lines, they committed no depredations, but conducted themselves respectfully towards the inhabitants, particularly towards Judge Moore and Col. Mix.

Although Gen. Brisbane, the commander of the advance division of the army, pretended to Silas Hubbell, a magistrate of Champlain, that the Indians were kept in arrear out of humanity; yet in a council of war at La Cole river, held by Sir George Provost and the war-chiefs, he was told in strong language of the propriety of their remaining in the rear of the army, and so determined were they that his excellency was compelled from necessity [75] to submit to their decision. At the same place, on the retreat of the royal army after their defeat at Plattsburgh, the officers of the Indian Department made a strong effort to obtain volunteers from among the Indians, by offering large rewards to retake the ships of war captured by the Americans, by the aid of the few remaining gunboats, but this application was rejected by their allies.

Thomas Williams, after this affair, says in his address to them: "Brothers, I have not deceived you in the result of the late campaign on the part of the red coats. I told you they would not succeed, but that a defeat would follow [76] such an attempt. Saranac (or Plattsburgh) is safe, and its strongholds are spangled with their flags, and the eagle and its stripes are floating in the air in all their glory. If the British army had remained four days longer at the place it would have been Burgoyned, and had I been with them, I should have fled in the night, as I did in 1777 at Saratoga, after the last battle with the brave Yankees. They beat the English then, and gained their independence, and be assured they will beat them again!"

His son John was in an honorable office in the British service, but soon followed his father into the United [77] States, with several others of the Caughnawagas. This son was a brave and fearless volunteer. On the morning of September 5th, at Beekmantown, he was in the advanced rifle corps, which opened the first fire upon the enemy, and as it advanced he disputed every inch of ground, until the corps reached the main force under General Mooers. The general action commenced by cannonading from the American line, by two hundred and fifty regular troops, under Major Wool, who maintained this position with great obstinacy until they were completely outflanked by the superior force of the enemy; and when compelled to retreat, [78] they did so in good order, disputing the ground for five miles with the advancing columns of the enemy. Col. Willington, leading the British column of Brisbane's brigade, was shot down within two miles of Plattsburgh, and this shot is supposed to have been from the weapon of John Williams, whose aim was sure of its object. We have not room to notice other feats of valor performed by this young man in the service of the United States.

The other son, Colonel E. Williams (the Superintendent General), when a general attack was made by the enemy at Plattsburgh, by land and water, had charge of one of the moveable [79] batteries, which played furiously and answering to one of the enemy's batteries on Ferris's Point, and at the close of the cannonade, he was slightly wounded.

It must not be omitted to mention here, that in all probability, he rendered an important service on that day, which saved from a complete discomfiture the American force, and the captivity of the forts and their defenders.[17]

After the surrender of the enemy's fleet and the recall of the royal troops from the battle-field, a council of war [80] was called by Sir George Provost at 3 o'clock, at which to sustain the honor of the army, and the British flag, it was determined to carry the forts by storm, at the dawn of the next day, and at the point of the bayonet. To effect this, scaling ladders were provided and eight thousand of the best troops were divided into three columns, commanded by Gens. Brisbane, Powers,, and De Rottenburgh, and three thousand of the regulars and one thousand of the light corps were selected to contend with American militia.

But in the mean time a *coup de main* was played upon Sir George, which completely disconcerted his former plan. [81] This was planned by Col. E. Williams, the confidential secret agent of the government, and approved by General Macomb and Mooers, who urged most earnestly to have the plan immediately carried into effect, and no means at the command of those officers were withheld to have it consummated. The plan involved danger and difficulty, but it was in the hands of a judicious and sagacious hand. With an eagle's eye, he foresaw the good that might be derived from it if properly executed, and with faithful and patriotic cooperators it was accomplished. By then, Sir George was alarmed at 5 o'clock, by a report that the Governor [82] of Vermont was on his march with ten thousand men, and ready to enter the village of Missisqui Bay, with the intention to gain his rear; that seven hundred bateaux (which were known by him to be at that place) were on their way to Plattsburgh, to take the troops, to descend with the fleet to *Isle aux Noix,* and that the Americans in his front were hourly expecting to be reinforced with eight thousand men of the best troops, while those on the ground were eager, in consequence of the defeat of his fleet and the retreat of his troops from the battle field, to follow him into the province. Gen. Man, from Franklin and St. Lawrence counties, was [83] reported as on his march with three thousand militia, to fall upon his rear that night or the next day, at Champlain; and the whole American force of the northern frontier as in motion to oppose him, rendering every hour of the greatest importance to his excellency. This unexpected intelligence alarmed Sir George, whose attacking troops had been recalled, in consequence of the loss of his fleet, and he most reluctantly gave orders for the whole army to retreat that very night.

This *coup de main,* played upon the British commander by Col. E. Williams, saved the defences at Plattsburgh, the honor of the American troops, and the [84] flag of the United States. It verified the military maxim that "with judicious management whole armies have been taken or defeated," but how far this important service is appreciated by the American government does not appear.

At the time of the event, and on the historic page, it has been boasted that the discomfiture and retreat of the enemy, was due to the bravery of the Vermont and New York volunteers; but every living man who had a knowledge of the affair must acknowledge *that there is a mystery* connected with the sudden retreat of the enemy, who with fourteen thousand of the best [85] troops, unaccustomed to fear and supported by a formidable train of artillery. They had suffered so little on the 11th, that his strength for battle with raw and undisciplined militia, remained unabated, and some other reasonable cause for his retreat must be found, than the heavy skirmish of that day. The light corps of the Third of the Buffs (as they were called) were only engaged and brought into action, the remaining force of ten thousand being only in motion when they were recalled.

In comparing the number of militia then in the field, against the best disciplined troops of England, they must [86] have yielded on that day, to such overwhelming force, and the victory would have been on the side of the enemy. General Brisbane wanted only twenty minutes with his three columns to carry the American works, but to the great mortification of this brave and active general, he was recalled. He remarked in the council of war, that it was his wish to retain the honor of the army, and if possible in some measure to retrieve the tarnished fame of the fleet, by attacking or carrying the American works, which he justly remarked were in an unfinished condition, and that in twenty minutes all [87] might be in the hands of his majesty's troops!

The author or planner was too modest to make it known as a pretext to raise himself in the estimation of the government. It is stated that this important affair had been *kept down* by Generals Macomb and Mooers, lest their own fame in the victory of Plattsburgh should be lessened in the public view. But the American government is too magnanimous to forget those who have rendered her valuable and important services like this! By this judicious measure, her honor was sustained, her troops, with immense quantities of property, were saved, and the whole [88] northern frontier was relieved from a troublesome enemy.

But to return to the biography of Thomas Williams. In December, 1815, he repaired to Albany, accompanied by his son, Col. E. Williams, to consult with Gov. Tompkins and Lieut. Gov. Tayler, on the propriety of his reminding the government of their engagements with him. He was advised to proceed to Washington and present his claims. With letters from these two officers, and from military officers at that place, and with aid of state funds, he proceeded to the capital of the union, where he was received with great cordiality by the president, and other [89] officers of the executive departments, particularly by Mr. Dallas of the state department, and Mr. Crawford, secretary of war. For want of suitable papers conformable to the laws, it was recommended to him to procure them, and the secretary of war was engaged to present them to congress; but they were mislaid, and the old and patriotic chief suffered much from the infidelity of the government towards him. He died without the compensation promised, and his aged widow is now an applicant for relief on his account.[18] [90]

Thomas Williams, having served his own people, the British and American governments, died in his native village, August 16, 1849. In person he was above the common size, with a countenance manly and speaking with intelligence. In his politics he was a strenuous republican, and by attaching himself to the American cause, in the war of 1812, he lost the graces of the British government in the Canadas. The functionaries in the Indian department [91] ceased not to trouble him on that account. His memory will be cherished by his American friends.

1 History fixes the date of this attack as the night of Feb. 20, by upwards of 340 Indians, under Major Hertel de Rouville.
2 During the residence of the Rev. E. Williams at Green Bay, a Winnebego chief related to him more than once of his having a hand in this murder. *Note by the Author.*
3 Snow-shoes.
4 Dr. Stephen West, of Tolland, Ct., graduated at Yale College in 1755, was licensed to preach about the beginning of 1758, and was ordained at Stockbridge, June 13, 1759. He continued to preach to the English in the forenoon, and the Indians, through an interpreter, in the afternoon of each Sabbath until 1775, when he relinquished the latter to Mr. John Sergeant, a son of the missionary. He died in 1819, aged 84. – *Holland's Western Massachusetts,* II, 587.
5 Stephen Williams was born at Deerfield May 14, 1693, graduated from Harvard in1713, and went to Longmeadow in Nov., 1719. He was afterwards a chaplain in three campaigns in the old French and Indian wars, and died, according to some accounts, June 10, 1782, in the 60th year of his ministry, and the 90th of his age. – *Holland's Western Massachusetts,* II, 78.
6 Samuel Williams graduated at Harvard University in 1740, received the Master's degree in 1785, and held the office of Professor of Mathematics and Natural Philosophy in that institution from 1780 to 1788.
7 Two editions of this work have been published. The first was in 1794, in one volume, and the second in 1809, in two volumes.
8 A tract equal to six miles square, near St. Regis, was expressly reserved out of the lands sold to Macomb, and only a tract of about 210 acres along Grass river, consisting of natural meadows, was repurchased from the proprietors by the state for the use of the Indians. The St. Regis reservation lies in the town of Bombay, Franklin county, N. Y., and originally embraced a tract equal to six miles square, the meadows above mentioned, a mile square on Salmon river, at the present village of Fort Covington, and a mile square on Grass river at the lower mills.

By successive sales these reservations have now been reduced to about 14,000 acres of choice land, a part of which is leased to whites for a term of years. – *Census of N. Y.*, 1855, p. 517. – Ed.
9 The Caughnawagas shared equally with the St. Regis Indians in the annuities stipulated in the treaty of 1796, until the war of 1812. A few years after, through the influence of Mr. Peter Sailley of Plattsburgh, a moiety of the annuity was restored to them, with the express understanding that Thomas Williams should receive $50 annually from their portion, as he had met with considerable sacrifices in consequence of the war. He continued to receive this until 1833, when they entered a protest, and he was not paid.

The above Caughnawagas have never been parties to any treaty or agreement with the state since1796; and other villages, representing the remaining "Seven Nations of Canada," have never been represented in any treaty with New York.

History will scarcely warrant the uncharitable allegation of the author in relation to the St. Regis tribe. – Ed.
10 In the War of 1812-15, the St. Regis Indians became divided in their attachment to the two governments, and though at first they professed to be neutral, numbers from both parties went off and joined the camps of the opposing armies. These parties have continued till the present time, and the distinction has become hereditary on the mother's side. The British Indians receive no share of the rents or annuities paid in New York, and the Americans none of the rents or presents paid in Canada. They however reside on either side of the national boundary that passes through their village, as convenience dictates, and mingle freely in the daily transactions of life in perfect harmony. There are about 530 American and 640 British Indians, who receive a share of the annuities and presents of their respective governments. – Ed.
11 St. Regis was founded as a Catholic mission, and has for nearly a century been the home of a resident missionary of that denomination. With the exception of about one hundred, chiefly Methodists,

these Indians are strongly attached to the Catholic church, and zealous observers of its requirements. On this account, the Rev. Mr. Williams had the confidence of but a small portion of the tribe among whom he had been so long a resident. He was accustomed to attribute much of the opposition he encountered, to the hostility arising from the two causes above indicated, and especially from the latter. – Ed.

12 At the time when the above was written (1852) the author was endeavoring to establish a school among the Indians upon the St. Regis reservation, but the enterprise did not meet with success, and was soon after suspended. A log building which he caused to be erected for his school was turned into a dwelling. – Ed.

13 Sir John was at this time Superintendent General and Inspector General of Indian Affairs in British North America, retaining that office till his death. He died in Montreal in 1830, aged eighty-eight. – Ed.

14 Judge Moore and Col. Mix of Champlain were permitted to be present on the occasion, and reported this to General B. Mooers as one of the most interesting scenes which fixed their attention at the commencement of the war. There was a great contrast between the negotiators in their appearance and dress. Sir John, aged about sixty-five, and Williams twenty-three or four: the former in scarlet and gold lace in abundance, with high military hat decked with lace and feathers; and with his broadsword; while the young American was dressed in a plain frock coat and round hat, with his elegant hanger and pocket pistols. But with his good sense and powerful and humane arguments Sir John had enough of it. After a good cheer the parties separated. – *Note by the author.* Ed.

15 The national boundary, as surveyed and marked by monuments, passes directly through the Indian village at St. Regis. The tribe is still divided into British and American parties, without reference to present residence, but according to the way they sided in the war of 1812-15. This distinction is hereditary, and transmitted from mother to son. Each shares in the annuities or presents of its own government only, but resides wherever upon the reservation his interests or inclinations lead him. Transfers may be made by consent of the chiefs or trustees, but it is believed this is not often done. – Ed.

16 NEW NOTE: The published book says this took place in 1817, but the author's manuscript has it in 1814, which is correct.

17 Historians will probably be inclined to differ from the author in some of these statements. – Ed.

18 The widow of Thomas Williams was, in 1852, residing on the St. Regis reservation, about eight miles from the village, and although over ninety years of age, walked regularly to church, with no other aid but a staff. She was apparently a full blooded Indian, tall and slender, but little bowed with age, and still able to attend to her domestic duties. She was a devout Catholic, and spoke no language but Mohawk. She has since died. – Ed.

Colonel Louis Cook in Hough's Later Books

The life of Colonel Louis Cook, as described by Eleazer Williams in manuscript and Franklin B. Hough in print, is nothing short of spectacular. Had he known of this story, James Fenimore Cooper might never have bothered writing *The Last of the Mohicans*. Cook experienced four of the most important colonial wars: King George's War, The Seven Years War, the Revolutionary War, and the War of 1812. He may have been the only person to have done so. There are two reasons why he is not a household name in America today, along with Paul Revere. First, he was half Native American. And second, he was half African. There is also a third reason: he saved America's butt. Well, kind of.

Had Sir William Johnson not died in 1774, there is a strong possibility that he, the silver-tongued Superintendent of Indian Affairs, might have maintained the unity of the Haudenosaunee, and got them all to fight on the side of Great Britain. His Mohawk wife Molly Brant and her brother Joseph did their best to carry out this mission, but many Oneida and Tuscarora famously joined up with the colonies. If they had not done so, the Battle of Saratoga might have gone the other way, and the war might have had ended differently. But Sir William Johnson did die, and poor Molly and Joseph were not up to the task of keeping everyone unified. A major reason for that was someone else who showed up who was very much alive: Colonel Louis Cook.

The Rebel of Caughnawaga already had the nickname of Colonel Louis, long before the Continental Army made it official. Molly and Joseph were no match for a sophisticate like Cook, who spoke several native languages in addition to English and French, and who was known to sing verses from a French opera in the forest before taking breakfast with the American officers at Valley Forge.[1] I'm not saying his panache won the Americans the war. But they did not lose.

Hough produced a book about the treaty negotiations that took place after the war, *Proceedings of the Commissioners of Indian Affairs, appointed by law for the extinguishment of Indian titles in the State of New York,* published in 1861. He revisited this nebulous man and found many interesting things about him.

Colonel Louis Cook was present, along with his Oneida and Tuscarora comrades-in-arms, when the United States entered into negotiations with not only the pro-American Haudenosaunee, but those that sided with Great Britain.

His name is given as "Lieut. Col Louis or Atyatoghhanongwia" in a listing of

Chief Warriors that attended a meeting with the Commissioners of Indian Affairs on September 4, 1784. In footnotes, Dr. Hough presents the official record of the commissions of the pro-American Oneida and Tuscarora officers as well as Colonel Louis:

The following Document embraces an official Statement of the Services of sundry Oneidas and Tuscaroras during the War:

War Office, Feb. 26, 1791.

The Secretary for the Department of War, to whom was referred the Petitions of several Oneida and Tuscarora Indians, by their Attorney, Cornelius Van Slyck, reports:

That on the 3d of April, 1779, Congress resolved, "That twelve blank Commissions be transmitted to the Commissioners of Indian Affairs for the Northern Department, and that they, or any two of them, be empowered to fill them up, with the names of faithful Chiefs of the Oneidas and Tuscaroras, giving them such Rank as the said Commissioners shall judge they merit; the Names and Ranks to be by the Commissioners reported to the Board of War."

That in pursuance of the said resolve, the following named Chiefs or Indians of said Nations were commissionéd, and Returns transmitted to the Board of War, viz:

Captains.
Hansjurie Tewahongrahkon,
Tewaghtahkotte,
James, Wakarontharan,
John Otaawighton.

Lieutenants.
Christian Thonigwenghsoharie,
John, Sagoharasie,
Joseph Banaghsatirhon,
Cornelius Okenyota,
Cornelius Kakiktoton,
Hansjoost Thaosagwat,
Totyaheahani,
Nicholas Kayhnatho.

That the Commissions granted as aforesaid, appear in the usual Form of Commissions granted to Officers of the Line of the Army, and specify that the Individuals before mentioned take Rank from the 6th June, 1779.

That on the 5th of June, 1779, Congress resolved, "That one more blank Commission be sent to the Commissioners of Indian Affairs in the

Northern Department, to be filled up with the Name of such faithful Chief as they shall deem worthy of that Honor."

In pursuance of this Act, it appears a like Commission of Lieutenant Colonel in the Army of the United States was granted to Louis Atayataroughta, giving the said Louis Rank from the 15 June, 1779.

That on the 11th of February, 1785, Congress resolved, "That it be, and it is hereby, recommended to the State of New York to settle with Captains Hansjurie Tewahangahtan, John Olaawighton, James Wakarantharaw and Lieutenants Nicholas Kayhnatsho, Cornelius Kakiktoton, Cornelius Okenyota, Indians of the Oneida and Tuscarora Indians, late Officers in the Service of the United States, and pay their Accounts in like Mannor as other Officers in the Line of that State."

In pursuance of said Act the State of New York made good the Depreciation of the Pay of said Indians to the 1st of August, 1780, and settled with them for their Pay to the 1st January. 1782.

That of the Indians who were commissioned by the Acts of Congress of the 3d April and 5th June, 1779, the following now appear by their Attorney, to claim the Benefits arising from the said Commissions, viz :

Lieutenant Colonel.
Louis Atayataronghta
   Captains.
Hansurie Tewahongrahkon,
James Wawakarontharan,
John Otaawighton
   Lieutenants.
John Sagoharasie, by his Widow,
Margaret Oginghtronte
Cornelius Hakiktoton,
Hansjost Thaosagwat, by his Widow,
Elizabeth Shetijo

It appears by the Evidence of Edward Johnson, that Hanjost Thaosagwat was killed on the Western Expedition under General Sullivan, and from verbal Information obtained from Captain Michael Connoly, of the late New York Line, it appears that John Sagoharasie died some Time in 1781, and that Lieutenants Christian Thonigwenghsoharie, Joseph Banaghsatirhon and Totyaneahani, deserted to and exchanged their Commissions with the British

That Lieutenant Colonel Louis Atayaronghta, has been settled for pay with for his Commutation *and for pay,* to the same Period that the State of New York settled with those under the Act aforesaid.

On this Statement the Secretary of War remarks, that, however much it may have been the Intention of Congress that the aforesaid Indians should receive the Half Pay, and the same Rewards as the Officers of the late Army, that the Claim is now precluded by the Resolves of Limitation, excepting as to the Lands which it appears they are entitled, and which it is conceived they may receive without any act of Congress.

All of which is humbly submitted to the House of Representatives.

H. Knox, *Secretary of War.*

—*Am. St. Papers, Ind. Treaties,* i 123.[2]

Colonel Louis Cook clearly deserves a book of his own. This might be the first time in history that a chapter of one book became two books, but first things first.

Dr. Hough includes a new biography of Cook in another footnote of *Proceedings:*

Colonel Louis Cook, or *Atoyataghronghta,* alias *Atyatoghhanongwea,* was born about 1740 at Saratoga, and is said to have been of half Negro Origin, his Mother belonging to the Caughnawaga Tribe near Montreal. He was employed with the French in the Campaigns on Lake Champlain, at Oswego and on the Monongahela; and in common with the Canadian Indians generally, yielded reluctant allegiance to the English in 1760. Hearing of the Disputes between the Colonies and the Mother Country, he made a Journey to Boston in the Summer of 1775, to learn the Merits of the Controversy. He evinced a deep Interest in the Cause of Liberty, and in the Winter following revisited the Camp with a dozen Companions, was kindly received by the Commander-in-Chief, and applied for a Commission, with the Assurance that he would raise four or five hundred Men for the Service. After some Hesitation his Request was granted, and he received a Commission to rank from June 15, 1779, appointing him a Lieutenant Colonel in the American Army. His residence in Canada becoming unsafe, he removed to Oneida, and remained usefully employed through the War, at the Head of a War Party of friendly Indians. In 1780, he visited, with others, his old Friends, the French Allies at Newport. After the Peace he removed to St. Regis, where he continued to reside till the War of 1812-15, when his martial Spirit again called him into active Service, and though Age had somewhat impaired his Vigor, the *Influence* which he had acquired among the Indian Tribes was great, and always actively exercised in Favor of those to whom he had been so long and faithfully attached. An Injury which he received on the Niagara Frontier led to his Death in October, 1814, near Buffalo. He was highly esteemed for his Integrity and moral Worth, and the State secured to him a small Reservation near St. Regis, besides granting Lots number 11, 34, 72, and 98 in Junius.—4th *Am. Archives,* iii, 301, *Sparks's Washington,* iii, 245, 260, 262; vii, 183; *Hough's Hist. St. Law & Frank. Cos.,* 182-198; *Balloting Book,* 140.[3]

Atyatoghhanongwia is another variation of Colonel Louis Cook's indigenous name, which has been given as Atiatonharongwen and Atayataghronghta in other official records. An entire chapter could be devoted to the many different names he was known by in various languages.

Hough's book on the post-war treaty negotiations has many other references to Colonel Louis Cook. His association with the Oneidas continued through the rest of the decade and into the next. Unfortunately, things went south for Colonel Louis, and I do not mean to Susquehannock country. He was too heavily involved with outside forces, and not the military kind.

Hough describes, in another of his lengthy footnotes, "Livingston's Lease for 999 years." This was an attempt by a group of influential men, most of whom lived in Sullivan county, to circumvent the constitution of New York State to secure a lease of all Indian lands in the state. Colonel Louis Cook is listed (under *Col Lewy*) as a witness to this deal, which was signed on November 13, 1787 by "Chiefs and Sachems of the Six Nations Indians" along with John Livingston and his associates. On January 8, 1788 they signed another agreement with "certain Indians claiming to Sachems, Chiefs and Warriors of the Oneida Nation."

Shortly after the "leases" were submitted to the Legislature, they were declared by that body to be *sales,* and therefore illegal. The Legislature then ordered the Governor, "to use the Force of the State, should it be necessary, to prevent Intrusion or Settlement upon the Lands so claimed."[4]

Hough includes a list of the eighty "adventurers," and then lets them have it:

In this List we find a former Commissioner for holding Indian Treaties, an acting State Senator, the Clerks of Albany and Columbia Counties, a future Sheriff of Herkimer and Oneida Counties, eleven past, seven present and fourteen future Members of Assembly, and others who had undeservedly shared the Public Confidence. It is but just to infer that some of these were misled by Falsehoods, or induced to lend Countenance to the Transaction through the Influence of bad Men; but to the greater Number History will attach a Stain of Dishonor, for which no Apologies can atone.[5]

The Commissioners of Indian Affairs, aware of the scheme that had almost been perpetrated, was about to enter into their own negotiations with the Senecas at Fort Schuyler, also known as Fort Stanwix. In a letter from their agent, John Tayler on May 16, 1788, it was revealed that Colonel Louis and those who signed the leases thought Livingston represented the State, and that Louis himself had been paid for his involvement:

Louis has his Note for two hundred pounds, as a Compensation for the Assistance he rendered in compleating the Purchase, but declared that he aided him under the impression that he was sent by the State. A Meeting with the Oneidas will be called by Livingston, and Presents made to them Louis and Schonondo will so fully explain the Intentions of the State, as to frustrate any thing that he can do, and Mr Kirkland will have little Influence at Oneida. In one of his Sermons to them previous to the grant of the long Lease, he observed that his Thoughts were too extensive, their Country so large that he could not collect himself, and urged the Propriety of selling a Part and then his Ideas would be more confined and he would preach better; they have discovered his Views and despise him. I have advanced the Messenger fifteen Pounds six Shillings in Specie, and sixteen Pounds in Goods. I have likewise sent a Boat laden with Indian Corn to the Oneidas in the Name of the Governor. I have further promised to Louis a Reward when the Treaty will be held at Fort Schuyler and have engaged him to return here with the Messenger who is to come to Oneida from Buffalo Creek, and to render any other Assistance that will be required of him.[6]

Peter Penet would be the next adventurer to appear on the scene, this time purporting to be authorized by the King of France. In actuality, he was a private merchant, and had been involved in supplying arms to the United States during the war. His dealings with the Oneidas split them into two factions. Colonel Louis sided with Penet, as did Peter Otsiquette, an Oneida who had visited France.

By the fall of 1789, the Oneidas who were opposed to Penet's plans complained to Governor Clinton about threats Colonel Louis made against them for not supporting him:

    Copy of a Letter from the Oneidas to his Excellency the Governor.

To his Excellency George Clinton, Esquire, Governor of the State of New York, and Commander of all the Militia and Admiral of the Navy of the same, &c., &c., &c.

Brother:
    We received your Answer the 16th of this Month, dated the 12th of September last, to which we are happy to hear the Truth that Mr. Penet is nothing else but a Merchant, pursuing his own Interest.
    We and our Sachems were all together and Colonel Louis was present when your Letter was delivered, but could not persuade our Sachems and Louis to make them believe your Letter; and tho' they believed your hand

writing, yet they still hold Mr. Penet that he is sent from the King of France, and Louis is trying to scare us and said that he would make us sensible in a few Days, and would make us sorry because we don't believe Mr. Penet. We are much surprised of his Interruption; and further he says in the Council, that he will make us sleep very fast, so that we cannot wake up again; and we look upon our Sachems, they are still the same as they were in the first of our Division or worse, quite contrary to our Opinion; and the said Louis blames us much, and said we did send for him from Canada the Beginning of the late War, therefore he thought then that we would mind what he would say to us; but we say he is mistaken about that. The Continental Commissioners of Indian Affairs did send for him. This said Louis has dispised the Governor and can't deny it; but when we told him he should not despise the Governor, he said he would do so before your Excellency, and he added and said to us: "You had despised Mr. Penet because you will not believe him, therefore you shall not expect any presents of him at his Return, and let Governor Clinton give you Presents more then you ever had; you think you are free People, but I say you are Slaves to the State of New York; but if you are free from the State, I myself will make you Slaves. Let your Minister, Mr. Kirkland, prove that you are free."

Brother:

We remember all our Transaction of the late Treaties; you always tell us that we are free People, and we look on our Nation are free People. Can Colo. Louis make us Slaves, when he is a Stranger to us? Can a single Stranger make a Nation Slaves? We think its too impossible. We never and cannot recollect whether we ever gave him Commission to reign over us as a King.

Brother:

We are little sensible that we have a little kind of Slavery. Our neighbouring Brothers the white People do not use us very well, our young Warriors were among them; when the white People saw our Indians they kill their Neighbours Hogs and told their Neighbours that the Indians did it, and so our People were put to Trouble for it. So Brothers we wish you would stop your People of serving us so.

Oneida, Octr. 28, 1789.

> JOHN JURY
> BLACKSMITH
> ISHADEKARENGHHES
> AKENTYAKHON
> ITANYEATAKAYON
> OGHTATSHEGHTE

>   ARIGHWAYAGENHA
>   SHAGOYAGHTORGHHERE
>   DEKANAGHTSIASNE
>   PETER OTSIQUETTE
>   AREARGHHOKTHA
>   OWYAGHSE
>   THASWENNAKARORAS

Attest, JAC: REED, Clk.[7]

By this time, Colonel Louis Cook had applied for a land patent near Akwesasne, and would soon make his presence known there. He continued at Oneida for a while. His home on Oneida creek eventually went to his son, whose name is sometimes given as Logan and Loran.[8]

Five years after he published *Proceedings,* Franklin B. Hough authored a book about Penet in which he included the letter of complaint by the Oneidas. It's full title was *Notices of Peter Penet: and of his operations among the Oneida Indians, including a plan prepared by him for the government of that tribe, read before the Albany institute, January 23d, 1866.*

Penet's plan for the government of the Oneidas contained twenty articles. It was approved by the "Sachems, Chiefs, and Head Warriors" on October 25, 1788. The second article reads as follows:

> ART. 2. Two men shall be appointed by the Grand Council, that are known to be men of principle and interest in the nation: they shall be invested with power to act and transact all business concerning the leasing and dividing the said land or lands into equal shares, to each person and family, and they shall be obliged to render a true and just account of all their proceedings, from time to time, to the National Council.[9]

After all of the signatures and witnesses are recorded, the document concludes with the following:

> The two men mentioned in the second article, to act and transact the national business, are nominated and appointed by the Great Council of the Oneidas, to wit: COLONEL LUE COOK, and PETER OTSIQUETTE.
>   Attested,   P. PENET, *Agent.*[10]

As much a dogged journalist as an historian, Hough stayed on the story. The revelations he uncovered about Colonel Louis Cook brought a new dimension to the individual he once described as "unquestionably the greatest man that has ever flourished at St. Regis, among the native population." He begins to emerge as someone willing to go along with the plans of outside powers, both public and private, to alleviate the Oneidas of the burden of having land to live on. And if his Oneida opponents are to be believed, he was not above using threats of violence to achieve his ends.

Reverend Samuel Kirkland's journal for 1790 has this to say about Louis Cook and the conflict among the Oneidas:

> Their disputes I would hope are amicably settled. The Presbyterian interest have obtained their wishes; & the others appear satisfied, except two persons, who cannot brook the mortification of disappoint, particularly *Lewis Cook,* the half-Negro from *Canada.* Tis nevertheless Governor Clinton's opinion that the oneidas will never enjoy peace, but be kept in a continual *boil* so long as he continues with them. And the Oneidas as a nation dispair of ever getting clear of him, as he hath married into one of their principal families & which family always had a fondness for the french.[11]

A few years after his Oneida opponents wrote their letter to the Governor Clinton, Colonel Louis and a delegation of chiefs from Kahnawake entered into negotiations with New York State. The end result was the "Seven Nations of Canada Treaty" of 1796. Is it any wonder that controversy surrounds that agreement to this day?

Hough included another brief biography of Colonel Louis Cook as a footnote in his book about Peter Penet:

> Col. Louis Cook, or Atyatoghhongwen, was a St. Regis Chief, who from hatred to the English, took a decided stand in favor of the colonies in the revolution, and led off quite a number of Caughnawaga and St. Regis Indians. He lived with the Oneidas several years, but when tranquility was restored to the northern border he returned to St. Regis. He participated in all the treaties made by the Canada Indians relative to lands in New York, and was employed the greater part of his life in the public service of his people. In the revolutionary war, he received a commission as Lieutenant Colonel. He again entered the service in the war of 1812-15, at an advanced age, and died of sickness near Buffalo towards the close of the war.– *History of St. Lawrence and Franklin Counties.*[12]

At this point, it would be safe to say that Franklin B. Hough closed the book on Colonel Louis Cook. There would be no separate volume about him as there was with Thomas Williams. He left it up to future historians to pick up his trail.

1 "Notes and Documents: The Autobiography of Peter Stephen Du Ponceau." Peter Stephen Du Ponceau and James L.Whitehead. *The Pennsylvania Magazine of History and Biography.* Vol. 63, No. 2. April, 1939. 221-223.
2 *Proceedings of the Commissioners of Indian Affairs, appointed by law for the extinguishment of Indian titles in the State of New York.* Published from the original manuscript in the library of the Albany Institute, with an introduction and notes. Franklin B. Hough. Albany, N. Y.: J. Munsell. (1861) 37-38.
3 Ibid., 39-40.
4 Ibid., 119-126.
5 Ibid., 120.
6 Ibid., 141.
7 Ibid., 353-354.
8 *The Navigators: A Journal of Passage on the Inland Waterways of New York (1793).* Philip Lord, Jr. New York State Museum. Albany. (2003) The location of Cook's home on Oneida Creek, near Stirling Road, has been surveyed by archaeologists. The name of Logan Cook appears on later maps of the area. Personal communications, 1998.
9 *Notices of Peter Penet: and of his operations among the Oneida Indians, including a plan prepared by him for the government of that tribe, read before the Albany Institute, January 23d, 1866.* Franklin B. Hough. Lowville. (1866) 24-25.
10 Ibid., 31.
11 *The Journals of Samuel Kirkland, 1764-1807, 18th Century Missionary to the Iroquois, Government Agent, Father of Hamilton College.* Walter Pilkington, Ed. Clinton, New York. Hamilton College. (1980) 197.
12 Hough, *Notices.* Ibid., 19.

ST. REGIS RESERVATION

*U. S. Bureau of Education Special Report, 1888,
Indian Education and Civilization,*
A Report Prepared in Answer to Senate Resolution of February 23, 1885
by Alice C. Fletcher Under Direction of the Commissioner of Education,
Washington, Government Printing Office
1888

Taken from a monograph on New York Indians prepared by Dr. Franklin B. Hough of Lowville, New York. "His work upon the census of New York State afforded him unusual opportunities to note the condition of those tribes and their relations to the civil authorities."

St. Regis Reservation.—The St. Regis Indians live on the south bank of the St. Lawrence, and own two large islands on the Canadian side in [562] that river,[1] where it is intersected by the line of 45° north latitude. The national boundary passes through their village, of which the greater part, as well as a majority of the Indian population of St. Regis, are in Canada. On the north side of this line these Indians own, besides the islands, a tract of land in the township of Dundee, county of Huntingdon, province of Quebec. Their reservation in New York lies in the town of Bombay, Franklin County, extending from the river eastward along the boundary about 7 miles, with a breadth of about 3 miles. After various cessions,[2] there remains a tract of about 14,000 acres of land, the most of which is level and very fertile.

    The St. Regis Indians are divided into British and American parties, the distinction not depending upon present residence or preference, but upon the differences that sprang up in the War of 1812-15, and which have been transmitted by hereditary descent, on the mother's side. By the consent of the chiefs of the British and the trustees of the American party, a person may be transferred; and a woman, upon marrying, loses her former rights and acquires for herself and children the rights of the party to which her husband belonged. A white man can gain no right in either party by marriage with an Indian woman, but his children acquire the rights of their mother. But a white woman is allowed to gain the rights to which an Indian husband is entitled.

    The British party receives rents from lands leased for a long period, and interest from invested funds. They formerly received from the English Government small presents of blankets, etc., but these have been discontinued. The American party receives by families and per capita an annuity of $2,131.67 from the State of New York. The United States has never had any direct dealings with these people or care over them, except in being represented by a commissioner at the first treaty (1796).

    The St. Regis Indians are descendants of a party of the Mohawk tribe, who were induced to emigrate to Canada by French missionaries about a hundred years before our

Revolution. They first settled at La Prairie, opposite Montreal, but a few years later removed 9 miles up the river, and settled the village of Caughnawaga, where a large number still reside. One branch from this colony removed to Oka (Lake of Two Mountains), on the Ottawa River, some 40 miles from Montreal, and in [563] 1760 another party emigrated under the lead of Father Anthony Gordon, a Jesuit priest, and settled at Ak-wis-sas-ne,[3] on the St. Lawrence, between St. Regis and Racket Rivers, and arriving on the 16th of June, they named their new establishment after the patron saint of that day, St. Regis.[4]

Being from the first a Catholic mission, by much the greater number of these people have remained in this faith. The Methodist Episcopal denomination built a church just off the reservation, near the village of Hogansburg, some thirty years since, and at a later period a neat Episcopal chapel and rectory were erected in the village, under the charge of the Rev. Eleazar Williams,[5] a member of this tribe. There were in 1875 ninety seven members and about two hundred usual attendants in the Methodist Episcopal Church near Hogansburg. There were but few, if any, of Mr. Williams's former charge, and since his death the premises have passed into the hands of an Episcopal society of whites. The Methodists have as a pastor a native Onondaga,[6] and services with them, as in the old Catholic church, are conducted in the native language, the Mohawk dialect of the Iroquois. Several devotional books [564] (some with music printed with the text) and a spelling-book have been printed at Montreal in this language under the direction of Catholic clergymen.

The St. Regis Indians depend chiefly upon agriculture for their support, and a notable improvement in this regard has occurred within a very few years from this fortunate circumstance:

In 1841 an act was passed allowing lands to be leased on the St. Regis Reservation for a term not exceeding twenty-one years. Under this privilege numerous leases were made of small tracts to white persons, who cleared lands, built houses, and made permanent improvements. As these leases expired the tenants were obliged to remove, and these farms came into the hands of Indians, who moved out from their village and took possession of the vacant premises. The very remarkable increase of population noticed within the last ten years (from 424 to 737) may be fairly attributed to the improved hygienic conditions and the abundance of wholesome provisions and pure air which this change occasioned.[7] There has been within this period no emigration of note, either to or from St. Regis, and a notable increase has been observed as well among those living on the Canada side as with those in New York.

Besides the ordinary pursuit of agriculture, in which most are engaged, the men find employment in cutting wood and in peeling bark for the tanneries of northern New York. The inducement for engaging in the latter industry was largely increased during the War by conscription and enlistments, which had rendered labor scarce. These people are good wood cutters and lumbermen, and many of them accounted faithful and industrious. In harvest and hop-picking time some seek employment with the farmers, and this tendency of mingling with the whites in various business affairs is notably increasing as the English language becomes better known.

In summer the business of rafting on the St. Lawrence was formerly an important industry. The hewn timber from the region around the upper lakes was brought in vessels to Clayton, N. Y., or to Garden Island, near Kingston, and there unloaded and made into rafts, which were conducted down the rapids of the St. Lawrence with great skill and success, and almost entirely by Indian pilots. With diminishing supplies, this industry has declined of late years. Fishing with nets is followed in its season by farmers owning the privilege in waters bordering their lands, and in 1875, fish were thus caught by farmers along the Raquette to the value of about $700. [565]

In the summer of 1875, the writer of these pages had occasion for the second time to visit every house on the reservation, for the purpose of obtaining statistics for the State census, and a period of twenty years had brought into use an industry which in 1855 was quite unimportant. In almost every house, the women were found engaged with much skill and industry in the manufacture of bead work, often as an incidental work to fill up the leisure moments of the day, but in several instances as a regular business and with hired labor. Fancy articles in great variety, made of bright colored cloth, on which designs were wrought by needle work with clear glass beads, are produced in considerable quantities, and in some cases a sewing machine was used to unite the cloth that forms the ground-work of the bead embroidery. These articles are sold by Indian peddlers throughout the country, and especially in places of fashionable resort.[8]

Basket work of considerable value is made and sold by the men, chiefly in winter, and in temporary camps among the white settlements, and remote from home, as the bulk of these goods is such that they can not be carried in quantities.[9] The trades of blacksmith, wagonmaker, carpenter, and shoemaker are found among these people, and a few athletic young men give exhibitions of their skill in running, and in playing the ball game of "La Crosse" at agricultural fairs and other gatherings.[10]

The lapse of twenty years brought many notable changes into notice, but none of these perhaps more striking than that seen on attending their church. On the former occasion the greater part of the worshipers sat on the floor, the men on one side, wrapped in white woolen blankets that covered their heads, and the women on the side opposite, wearing blue broadcloth blankets in like manner. The latter wore much beadwork and other rude ornaments of their own contrivance. The church is now (1875) provided with seats,[11] and the dress and deportment of either sex would scarcely be noticed as differing from that of a well-behaved congregation in a country church. The styles of fashion are imitated according to the means or taste of the wearer quite as fully as among the white population.

These people evince a fondness for vocal music, which is taught from [566] books printed in their language, and portions of the Catholic service are sung alternately by male and female voices with great harmony and pleasing effect.

The English is, however, the only language taught in the schools, of which one is supported by the Canadian Government, and two by the State of New York. Those who live upon the islands are practically deprived of opportunities for education, and there is but little care taken by parents to secure punctual attendance where opportunities are near. This indifference to learning appeared partly due to careless teachers, who took little interest in their charge. It can scarcely be doubted but that an earnest teacher would succeed by visiting families, offering little premiums, and otherwise seeking to enlist an interest in the school. A scale of wages which, from a minimum barely sufficient for support, should rise in proportion to actual attendance to a full and ample allowance for a full school would, we believe, under competent supervision, begin before long to yield the best result. The schools upon this reservation appear to have had little encouragement from the missionary who has been so long in charge, and this influence may have led to the indifference too plainly evident.

Another difference was observable in their traditional regard for ancient customs. In 1855 they gave with willingness answers to the voluntary question as to the particular band (Wolf, Bear, Turtle, etc.) to which the family belonged. In 1875 it was soon apparent that the inquiry would offend some and would be ridiculed by others as concerning events that had passed away. There is still, however, a trace of these distinctions in the form given to loaves and cakes prepared for church-day festivals, and there is probable no one among them whose "band" is not still known among the old people.

The greatest hindrance to prosperity at St. Regis is the want of certain boundaries to their lands and the assurance of individual right in their possession. No regular surveys have been made except in running the boundary line and in laying out roads, and although custom has given right of possession, which is generally respected, and may be bought and sold among themselves,[12] not one among them has an acre of land for which he could show a written title, and but very few a corner fixed by recorded survey. The State of New York owes it as a duty to these people to cause a just apportionment and survey to be made, and separate recorded titles to be given. If it is deemed best to forbid for a time the sale of these lands except to Indians, let this be done; but the time is not distant when the principal of their annuities might be paid, and their lands given, as has long since been done at Oneida, in full and absolute free-hold, to individual owners.

There would be active opposition to this from many of the more wealthy and intelligent, who already hold more than their just share, [567] and would vehemently denounce any plan of apportionment. But this should not deter the State from dealing justly with all, and if any are deprived of improvements which they may have made there would be no difficulty in equalizing the value by requiring payment from those who received them.[13]

The British party are still governed by chiefs. The American party, at an election held annually on the first Tuesday of May, choose one clerk and three trustees, whose powers are defined by law. None but males of the age of twenty-one, and living in this State, are allowed to vote; and besides this, the voter must have the qualifications recognized by custom, which excludes from voting any member of the British party, although he may be permanently living on the American side. Parties spring up among them at these elections founded entirely upon local issues, such as the policy of leasing land, etc.

    A record is kept by the clerk, showing who are entitled to annuities, and this practically amounts to a registration of births, marriages, and deaths. The population is scarcely affected by migrations to or from other Indian settlements, although a friendly acquaintance is maintained with their kindred at Oka and Caughnawaga.

1   Cornwall and St. Regis Islands.
2   The following treaties have been held with this tribe for the cession of land:
1796. May 31. At New York City, when they ceded all their lands, except a tract equal to 6 miles square at their village, a mile square on Salmon River (now Fort Covington village), a mile square at the lower mills on Grass River, and the natural meadows along the same.
1816. March 15. Sold the mile square on Salmon River and 5,000 acres from the east end of the reservation.
1818. Feb. 20. Sold another tract of 2,000 acres.
1824. March 16. Sold the mile square on Grass River.
1824. June 29 to Dec. 14. Sold land at and near Hogansburg, 1,144 acres.
1825. September 23. Sold 840 acres east of St. Regis River.
1845. February 21. Sold the natural meadows, found to contain 210 acres.
3   This term signifies "where the partridge drums." This was not from any unusual abundance of these birds in this region, but from the circumstance that in winter the river here forms solid ice, while from the rapids above, which are never frozen, great masses of ice will come down, and passing under the solid ice, produce the noise that has suggested the name. In intensely cold weather the floating ice will sometimes pack so as to raise the water and overflow the village. The river has been known to rise 15 feet in as many minutes, and the current, setting back up the Racket River, has swept bridges and dams away *up-stream*. This calamity, coming in the depth of winter, has occasioned much misery and loss of property, but is fortunately not of frequent occurrence. It usually lasts several days at a time. These overflows of January 24, 1854, January, 1859, and January 24, 1867, were memorable. The latter continued a fortnight and destroyed fifteen buildings.
4   The incidents which led to this emigration are related in Hough's Hist. of St. Lawrence and Franklin Counties, pp. 110-124. Gordon died in 1777, and the station was some years without a missionary. The present incumbent (Rev. Francis X. Marcoux) has been stationed here since 1832.
5   Much was said a few years ago about the identity of this man with Louis XVII of France. The story is generally regarded on the reservation and in the country adjacent as a fiction of his own invention.
6   Most of the Methodists reside in a neighborhood together around Hogansburg and on the road to Massena. They are thrifty farmers, with good buildings and well-fenced fields, and a stranger passing their premises would scarcely notice a difference between their farms and those of their white neighbors. In other parts of the reservation are farms of people not of this sect that show abundant evidence of good management and ample means. As they pay no taxes they enjoy an advantage over the whites, and at the same time are fully under the protection of the law. They can scarcely be called a burden upon the county, as they support their own poor, and it is very seldom that an Indian finds his way to the county poor-house, or that he receives temporary aid from the town. The question of charity is disposed of in a very primitive way at St. Regis. A widow or orphan children left homeless by the death of the head of a family go to live with some relative or acquaintance without any attempt at assessment for their support. It was pleasant to notice how kindly they were received, as if an original member of the family.
7   The number that shared in the State annuities was 666 in 1869, 671 in 1870, 695 in 1871, 709 in 1872, 718 in 1873, and 711 in 1874. The number of families on the American side in 1875 was 156, of whom 39 were of the British and 117 of the American party. Owners of land, 133; adults, 157 males and 139 females; unable to read and write, 98 males, 100 females; read more or less easily, and some only in Iroquois, 58 males, 39 females. The number of St. Regis Indians under charge of New York agent in 1884 makes 937.
8   Bead work was reported in 1875 as made in forty-five families, and to the value of $3,792. The greatest amount in one family was $300, in two cases; in two instances it was $250, in one $200, in two $150, in one $110, in seven $100, in one $90, in two $80, in three $60, in one $54, in twelve $50, in two $40, in one $35, in two $30, in one $20, in three $15, in one $10, and in one $8.

9   In nineteen families basket work to the value of $1,954 was reported.

10   One young man had made twenty dozen sets of bats for playing "La Crosse," worth in all $160. Two farmers reported made, for sale, one 30 and the other 200 bushels of lime.

11   The wood-work of the stone Catholic church was burned April 1, 1866, and the interior, since rebuilding, is still in an unfinished state. Three interesting paintings, representing St. Regis, St. Louis, and St. Francis Xavier, which had been given to the church by Charles X, King of France, were lost in this fire.

12   The usual price of land, when sold among themselves, is about $10 per acre. If offered free of incombrance, most of it would sell readily at $50.

13   An act passed April 19, 1858, and amended April 15, 1859, made provision for a survey and division of the lands, but from causes unknown nothing was accomplished by the commissioner appointed, nor was any published. A clause in this act leaving it optional with any person to accept or not the land allotted to him, would probably defeat any effort that might be made tending to a settlement of rights, as nothing short of entire unanimity would ever close the business, and this could never be expected. Under the present law, land may be leased for ten years to Indians, by the trustees, with the consent of the State agent, and the farms formerly cleared by whites are thus held. No wood or timber can be sold without the written consent of the trustees, but the supply has already been reduced to below that needed for their own wants.

Franklin Benjamin Hough

by Henry S. Graves
Dictionary of American Biography
Volume 9 Hibben - Jarvis
Edited by Dumas Malone
Charles Scribner's Sons, New York
1932

HOUGH, FRANKLIN BENJAMIN (July 22, 1822-June 11, 1885), forester, physician, was born in Martinsburg, Lewis County, N. Y., the son of Dr. Horatio G. Hough, the first physician to settle in the county, and Martha (Pitcher) Hough. He was christened Benjamin Franklin, [251] but when he was eight the order of the names was reversed. He was prepared for college at Lowville Academy and later at the Black River Institute at Watertown, N. Y. In 1840 he entered Union College with advanced standing, graduating in 1843. After a year's teaching at the Academy of Champion, N. Y., he became principal of Gustavus Academy in Ohio, but in 1846 he decided upon a medical career and entered Western Reserve Medical College, where he received the degree of M.D. in 1848. He then returned to New York state and practised medicine in Somerville.

Hough was interested not only in scientific studies, but also in historical research. He collected local historical data and edited documents of the Revolutionary and Indian Wars. In 1854 he was chosen to direct the New York state census and carried on this work in Albany while continuing his work as a practising physician. In the early part of the Civil War he acted as inspector of the United States Sanitary Commission. In 1862 he enlisted as regimental surgeon of the 97th New York Volunteers, serving until Mar. 10, 1863, during the Maryland and Virginia campaigns. After the war he settled in Lowville, N. Y. He superintended the New York state census of 1865 and edited a *New York Convention Manual* (2 vols., 1867) and an annotated copy of the prevailing constitution for the use of the convention assembled in 1867 to revise the constitution of New York state. He was then called upon to supervise the census of the District of Columbia in 1867, and subsequently he was selected as the superintendent of the United States census of 1870. These census studies revealed to him the rapid depletion of the nation's forest resources. He recognized the danger of the popular impression that the timber of the United States was almost inexhaustible and undertook to place before the public the need of action to check the destructive agencies that were operating to devastate the forests. At the meeting of the American Association for the Advancement of Science in Portland, Me., in 1873, Hough presented a paper "On the Duty of Governments in the Preservation of Forests." It resulted in Hough's being appointed with George B. Emerson [q.v.], to prepare a suitable memorial to Congress. The report of this committee advocating the enactment of laws to encourage forestry was indorsed by President Grant who transmitted the plan to Congress in February 1874. Two years later Congress took action and Hough was chosen to investigate the consumption of timber and the preservation of forests, receiving the appointment as forestry [251] agent in the Department of Agriculture on Aug. 30, 1876.

Hough's first report was completed in December 1877. In 1881 he received a new commission carrying a larger appropriation from Congress. His work included travel in Europe where he studied the German system of forestry and of forest education. During the next two years, he issued his second and third official reports. This investigation, covering the timber and forest products of the whole period of our government, aroused wide international interest and was awarded a diploma of honor at the International Geographical Congress in Venice a few years later. When Nathaniel H. Egleston was appointed the chief of the division of forestry in 1883, Hough remained as forestry agent to assist in the preparation of the fourth volume of the official forestry reports. In March 1885 he drafted a bill for the New York state legislature which created a comprehensive forestry commission for the state. Some of his more important books are: *A Catalogue of Indigenous, Naturalized and Filicoid Plants of Lewis County, N. Y.* (1846); *History of St. Lawrence and Franklin Counties, N. Y.* (1853); *History of Duryee's Brigade in 1862* (1864); *Washingtoniana, or Memorials of the Death of George Washington* (1865); *American Biographical Notes* (1875); and *Elements of Forestry* (1882). He has to his credit seventy-eight publications, including government reports and bulletins on history, meteorology, climatology, education, law, and civil records. In addition to these he edited numerous colonial documents and translated Lucien Baudens' *Guerre de Crimee* under the title: *On Military and Camp Hospitals* (1862). He published the first *American Journal of Forestry* in October 1882, but he was forced to abandon this project within about a year on account of lack of subscribers. He was also interested in geology and is said to have discovered the mineral known as houghite. Although he was not a professional forester, his contribution to the forestry movement was outstanding, particularly in educating public opinion toward a more conservative use of forest resources. He was the first federal official in forestry, and he efficiently prepared the way for the work of his successors. On July 9, 1845, Hough married Maria S. Eggleston of Champion, N. Y., who died on June 2, 1848, leaving an infant daughter. On May 16, 1849, he was married to Mariah E. Kilham of Turin, N. Y. They had eight children.

[T. H. Fearey, *Union Coll. Alumni in the Civil War* (1915); B. E. Fernow, *A Brief Hist, of Forestry* (1911); "Franklin B. Hough," *Am. Forests and Forest Life,* July 1922; F. B. Hough, *Hist. of Lewis County,* [252] *N. Y.* (1860), and *Letters and Extracts from Testimonials Accompanying the Application of Dr. Franklin B. Hough for Appointment as Superintendent of the Ninth Census* (1870); R. B. Hough, "Incipiency of the Forestry Movement in America," *Am. Forestry,* Aug. 1913; *N. Y. Geneal. and Biog. Record,* Apr. 1886 ; J. H. Hickcox, "A Bibliog. of the Writings of Franklin Benj. Hough," *99th Ann. Report of the Regents of the Univ. of the State of N. Y.* (1886).] H. S. G.

Made in the USA
Columbia, SC
05 November 2024